Yours truly
George M Dawson

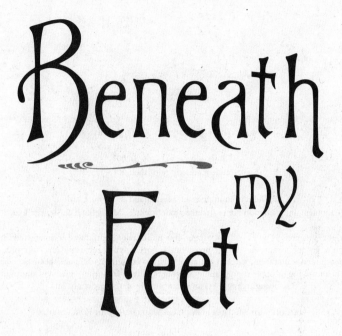

Beneath my Feet

THE MEMOIRS OF

—

GEORGE MERCER DAWSON,

WITH

PHIL JENKINS.

EMBLEM
McClelland & Stewart

Cloth edition published 2007
Emblem edition published 2008

Emblem is an imprint of McClelland & Stewart Ltd.
Emblem and colophon are registered trademarks of McClelland & Stewart Ltd.

LIBRARY AND ARCHIVES CANADA CATALOGUING IN PUBLICATION

Jenkins, Phil, 1951-
Beneath my feet : the memoirs of George Mercer Dawson / with Phil Jenkins.

ISBN 978-0-7710-4333-8

1. Dawson, George M., 1849-1901.   2. Geologists – Canada – Biography.
3. Scientists – Canada – Biography.   4. Explorers – Canada – Biography.
I. Dawson, George M., 1849-1901 II. Title.

QE22.D28J45 2008   551.092   C2008-900903-7

We acknowledge the financial support of the Government of Canada through the
Book Publishing Industry Development Program and that of the Government of Ontario
through the Ontario Media Development Corporation's Ontario Book Initiative.
We further acknowledge the support of the Canada Council for the Arts and the
Ontario Arts Council for our publishing program.

Typeset in Van Dijck by M&S, Toronto
Printed and bound in Canada

This book was printed on acid-free paper that is 100% recycled, ancient-forest friendly
(40% post-consumer recycled).

McClelland & Stewart Ltd.
75 Sherbourne Street
Toronto, Ontario
M5A 2P9
www.mcclelland.com

1 2 3 4 5   12 11 10 09 08

I turned the page and slowly read
The yellow paper stained and old
Marked what leaf was fairly writ
Which was blotted and half told
Of weariness or grief or joy
The hand had felt in its employ
and where, at length, the pen was stayed
and life's last entry weakly made.
The story of a life was there
An echo of the old refrain.
I knew I would not find enscribed
The thoughts of night, the words of prayer
The looks of love or hate and all
That made life truly dark or fair
All, all had faded in the night
Save what poor outline here was spared.

GEORGE MERCER DAWSON.
written on the shore of Francois Lake,
British Columbia, 1876

Contents

—

LIST OF ILLUSTRATIONS   IX

BY WAY OF EXPLANATION   I
BY WAY OF INTRODUCTION   3
THE AGE OF GROWING   6
THE AGE OF LEARNING   36
THE AGE OF THE LINE   74
THE AGE OF THE WEST   145
THE BRIEF SPAN OF THE HEART   253
THE AGE OF THE NORTH   274
THE AGE OF THE DESK   306

BY WAY OF ACKNOWLEDGEMENT   348

LIST OF ILLUSTRATIONS

—

James Dawson   9
George Dawson, aged ten, Montreal   9
Anna Dawson, aged eleven, Montreal   9
Fossil drawings   31
Group portrait, Montreal   31
The *Lake Erie*, sketch   38
Lecture notes   38
Map of the North American Boundary Commission route   77-79
The North-West Angle Monument, Manitoba   88
The North American Boundary Commission, North-West
    Territories   88
Odometer party, North-West Territories   129
Waterton Lake, North-West Territories   129
The Wanderer, watercolour, British Columbia   218
Haida village, Queen Charlotte Islands   218
The Athabasca River, etching   247
Fort McLeod, British Columbia   247
European sketches   268
Map of Yukon survey route   279
Telegraph Creek, Yukon   280
Gold prospector, Yukon   280
Indian crews, Yukon   295
Pelly River, Yukon   295

Geological Survey, Ottawa   308
Geological Survey museum, Ottawa   308
Family gathering, Métis   333
Victoria Chambers, Ottawa   333

The illustrations on the following pages are the personal works of Mr. Dawson: 31, 38, 218, 247, 268, 280, 295

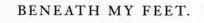

BENEATH MY FEET.

BY WAY OF EXPLANATION

—

I FIRST ENCOUNTERED the subject of this book, George Mercer Dawson, in 1988, on the wall of a small rural museum in southern Saskatchewan, near the United States–Canada border. A photograph, dated 1874, portrayed a group of men involved in the Joint Commission charged with mapping the border in that and the previous year. Twenty-four-year-old George Dawson was a Canadian naturalist, botanist, and surveyor with the Commission. In the photograph, Dawson stands among a group of large, bearded Métis guides, all of whom are a good foot and half taller than he.

Intrigued, I did further research and discovered that all of the Dawson family correspondence was catalogued and indexed at the McGill University archives in Montreal. This treasure trove was the result of George Dawson's father, John William, having been the Principal of McGill for almost forty years. There are around five thousand of George's letters in grey archival boxes, from the letters he wrote to his grandfather as a boy, to one he wrote to his beloved sister Anna only a few days before his death, when he was head of the Geological Survey of Canada. As well, there is a wealth of his photographs, poems, diaries, journals, and sketches.

Clearly a book was in order, a biography. There was already a fine retrospective collection of his letters published by his niece, and a couple of slim life stories aimed at adolescents, but no comprehensive telling of the tale of this extraordinary Canadian. And so it began.

In the telling, however, I soon became aware that an unusual approach was needed. George Dawson was a wonderful read. He was a writer – in his personal letters and even in the published reports of his travels – of endearing wit, evocative description, and illuminating fact. I found myself quoting from him every other sentence and realized that, for the reader, this rhythm would be like riding a cart down a corduroy road. Better to get out of his way.

When I returned to the letters and laid them out in a narrative line forty-five years long, it emerged that Dawson had almost told his own life story. After leavening in his descriptions of his professional career, I could see he had effectively written his memoir; it had simply never been assembled. So, I appointed myself his ghost writer – although he, not I, was the ghost – and the memoir grew. Dawson himself had suggested, in a letter written near the end of his life, exactly such a course for a first draft autobiography his father had not completed, advising that "a literary man be brought in to knock the thing into shape." To provide a frame for his story, I added, taking as much care as possible to build only on the facts, an opening in which Dawson describes starting the memoir, and gives his reasons for doing so.

In creating a coherent narrative, parts of some letters were moved to the times they described, similarly there was some rearrangement of his more thoughtful notes to ensure a narrative flow. Key events during his life on which I could find only passing comment, such as the death of Darwin, were expanded. Finally, I inserted samples of Dawson's nature poetry, and a small selection of his vast output of photographs, watercolours, maps, and notebook sketches.

Every fact in this memoir is Dawson's fact, as is every description of his travels. I would estimate close to ninety-five per cent of the book is written in his own words, tidied up to best tell the story of a man who led a heroic life, and who deserves to have his story on as many bookshelves as possible. Thank you, George, for your literary legacy.

BY WAY OF INTRODUCTION

April, 1900 Ottawa

—

WERE YOU TO TAKE the measure of me, pass a surveyor's line from my toes to the tip of my head, it would record the height of a lad of twelve, though I am now past fifty. However, had the string been secured to my ankle in the May of 1869, when I set sail from Montreal for England to become what I am now, a natural scientist, it would have unspooled many thousands of miles, tracing a line of travel through the New World and the Old, and arriving here, anchored to the leg of a desk in the offices of the Geological and Natural History Survey of Canada. The desk where I now struggle to start a literary assay of my days.

I have had the fortune to publish many papers on the personality of the good earth, reports on glaciers, dinosaurs, Indians, gold, and coal, and I have kept pace by pace journals of my travels, compiling them into reports that stretch along the shelves of the Survey library. I could place several volumes of minor poetry alongside them, and yet the commencement of this memoir has been a hard vein to mine.

It is not, to be sure, lack of time that has held me back. True, the affairs of the Survey keep me welded to this chair, until I fear I shall fossilize one night and my colleagues discover a seated statue on the morrow. But such endeavours do not fill a day. I rise as the sun does, no matter where I find myself awakening, and I keep the moon good company, so the day has hours to spare for me. And, I must confess, I am in a state of ennui. Boredom's child, restlessness, is a constant tug at my heel. Perhaps in this expedition into memory I will find relief.

Sitting here with a lamp burning and the inkwell open, I feel again as I did as a child, confined on the wrong side of a window, willing strength back into my spine that I might stand up, walk out, and not cease until I had answered all of nature's questions. Instead, I find myself a reference point on the journey of others in this institution. Petty problems are the pebbles of my days, a mound of them piled around my feet. I look into the eyes of an anxious junior surveyor and maintain courtesy, even as I see with my mental eye the wild black glare of a stampeding buffalo as I raise my rifle. Or, attending a departmental meeting, I feel I am standing once more in a swarm of locusts thick enough to choke an ox.

But I am pinned here, a lepidopterist's specimen, a thing that once flew but now is cocooned in ledgers and memoranda. Denied extended trips into my beloved western wilderness, I am resolved instead to make an internal expedition across my own history. My father, a man who wrote almost without fail every day of his life, once admonished me for not turning my "power of writing into more popular and widely useful channels than reports." He flatters my penmanship, I think, but I do so tire of reports, and so in these pages I shall grant Father his wish.

There is a sadder reason for breaking my desire to leave my inner life unrecorded. My younger brother Rankine, whom I continue to love fraternally but have lately been pressed to like, is in London making terrible plans to publish our poor father's rough and unready memoir. Sir William Dawson, my dear father, gone to his beloved God six months ago, deserves much better and yet, despite having the rest of the family ranged against him, Rankine proceeds, as he has always proceeded, from the conviction that his own wallet is his truest compass. I fear he may one day try the same dreadful ruse with my own biography, after I am gone to dirt before him, as I surely will be. So, this account of my days and thoughts, told in my own words, will, I pray, grant me a kinder fate. As I begin writing, it is April, 1900, the first Spring of a century that promises to be a parade of scientific wonders.

THE AGE OF GROWING

—

OF MY EARLY DAYS in Pictou, Nova Scotia, I have no sharp images embedded within – excepting one. It involved myself and my Grandpapa James, who had come to Canada from Edinburgh just a year before the British-American war broke out, and who was many things by necessity. A printer, a bookseller, a ship-owner, but in his heart and mind I believe he was a natural scientist. To have grown up in Edinburgh as he did a century ago, and being blessed with even a modicum of curiosity, rendered that almost unavoidable. Grandpapa was a young man when James Hutton published *The Theory of the Earth* in that volcanic, walled city, a copy of which I possess and treasure, and in which Hutton writes "this world has neither beginning nor an end," a rather large proposition which some say led Mr. Charles Darwin to his conclusions.

Pictou, washed by the sea, was a geologist's dream, blessed with a fossil beach nearby flooded with specimens. My father, under Grandpapa's tutelage, had rambled its rocks and brought home his keepsakes, and in my turn I know I did the same. I believe I can see myself through history's lens, on a beach, looking down at a flat broken stone, and seeing upon it the skeleton of a fish, etched by time. I pick up the wondrous thing and run along the sand back to Grandpapa, where he patiently talks to me of its making, and of God's design for our Earth. This is the only authentic memory I can credit to my time in Nova Scotia, but I certainly cannot dismiss its importance; half a century later I am here, in an office which bears the wording DIRECTOR–GEOLOGICAL SURVEY OF CANADA on the door.

I was not my parent's first child, though I became the eldest. Mother later told me, when I was a young man and close to death myself, that my brother James Cosmo, who bore my grandfather's name and that of my father's deceased brother, was born in 1848 and died at the age of seventeen months when Mother was already bearing me. The baby James, running about the house, saw a pot of beans destined for the garden and ate one. Soon he began choking, sufficiently that a doctor was fetched but nothing in the way of blockage could be found. The boy grew feverish and a week later died, after which the bean was discovered in his lung. I was born not a month later in Grandfather's house in Pictou, on the first day of August 1849. Soon after that Father took Mother for a walk, and pointed out a pretty house, and asked if she liked it. She said yes, and Father then said it was theirs, he had already purchased it. I remained in that house till the age of five.

(My father had also lost someone while still a boy – his younger brother. James was cut off, while still a lad, by scarlet fever, which at that time was remarkably prevalent and fatal. The uncle I never met was a favourite with all, less diffident than my father and the two young men were constant companions. Almost six decades after the terrible loss of his sibling, Father told me, there was but one incident between them of which he still repented. One day, not long before James was seized with the illness which proved fatal, he asked Father to assist him with a difficult piece of Latin translation. Being busy with some affair of his own, Father refused his brother, and James went away disappointed. Not many weeks later he died. Perhaps by way of a warning, Father drew from this sad story the admonition that such little acts of unkindness may form bitter drops in the cup of life, even if repented of and forgiven.)

Pictou, when my father was born there, was a harbour of some local importance as a trading place, with a population of about two thousand souls. The shores of the pretty landlocked inlet received the waters of three rivers, and were originally occupied by Micmac Indians. The early French explorers left only a few graves by the waterside, and a rudimentary Catholicism implanted in the minds of the natives. It was colonized towards the end of the 18th century by immigrants mostly from Maryland, families of Scottish, Presbyterian descent. Either with them, or shortly after, came a few Negroes, still held in slavery but soon emancipated. The next wave of settlers were the Loyalists, driven north by the American War of Independence, then larger numbers of Scottish Highlanders dispossessed in the clearings, followed by a sprinkling from the Irish exodus. To this substratum were added various individuals, people who had seen better days and brought with them the remains of an earlier culture, and perhaps the dregs of bad habits which had ruined them elsewhere. Pictou thus held both persons of good education and of reputable antecedents, mingled with all sorts of waifs and strays down to the recently emancipated Negro and the poor Micmac deprived of his lands and degraded into becoming a gypsy and a beggar. These were all my father's neighbours as a growing boy and, a generation later, their sons and daughters were mine.

My father, when I was born, was the Superintendent of Education for the province, a position he had taken on the urging of Charles Tupper, who was also Edinburgh educated, and eventually became Prime Minister, if only for less than three months. When he was offered the post of Superintendent, a new position, Father was inclined to refuse it, as he was busy working up the local geography and preparing papers for the Geological Society of London. Premier Sir Joseph Howe would take no refusal however, and thus Father began an entirely new career of a most active and exacting nature which, being peripatetic, took him frequently away from home.

In 1853, when I was but four, a gentleman by the name of Sir Charles Lyell boarded a steamer bound for Nova Scotia, and Sir Edmund Head, then Governor of New Brunswick, was aboard the same ship. Both men proved fortuitous to Father in the next

My grandfather, James Dawson,
who immigrated to Nova Scotia in 1811.

Myself at ten years old.

My sister, Anna, aged eleven.

two years. Sir Charles was already known to my family. It was in the summer of 1841, by an act of providential coincidence (or so he considered it) that Father met the great geologist, a man whose friendship followed and assisted the early years of his career, as later on it did mine. Sir Charles Lyell was a genius who was the guiding mind of his time in geological theory, and he was visiting Nova Scotia as part of his wide-ranging researches when he heard of a young geologist and arranged to meet him. Father was then twenty-one and Sir Charles (who was actually not yet then a Sir) was more than twice his age. This was an event that must have awed Father, since Lyell's *Elements and Principles of Geology* gave form to the modern science, and the three volume edition had been a lightning rod in Father's scientific advancement.

By the time the two men got together that summer, my father was himself already well on the path to becoming a great scientist. It is not given to all men to remember the moment they find that portion of Creation to which their intellect and powers of study are best suited, but Father did, when he was still a schoolboy. An excavation in a bank of earth not far from his schoolhouse exposed a bed of fine shale, from which the boys discovered they could fashion home-made slate pencils. While digging out a flake of stone, he was surprised to see on it a delicate tracing in black of a leaf, like that of a fern. When he showed it to the Rev. McCulloch at the Pictou Academy he was informed that it was a fossil, and that the leaf was a real one embedded in the stone when it was being formed. Consequently some of Father's specimens ended up in pride of place in the school geological display cabinet, and so vindicated his pursuit, for the other boys had repeatedly derided him for his unathletic hobby. From that time on he became a zealous geological collector, gradually extending his researches out to all the cliffs within reach, and even into the ships' cargoes of limestone imported to supply the lime kilns near town. Wider and wider afield he went, to the coastal cliffs and grindstone quarries of South Joggins, where he suppered and slept alongside the quarrymen and beheld entire erect trees represented in sandstone casts in the cliff walls.

Father was able to show Sir Charles his hard-won collection of geological and mineral samples and, on an excursion to the Joggins beach, Father and Sir Charles were so fortunate as to discover the remains of the first reptilian animal embedded in a coal formation in North America, as well as coming upon the first known landshell from the Palaeozoic period, the age when the fishes and the amphibians made their appearance upon the earth. The young scientist and the master corresponded, and then a dozen years later, Sir Charles returned.

The two men went again to Joggins shortly after Sir Charles's arrival on that second visit, and then a year later, Sir Charles wrote to Father in a matter he imagined would be of some interest to him, which indeed it was, and how different my life would have been if its suggested course had been fulfilled. It seemed that the professor of Natural History in Edinburgh had been removed by death, after only one year, from the position, and Sir Charles wanted Father to become a candidate. Father had actually gone to Halifax to take his passage for England by Cunard steamer when a message arrived to the effect that the appointment had been hurried through in favour of the candidate of the Biological department at the university.

Almost simultaneously with the news of the failure of the Edinburgh candidature, a letter arrived in Pictou from the Board of Governors of McGill University in Montreal, a place Father knew little of except that it had some reputation as a medical school, offering him the position of principal. He soon learned that it was Sir Edmund Head, who had been promoted to the office of Governor General of Canada, who desired that Father go to Montreal, a recommendation which both startled and disappointed the McGill Board, who had hoped for some man of mark from England. Sir Edmund was a zealous university reformer, and a man of high literary gifts, and his endorsement of Father carried sufficient weight to be persuasive. Father, as previously arranged, spent a summer in Scotland to attend a meeting of the British Association for the

Advancement of Science, and when he returned in September, Mother, with myself aged six, my sister, Anna, then almost four, and brother William but a summer old, met him at Halifax and we all boarded the steamer for Montreal. Grandfather, when he could close up his affairs and Father was well settled in his new life, was to join us there, but this, as things transpired, was much delayed.

My earliest, solid memories of Montreal are of a mountain rising up behind our home, Mount Royal. It was early October when we came off the steamer at Pier Eight and took a carriage through the city towards the mountain. We saw our new home in a dimming fall light, but even in fullest summer sun it would have been disappointing. Mother was anguished by the sight of two blocks of unfinished and ruinous buildings standing amid a wilderness of excavators and masons' rubbish, overgrown with weeds and bushes. The grounds were unfenced and pastured at will by cattle, who not only cropped the grass but browsed on the shrubs leaving unhurt only one great elm, the Founder's Tree that still stands, and a few old oaks and butternut trees, most of which long ago gave way to the new buildings. A circuitous and ungraded cart track was the only access up from the town, impassable at night.

We had intended straightaway on arrival to take up quarters in our promised residence, the east wing, but the retiring Principal, and his furniture, remained still within it, in mid-evacuation, and so we children were installed at the St. Lawrence hotel with Miss Geddes, our governess. The completion of other buildings had likewise been arrested by lack of funds, and the students and professors were housed in a brick building nearer the town. Father, in a speech he later gave to the faculty, portrayed the campus then as being destitute of nearly every requisite of civilized life, with a bank of rubbish and loose stones in front and a swamp below.

The day the house came empty Mother went at it with two char women from the town, and a home began to emerge from the dust and disrepair. An old mahogany sideboard had been left, and Mother bought it and revived it, and it remains in the family. Our furniture arrived from Pictou the same day as a herd of tradesmen began their work, and it was into this chaos that we children decamped from the hotel to our rooms. The smell of plastering, painting and wall-papering, if happened upon by chance, is for me the aroma of youth.

Our first Christmas in Montreal Father was away in Toronto, the seat of government that year. Since the Parliament buildings in Montreal were burnt down by rioters a few months before I was born, government had pendulumed between Quebec City and Toronto, and was sitting in Toronto when Father set out for it across the icy St. Lawrence in a canoe, by way of Albany, Niagara, and Hamilton. He made himself known to many of the Members and was able to thank Sir Edmund personally for his appointment. Then, no sooner was he back than a fire, a regular occurrence in all formative towns, burnt down the uninsured Faculty of Arts build-ing at the rear of our quarters, Father losing a large part of his private collection to the flames. Meanwhile the students moved in to temporary buildings around us, and their toing and froing between classes was the rhythm of my early years.

Our besieged home gradually took on an order, its interior being Mother's bailiwick, just as the University was Father's. My mother as I know her now is devout – her days always begin with porridge and prayers – somewhat reserved and, when the opportu-nity presents itself, joyous, a combination not as uncommon in the Scottish as English opinions of us might suppose. At the sound of music she is likely to take up the rhythm with her movements, as though holding back on the urge to take the dance floor. She enjoys the company of bright colours, scarlet in particular, and I do not recall being in a room of her decoration that did not contain a little or sometimes a surfeit of that colour. She has maintained her abil-ities as seamstress and watercolourist, both of which she passed on to my eldest sister, although only a portion of the talent in water-colour reached me.

Mother determined as quickly as possible to provide us with a home that was a reflection of herself and her family. The drawing

room settled into browns and yellows, Mother's hands as a seamstress and crocheter evident in the drapes and cushion covers, and
the grand mirror over the fireplace watched us all come and go.
From the hall, two doors admitted to the library, the windows
hung with vermilion curtains, and all the space twixt floor and
ceiling filled with books. Between two windows giving to the east
was a grey marble fireplace. At the far end of the library a set of
double doors opened to the dining salon. These were opened to
announce dinner to Father, and he would take his place at the head
of the table, and after prayers perhaps recite some of the latest
publication by Mr. Dickens or a poem, while we stared at the ironstone service with patient hunger, waiting for the laden dumb
waiter to arrive from the pantry. At breakfast there were prayers
for all in that room, the maids included, plus a psalm or a short
Biblical reference.

The desk at which father must have spent half his life sat in
the middle of the library, one drawer filled with medicinal barley
sugars for us and peppermints for him, and a brace of leather
chairs faced the desk, in one of which of an evening Mother often
sat stitching and listening to Father's recital of that day's literary or religious composition.

When Father left for the day's work and teaching at the
University, Mother would go down to the ground floor to visit cook
and the laundry and the locked store rooms of barrels, boxes, and
bushels of St. Lawrence apples and other comestibles. There was
never, never any alcohol of any sort in the house, for my parents
were abstinent, as was the household. Even at New Year's, when
Scottish custom dictated the welcoming dram, tea and coffee were
the only order, and the gentlemen were offered nothing as they
were received by the ladies in the parlour. I must say this made us
quite singular about the city at the time. Two floors above the store
rooms there were the bedrooms, and Mother's boudoir where she
would go after visiting cook to draw up lists and complete her correspondence. Behind her chair as she wrote hung a portrait of the

family tree, a plum tree with miniature family likenesses within each plum. My room was more to the back of the house, and beyond its windows stood the mountain.

Mount Royal, anciently rising seven hundred feet above sea level behind the chaos of our own stones, was my playground and my first instructor into the Earth's secrets. I learnt from Father even before I learnt all my alphabet that along the path the students took across the college grounds to their lectures, magma once flowed when the progenitor of Mount Royal erupted in a cooling world, and then was sculpted down to its present outline. Mount Royal was also the subject of the first of my poems to be published praising the natural world, in *Grip*, a Montreal comic paper claiming a firm grasp of the juvenile mood. The ode, as I recall (I am cursed with a fine memory for my own verse), involved two frogs, one young and therefore foolish, the other wise with years, discussing news of a park coming to Mount Royal. The senior frog sagely concludes both frogs will be in the Creator's embrace by the time the Committee charged with planning the park has reached any definite consideration. "Upon Mount Royal's wooded height," was the poem's opening line, I believe, and it serves well as the opening line of my remembrance of my young self, when I was a tadpole. The park, of course, a splendid design by Mr. Olmstead, who gave New York its central – and flat – designed acres, did not appear until four decades later. No doubt long after both frogs had passed on.

(I have had occasion in my researches for these pages to read my earliest diaries, and I notice my handwriting has become less clear with time. There is import in this, no doubt. I note also that the habit of Capitalization of nouns that normally do not take them still lingers in my pen, a grammatical flaw I inherited from Grandpapa. An example: A dedicated gardener, Grandpapa begrudged the Nova Scotian Fall and Winter their tyranny of the calendar. He far preferred Spring and Summer, enjoying the company of their warmer personalities during the rise of the greenery, and taking to the sea with me in our rowboat. In the Spring of 1856, saddened by our departure, Grandpapa wrote me often, at least biweekly, and in one letter reminded me of the pleasures of watching the coming of seed to Perfection. Of course there was the attendant admonition that "if you do not sow, neither can you reap." He also warned me of the wisdom of getting Parsnips and Carrots early into the ground. "Aunt" Agnes, Grandpapa and Grandmama's housekeeper, likewise in one of her notes, imagined us walking the streets of Montreal and coming upon a "Dashing Confectionary" and how "Nice and Sweet" it would be to consume its wares. Agnes occasionally enclosed a three pence piece for each of us, to be "speedily spent on sweets," which it was. My palate was sweeter then than now; I am longer in the tooth and also, it would seem, more bitter in the tongue.)

Grandpapa was my first steady correspondent, and I looked forward to his missives in those unsettled days, the words on the page like lines of rigging stretching from my precarious crow's nest back to his safe deck. I have them bound in ribbon, and here is one written to me from the deck of one of his ships, telling me that "While sailing today the mate caught 22 cod, which we will have for supper. You say that you have bought a drum with the money I sent you, that I think indicates that you are likely to make a noise in the world." He was anxious that we write and spell well, and leavened his homilies, such as "obedience makes you happy" with stories of white porpoises in the St. Lawrence (he meant beluga whales) and immense log rafts the size of one of his farm fields with nineteen temporary houses upon it, and men in snowshoes who tumbled forward into the snow so far that only the bottom of the shoes could be seen. I wrote back about finding pretty snail shells on the mountain and baby William having the chicken pox.

In our early days at McGill, the natural calendar unfolded for me at Father's boot heels, as I followed him outdoors in the after-noon having, as Mother had bidden me to, read my twelve Biblical chapters and absorbed another portion of the Psalms.

Through Father's efforts a welcoming hedge of sweet briar soon stood guard before our apartment's door, and the garden gained form and pattern. Hundreds of trees that would one day tower over me went into the still raw university grounds as saplings, treelets no higher than my boot tops, planted by teams of men shouting to each other in French, my first acquaintance with the tongue. "Natural investment," Father called it, this forging of an ordered landscape, a phrase that could apply equally, I now realize, to his concern for a growing family. Most certainly my father's, and his father's abiding curiosity into the design of Nature, which they knew is divinity made incarnate, is my inheritance, and one I have striven to pass on.

Spring saw us wishing away the last handkerchiefs of snow from the grounds, and out we went down the path to the garden, or around behind the Arts Building where there was a small cliff of rock and a stream from which Mother would every day draw a pitcher of water for the dinner table. Soon the birds came to the mountainside and the minnows to its unfrozen streams, as though in answer to the same invitation from the ringing of the bells on the lilies of the valley. Father graciously studied with serious gaze my weekly ration of fossils pried from the mountain, be they true and false, some were true fossils, most of a pattern able to trick my young eye into believing here was the trace of a life, where in fact none existed. We planted the vegetables in rows side by each, Father restraining his pace so as to remain level with me as we made and refilled the holes. In late summer and through the winter we ate our crop from our plates, the day of their planting (I called it their birthday) still fresh in my memory.

An occasional sortie with my dear sister Anna to the summit of the mountain, the top of my world, laid Montreal at my feet, the silent St. Lawrence running west to east and the mast tops just visible. When we returned we always collected a bagful of snail shells and then fashioned bouquets of adders tongues and trilliums, the latter straining to flower and carpet the forest bed before the canopy's umbrella closed over. One day in May, when I was seven, we returned to find a water tap installed in the kitchen and a water closet also within, and were able to wash our hands and

gain intestinal relief in the same room, without leaving the building. By high summer there were ripe currants on the bushes Father
had transplanted from Pictou, and the bull had run with all the
cows in his field, including the cross-cow, Agnes, named after
Grandpapa's housekeeper. As Fall descended the acorns dropped
down to the ground and were ignored; not so the butternuts that
seemed to be caught by boys with outstretched hands even before
reaching the earth; Father fenced in the healthier trees the next
year, which certainly reduced the boys' booty but did not entirely
keep them out.

Then came my own fall, or rather stumble. In due course, like
the sons of the other professors at the University and of the
English townsmen, I had enrolled at the High School Department
of McGill College, and made the short walk to Burnside Hall on
Dorchester Street each day to attend classes, taught by an
Englishman and a Scot. I was as robust as any other boy there and
it was my sense of adventure, rather than any timidity or hesitation, that caused my misfortune. The High School was near to
several ponds, the largest of which we boys had dubbed Lake
Inferior. At almost every noon break in that Fall term of 1859,
we would pole across the pond and back on a raft the seniors of
previous years had lashed up and we had enhanced, imagining
ourselves shooting the Lachine Rapids with an Indian guide, which
role I usually took. I cannot say whose elbow pitched me forward
that day, and I am sure it was accidental, but in I went, the sound
of laughter and splashing commingled above me. My chum O'Hara
caught me and put me back in the medium my lungs preferred, and
I was relieved of my duties as guide till we made shore. With some
twisting and dog-like shaking I reduced the stream of cold water
running into my shoes to a drip, and returned to classes as well tow-
elled as time allowed. By the time I walked home I was no soggier
than a blotter, but it was still apparent that my apparel was worse
for the wetting and Father guessed directly what had transpired.
Mother provided both a reviving scalding and, when I awoke from

a troubled nap, a mild scolding which was, I could tell by its tone, a mask for concern at the length of time I had remained within my damp garments. Some part of that chill made its way into my bones and could not be entirely warmed out.

At first, after the shivering and sneezing had passed, my recovery seemed complete. Come the week's end, I would plunge outdoors at a moment's permission, heading for town beside Mother, brother William's hand hardfast in mine if shopping were the day's order, returning once with – why do I remember the exact number? – thirty-eight marbles which I was able to amplify in a game at school to over one hundred. Other times, feeling over-whelmed with energy, myself and O'Hara would team up and cheer for a favourite in the student snowshoe races, then race ourselves on shoes over the same course, O'Hara the fleeter, myself the more determined, the spoils divided as they are in life between the nat-urally gifted and the determined drudge.

We cannot remember the moment in childhood we first told a lie, or were told one, nor can we pinpoint the exact time and day when we realized we would one day die. Likewise, I do not remem-ber when the first headache, the first of so many, seized me making it feel as though my head were turning to stone, thought by thought. I know now that it, and its later companions, were the result of the bending torque being applied to my spine as it weakened, as though I were being malformed by igneous intrusion.

The headaches were the precursor of a general malaise that kept me home from school sporadically and then constantly. When it became clear that I was likely to be ill for some time, Father arranged for a tutor, a Miss Macdonald. She was a woman of great patience, but she would sometimes complain of the need for rep-etition of her instructions, assuming simple distraction on my part. In fact a fog of pain was upon me that her words could not penetrate, and it dammed my lines of reasoning.

As winter began to withdraw, so did the headaches and now the pain in my lumbar advanced. At first the general opinion was that they were growing pains, the sort a ten-year-old might expect! But I had only to begin a game of marbles or a game of Birds in the Bush, go hawing or set out cuttering and sleighing and the pains would commence. Excitement itself, it seemed, raised the pain to another level. On the increasingly rarer trips across the field and into the town, such as those Father took me on each Saturday to buy flounders from the fishmongers, I was often free of strain, letting my eyes soak in the details of a world so much larger than my room, my bed. But when we would slit open the fish and examine the stomach's array of shells, the excitement this induced – as it would in any boy, surely – triggered the throbbing in my forehead, over the left eye. Calm returned later, when the shells were added to a big wooden storage box Father brought back from Labrador, and I classified them over and over, first by colour, then by origin, then by size, and so on.

It was in that Spring that I was given a magic lantern by Grandpapa. I can conjure the delight I took in preparing slides to feed it, and I can recall the recipe for Red, "dragon's blood and spirit," producing a colour of arterial splendour. Father gave me a prepared slide relating to the human skeleton and though anxious to display it to my sister after tea, a headache took the chance away, and Mother played a little music to me and bathed my feet in warm water to try and cure it. Projected later onto the wall of my room, the bone figure was of a perfect posture.

And so began the years of the doctors. The trouble, as it were, was behind me, in my spine. The chill of that tumble in the stream had percolated into my support system, and the result was curvature. It was incremental, a weakening of bone in one spot relative to another, the waning vertebrate members bowing before the pressure of the stronger. After the first winter it seemed I might have turned back towards my former health, but it was a mirage, and over the months of my eleventh year (an ironic number, consisting as it does of two perfectly erect lines) I took on the aspect and outline of the question mark residing at the end of a sentence.

Sentence it was, for I became a creature of the indoors, no less than a convict, one such as poor Abel Magwitch of Mr. Dickens' *Great Expectations*, met by Pip in the marshes and who later dies in hospital. I was determined, once the length of time required to overcome my fall towards death was clear to me, to follow Pip's fate, not that of Magwitch, and to make of my room at McGill a preparatory cocoon for my emergence as a moth, bent but capable of flight.

I have always undertaken to blur the boundary between indoors and outdoors, by importing as much of the latter into the former as possible, so that it might receive intimate scrutiny. Scrutiny reveals secrets, and hence placement in Nature's catalogue, which I have striven my whole life to compile. This habit commenced when it became my mission to catalogue the Creator's wonders, a task of course that would never reach completion. To my knowledge no one has ever complained to a physician of an overfull memory, one unable to take in one more item, so I had no fear of surfeit.

In that room, I dedicated my remaining years – not knowing how many there were, whether they would accumulate to a famine or a feast – to rendering the unknown familiar, and instructing curiosity to always be my guide so that, at the very moment before passing into the Creator's good morrow, with death a blink away, I might be handed a mystery, and strive to unlock it even as the last breath rose out of me.

Two happier incidents come to mind when I comb those first long months of debilitation. The remains of the Indian village on the college grounds were in the process of being unearthed that spring of 1861. They had surfaced when sand was required to assist in the construction of Molson Hall. The workmen were in the employ of Mr. Edmond Dorion, and as they dug they turned up fragments of human bone, which they simply reburied elsewhere on the site. Further excavation, however, revealed the remnants of multiple cooking fires, and such objects pertaining to daily life as pipes and pottery. Mr. Dorion, who was aware of Father's position and knew him to be a man of science, consulted him as to the mystery the ground had released. Father, realizing that here was an Indian settlement of considerable age, right on the grounds of a University, was able to proceed in an orderly fashion with the requisite archeology. Mr. Dorion was persuaded to donate those artifacts already in his possession to the Natural History Society of Montreal, the country's senior scientific body. On more than one occasion Father allowed me to walk slowly with him to the site of the excavations over which he and Senator Murphy, a fellow member of the Society, presided. Indeed, I feel sure Father considered it essential that I see the painstaking labour involved in archeology, or any "ology" for that matter, and chance had provided on our doorstep one of the first such thorough excavations in Upper and Lower Canada. Though I did indeed witness the stooping toil, I also recall the fascination of holding and regarding a fragment of pottery, imprinted with chevrons and small circlets, and imagining its manufacture and place in the daily life of people who had lived an unknown number of generations before me, yet in the same place. Father eventually expressed a reasoned belief the site was none other than Hochelaga, the Iroquois longhouse encampment visited by the French explorer Jacques Cartier well over three centuries earlier. Cartier, as I had already learned, had stood on the mountain directly behind our house in the year 1535, and beheld the confluence of the Ottawa and St. Lawrence Rivers, the former seeming to him auriferous, or golden, the latter argentiferous, or silver.

For a few months in the summer of 1860 I was returned by ship to Pictou, there to convalesce under Grandpapa's watching eye, although I see now that there was relief for my parents in the action too. The birthday party Grandpapa laid on for me in Pictou, the place I was born eleven years prior, shines like a candle in a dark room. Grandpapa must have been sixty then, being as old as the century, and a widower, for Grandmama had died before we left for Montreal. The young always see the old as older, but Grandpapa did in fact carry himself as an older man, for he had run into the wind most of his life and the years had bent him as the months had bent me. When the party subsided, and I lay in bed with excitement as a blanket for my pain, Grandpapa came and told me a story:

My great-grandfather was present, our family lore has it, as a stripling on the side of the Pretender at Culloden Moor. He escaped that dangerous day, married a Protestant woman, and later went over to her religion. The children, including my grandfather James, one of the younger sons, were all educated as Presbyterians. Great-grandfather Dawson was a burleyman in Banffshire, by which I mean that he was an appraiser of grain, and he was regarded in his parish as a man of vigorous intellect. He lived to a great age. His wife, my great-grandmother, was an eminently pious woman, earnest in the careful training of her children.

Grandfather James Dawson, being a younger son, was not destined to inherit the farm, or to received a liberal education that would fit him for the legal profession. Rather he had to be content, when his time came, to be apprenticed to a tradesman in the neighbouring town of Huntley, where he was drawn to two of his work mates who stood out as decidedly pious. Grandfather met with them once a week, in the evening for mutual prayer. He was admitted at the age of nineteen into the church, and subsequently spent his savings on books of high class and read them with care. He became a dissenter in religion, being repelled by the loose and ungodly lives of some of the clergy and, when free of his apprenticeship, this dissent and his love of independence prompted him to emigrate to the New World where a promise of employment awaited.

It was a journey of almost two hundred miles, made on foot from Keith, his home in Banffshire, up through the Grampians, down into Perth, and along the valleys to the departure dock at Greenock. There was not enough money in his pockets to pay for both him and his luggage to make the journey to Greenock together, so the luggage travelled in style while he paced out the distance. Accompanying him were three other hopeful young men

in similar circumstances with barely sufficient provisions and cloth-
ing on their backs. In twelve days he was at the dockside, and there
waited twenty-one days for a packet ship to take him through the
Firth of Clyde and beyond old Scotland.

After a voyage of five weeks his ship cast anchor in Pictou
harbour on May 19th, 1811. Grandfather was twenty-two years old,
and had but the proverbial guinea in his pocket. His contracted
employment completed, he established himself in mercantile business on his own account and fell on prosperous times as a merchant
and a ship-owner. He married Mary Rankine, in 1818, who was then
living in Pictou with her brother William Rankine, who had come
ahead of her to Nova Scotia from the parish of Lonerig in Scotland.
My father, the first of two sons, was born two years later, in October.

Throughout his life Grandfather was ever influenced by a
strong sense of duty, ever ready to do good when he had opportunity, and too independent to conceal his opinions or to cringe to
men in place and power. He retained a warm sympathy with movements in favour of Christian union, peace, free trade, and the
abolition of slavery. He became active, against much opposition, in
establishing a temperance society in Pictou, the second in British
North America, I believe, and temperance was part of my father's
inheritance. Father's early home had much in it to foster the study
of nature, and his parents encouraged such pursuits, as they did in
his brother James, the younger by three years. In the year that the
second boy arrived, Grandfather, with many others in that part of
the world, was reduced almost to ruin in the great commercial col-
lapse of 1823. Thus, when my father was in his formative years, the
condition of the household was that of a hard and honest struggle
to maintain a respectable appearance. With all that, both his
parents were willing to make the educational interests of their
boys the first charge on their resources. It was a maxim of my
grandfather's, oft repeated along the generations, that it is better
for a child to receive training, which no man can take from him,
than to give him property, which might be dissipated or lost.

When I returned to Montreal from that Pictou sojourn, I was no better in body though my spirits had revived in the Nova Scotian salt air. Mother sought to minimize my day-to-day pain with common maternal care; simple warm water and a gentle touch, in the hope that constant concern could halt and then reverse the damage already done. Soon, as the confinement lengthened, it was the habit of Anna and William to import the outdoor plants that caught their eye, including some from the mountain that had been plucked with their own hands. Rather than merely press, label, and file the specimens, I began to root out their, as it were, personalities and to assign their attributes to my own. I appreciated the defence mechanism of the sensitive plant, which whenever you touch it, curls up. Likewise, as I built my collection of the pressed leaves of trees I posed this question. Were I a tree, which should I favour appearing as: the smallest of the species, mould, rather than the biggest, the palms? I fear I may have leant even then towards mould.

Father was beside me, it seemed, in his every spare moment, decanting for me the events of his day, bearing specimens that required study, filling the shelves with books that did not remain unopened long. I can see him now at the bedside (it must have been in 1863 or thereabouts, because I recall Rankine as a baby less than a year old wailing away in another part of the house), recounting the details of a lecture he had delivered the previous evening entitled "The Duties of Educated Young Men in British America," a subject dear to his heart. As I counted myself among the ranks of those young men, I was all dutiful ears.

I believe that if he could have, my father would have straightened my failing spine with his own loving hands. Knowing that he could not, he sought the specific key of knowledge that could spring me free of the closing vise that so threatened my posture. With a scientist's determination he pursued the most righteous combination of place and person to arrest the decline, to brake its progress and bring me back to health.

It was as part of this pursuit that we travelled by railroad to Cape Elizabeth in Maine, where, once the family was settled in, Father and I carried on to Boston. Father had arranged for me to visit yet another doctor. The first time I saw Dr. Buckminster Brown I recoiled, for I was viewing myself as I might one day be. Dr. Brown's right shoulder was ahead of its sinister counterpart by a hand's width, and his dorsal muscle had ridden up so that he appeared to be swimming through air and in constant mid-stroke. To look into Father's eyes the doctor was obliged to rotate and look up along his own forehead, and it was in this position that he asked Father what treatment I had received thus far, and on being so informed, he sighed. His diagnosis, after examination, was Pott's Disease, a tubercular invasion of the spine which could be cured using a device he could guarantee would have effect, for he had evolved it both by and for himself. It was a bracing system capable of tightening by increments, and it was a horror that I choose not to mention again, but it had a singular virtue. It worked, and arrested the advance of the disease.

—

FREEDOM TRULY CAME the day Father walked into my room in May of 1865 – I was by the window, sitting up, watching a robin conquer a worm – and announced a grand adventure. Anna and I were to accompany him by steamer to Britain. I would see the Scotland Grandpapa had left as a young man to make his fortune in the New World, and walk the streets of London that Mr. Dickens so vividly described in *Great Expectations*, and I would turn sixteen there. Indeed that book accompanied me across the ocean and all that summer. Ten years after we had come into Montreal, I left by the same river, sighting the snouts of Quebec's cannons on the ramparts and saluting the power of the falls at Montmorency that leapt mightily towards us, then succumbed to gravity. We sailed from lighthouse to lighthouse down the river, then, in the

Gulf, the jealous fog kept Newfoundland and Labrador from our sight. Out on the ocean, icebergs and whales were the only surface distraction. After five days without glimpse of another ship, a steamer making for Quebec passed us, and soon after we made the lighthouse on Tory Island just after dawn. When we came up on deck that morning we were in sight of the Irish coast, and Anna and I stayed at the rail as we began to enter Loch Foyle, and Green Castle and the fort near it slid by, the former all covered with ivy. Opposite the telegraph station a pilot came on board, we fired a cannon, and a steam tender came alongside to collect the passengers for Londonderry.

That accomplished, we crossed the Irish Sea without encountering the fouler kind of weather it can provide, and came up from breakfast just as we were entering the Mersey estuary. The docks at Liverpool were functioning as some great unified machine and there was not an idle soul to be seen. In the Liverpool Public Museum, I stared down at the model of the city, a real city such as Montreal might one day be, and felt the urge to reach London, as soon as possible. The train that left Lime Street Station to take me there seemed anxious to grant my wish, and long past nightfall our train pulled into Waterloo, and the frantic sightseeing began as London and I became acquainted for the first time. Besides the usual magnificences we ventured into Westminster Hall and into a room which opened off it, the Divorce Court, and Anna and I paused awhile to hear a case in progress, which was much like viewing a rare animal at the Zoological Gardens.

And then it was time for me to leave London while Anna and Father remained in the South, and go northwards to Scotland on the Express. My recollection of York, a way stop to change trains, is of a cathedral, a very fine one, less stocked with monuments than Westminster but more imposing by a degree, loftier within and more suddenly come upon. My memory for relics can summon an ivory horn donated by a Saxon Prince, and there was the pleasure of promenading on the back of the Roman walls that ring the town, a rare treat for a Canadian unused to antiquities forming the casual fabric of the landscape.

Reaching Scotland was a homecoming to a place I had never been, although its coast and castles, as related in Grandpapa's stories, already filled my head. Father had rented a house for myself and the Bell family, Mother's people, at North Berwick, just to the west of Edinburgh, and the greater part of my time there was spent fishing, boating, and searching for shells and sea creatures, particularly when the tide was a long way out, when we got sea urchins and razor fish.

The sea was my sandbox that Scottish summer, which was filled with energetic male cousins, Alfred, Charles, and Frederic, who gave me no compassionate quarter, for which I was grateful, although no doubt Father had prepared them for meeting me. The illicit borrowing of boats and fishing for mackerel made a sailor of me, and I discovered a strong sea stomach, an asset I was thankful for in later years. Collecting the stamps from Anna's letters of her doings with Father and drafting my replies kept me occupied during my afternoon rests. Cousin Alfred was a fine shot even then, and we spent hours were engaged skinning the solan geese and norries he brought down. I'm sure it is not how it happened, but the glorious holiday seemed to end quite abruptly, Father and Anna coming in unexpectedly to fetch me, and in no time we were on a train for Liverpool, on board the steamer and from thence . . . home.

For our holidays in the next two summers we went to the south shore of the St. Lawrence, to Cacouma, close to Rivière-du-Loup. The river here was wide and smelt of salt — a change from the deadening stench of Montreal's stretch of the waterway. That was the summer of a great heat wave, one that had people dropping dead in the cities, as Father informed us in a letter, and there was a general resistance to travelling overland. The river steamers enjoyed a robust trade, with many a bleached city dweller running down to Quebec from Montreal for the sheer relief of the breeze on deck. I was by then a veteran observer of the change in landlubbers once they got their feet on board ship. They would immediately claim proprietorship of the steamer, and take credit for all it did well, commenting in a stage voice, "Ah, we are getting up steam," as the rumble began below deck. Of course, if anything went wrong, it was all the captain's fault, including the weather. For example, at Murray Bay, where half the register would disembark, it was invariably raining furiously, and all the people who landed there got thoroughly wet to the skin, or even deeper. They would turn and blame the nearest crew member for the inconvenience.

The house at Cacouma was modest and comfortable, as best suits summer accommodation, with a river view for distraction. Between the house and the shoreline a medley of stones posed at an angle, as if anxious to look in at our front windows. Unfortunately the view was not all-encompassing; the man who converted the cottage for summer people had placed the ice house directly between us and the best vista, and the milk house between us and the next best, on the principle that we might otherwise have too much of a good thing.

Despite my return to health – apart from the occasional headaches, guaranteed now to disperse before sunset – Father remained overly solicitous, the more so because I was downriver and out of his sight. He insisted a hand carriage be found that could act as my second in the case of a sudden duel with fatigue. In my daily letter to Montreal from Cacouma I told him that, with regard to hand carriages, if he could locate one suitable for running up and down precipices and through woods full of spruce scrub it might also do well to carry water for my aquarium. In those youthful, remedial summers I always found books a better mode of travel than any wheeled contraption. I read for betterment and for the future – Issac Walton's *Compleat Angler*, Dickens' *American Notes*, *Dingby Junction* and Dicson's *New America*. I was inclined to be arch in my letters in those days, and Mother, leaning over my shoulder, felt free to both read and pass comment, particularly if she sensed rudeness, a vice she abhorred. Postscriptive comments such as "you may distribute my love, but only to those who will value it," something I was inclined to add to Anna's letters, would bring tutting.

The return mail would arrive mid-forenoon, and Rankine, now an energetic four-year-old, would walk over at Mother's hand to fetch it, while Anna looked after our new sister Eva. One of my naturalist's projects for that season was to rear moths from silk-worms. An issue of *American Naturalist* sent by Father explained how. The comparison between the journey from worm to moth, and the years spent indoors and my release as though born a second time did not escape me, and no worms were ever so well-tended.

Those Summer days on the river side were serially similar, a line of flags blowing in the same prevailing breeze. The worms were turned and I rose late from my bed and later returned to it, tired from maintaining the pretence of having a normal young man's quota of energy. Sometimes I was forced to lie prone in the garden as the sun went down, inert as a fish. In fact I have suddenly remembered a man who came one afternoon with a very large fish which he was selling in pieces from door to door; it must have been six feet long when it was whole. He had caught it down near Isle Verte the day before. I suppose it was a sturgeon.

Of all the settlements along the St. Lawrence, Tadoussac, where we passed the summer of 1868, shines brightest in my memory. Yet our sojourn there did not start well. The *Union*, our steamer out from Montreal, ran aground in the dark on the first night, before we had even reached Murray Bay. After stoking the engines to their strongest torque, the captain applied some rudimentary physics to the problem, hoping for a reaction when he bade us all gather at the opposite end of the boat from the one held fast, employing the principle of see-saw. We stood in the smoky air, the male passengers discussing their own, surefire solutions, while the captain reversed the engines. She was too fast on, so for safety the steam was blown off and the fires put nearly out. Boats were put down and made ready. Then, all the ladies and some of the gentlemen put on the long cork belts. At midnight, all the stateroom doors had to be opened as the

A set of my fossil drawings.

William, myself, Anna, Father, and Mother on the steps of the east wing at McGill.

tide was falling and they began to jam. In case the ship fell over, all the lamps were put out and a few candles substituted.

Dawn found us in the self-same position, and I began to fret for my belongings; I had brought fishing rod, aquarium, telescope, microscope, jar of spirits, a Jew's-harp, and, wrapped in an oilskin, the rifle Father had bought me. (This last item was his subtle way of pointing me in the right direction, as no self-respecting Canadian naturalist entered the wilds unable to collect specimens.) We retired to the boats, and the absence of our weight on her back lifted the ship and we reboarded and continued. The next day, Rankine lost his felt hat overboard and all day afterwards was pointed out to the other little boys by their mothers as an awful example — "the boy who lost his hat." His face remained red the rest of the trip, not with embarrassment but mute anger, the two shades of rouge appearing the same to the outside eye. It was the first time I saw him display his cold temper, which in the days following would lead to rejection of any suggestion of a path to cheerfulness.

One morning, towards the end of that vacation, Father roused me with the birds and we ventured outside, collecting my rifle as we went. Learning to release my weapon had not been a priority — I still find them only a bearable tool, devoid of the fascination they hold sway over others — but Father insisted on a preliminary trial alongside Mother's kitchen garden. I was a young man of seventeen, and it was time I awakened the hunter within. We riddled an unfortunate little box and cut a row of peas into salad, but I did gain sufficient accuracy to be able to select which tree I might wound first, were I called on to slaughter a forest. I relayed this news to Aunt Dora in Scotland, who thought me too young to be in armaments, telling her that my gun sent its kind regards.

When the others returned to Montreal, Father to prepare for the coming semester at McGill, I stayed on at the Hotel Tadoussac till the end of August. It seemed as if the better families from several blocks of Montreal's Golden Mile were there too; Mrs. Ogilvie who lived on St. Catherine Street, with her two children and sister from Upper Canada; young Master Redpath and his wife. Miss Ogilvie was very nice but had rather a fishy expression, her sister ditto. Miss Windham was ensconced with two governesses, one for each of the youngsters, the littlest miss being an awful tomboy and the brother one of the crossest, noisiest, most spoilt youngsters ever.

The days at Tadoussac blend together, like a series of photographs might to simulate motion, but one day in particular is fixed. Why this day holds on when the others have fallen to the back of my memory I know not, but it does. Perhaps it was the first when I felt truly well for all of the sunlit hours, not just some brief part of them. In the morning I had a nice sail in a birch-bark canoe all about the bay in search of extraordinary seaweeds, then a picnic on the Saguenay and, when we had stopped for a bit of a peruse, I was attracted by and collected a beautiful moss, and later admired a large wild-cat killed by some gentleman while fishing. At the nightly concert, when my turn came, I explained and named the shells I had retrieved on the beach, and my lecture went off very nicely. Sharing the playbill with me, one might say, was a Mr. Holmes, who sang the NEGRO MEDLEY IN COSTUME and was encored. He was an American on his wedding trip. The gossip concerning his marriage reached even my uncalloused ears; he was thirty-five and his bride only fifteen. Her cruel parents would not consent, so she went out to go to Sunday school one day and ran away with him. This I felt to be not scandalous but romantic, and I learnt the lesson that gossip springs deepest from envy, not moral superiority. Mr. Hoovey, who seemed to me then the oldest man alive, sang two of the queerest old songs I'd ever heard in the queerest manner possible. The performances ended with a gentleman who read well and gave selections from Dickens. There was dancing till late, which was naturally beyond me, and I stayed up till twelve looking at the stars, and, as one does after prolonged gazing at the heavens, at my possible future.

—

SUMMER'S LEASE hath all too short a date, and I returned to Montreal and dutifully began classes at the University. After all those years of tutors, I was now at a desk in a room full of other desks, each with a fellow student behind it. I was in advance of my classmates in the natural sciences, as was expected, but in the remaining disciplines I was an average student. While I worked hard to fill those cups which were low, there was some adjustment to be made in being part of, as it were, a collective noun and, it has be said, a competitive one. Added to that was my last name, which not coincidentally was also that of the Principal.

The studentry had surpassed the hundred mark in number when I attended, and the educative buildings that formerly had stood separate alongside our rooms in the east wing were now linked by smaller passageways inserted in the gaps. The William Molson Hall was now attached to the western flank of the Main building, so I could travel from my room to the Chemical and Natural Science laboratories without breaking into daylight, and with few stairs or great distances to exhaust me. I was a young man among young men, perforce less sporting but in a constant mood to learn from the better minds around me.

I completed the year without any great measure of anxiety, and in June was away again on the steamer down the St. Lawrence, this time only as far as Caocoma with Mother, the rambunctious Rankine, and the equitable Eva, who can then have only been four but whose quiet nature was already evident. That summer was in a way the end of my childhood, for as I knew then, at the end of the season I would sail down the river again and keep going, all the way to London, where Father had arranged through his old friend Professor Lyell that I should attend the Royal School of Mines. There was nothing to compare with it in our country, and Father knew that an education there would fit me for a future in a Canada where coal would be centre stage. Father had his ear to the ground, and he could hear the railways rumbling westward, where it was suspected there were great reserves of fossil fuels that it would take well-trained men to locate.

So there was one more summer at Caocoma, that last idyll of 1869. The postcards my memory sends me of those swiftly passing months are of alterations and improvements to the structure of the house, and an old man with a smiling face under a towsy wig walking right into the middle of them and setting up a peek show, and refreshing us with the sight of fifteen grubby pictures of Europe's great palaces for "deux sous par tete," two cents a head. Of writing every day to Anna to try and evaporate the dullness of not having her there; she was eighteen and taking her examinations, and would join me the moment they were finished. Of a scarcity of meat and an abundance of fish, either a salmon, a shad, a herring or two, smelts, tom cods, or sardines turning up on every plate, morning, noon, and night. At the end of a day's search on the beach, Mother would enter some new example of seaweed pressed into the album she kept, which had this verse in it that I still know by heart.

> Call us not weeds
> For lovely and bright and gay tinted are we
> And quite independent of culture or shower
> Then call us not weeds
> We are ocean's gay flowers.

In September I packed my rod away, and returned to Montreal. The day came when I was standing at the door, the carriage before me, my bags within, and I lifted my eyes up to the window that had only looked one way a few short years earlier. Like Pip in *Great Expectations*, "I only wondered for the passing moment, as I stopped at the door and looked back, under what altered circumstances I should next see those rooms."

THE AGE OF LEARNING

—

AS I MOUNTED the ramp onto the ship that was to carry me to my vocation at the Royal School of Mines, I knew that I was now headed into a new stratum. It was October 1869, and London was the centre of the world, a place where the best of men went to come into their own, and thence return home to employ the tools of study and knowledge in revealing a country to itself out over the sea of ignorance. The times were rife with great men making great strides, but in truth, I felt like one of those frogs in my adolescent poem, most certainly the younger, lifted from his own comfortable pond into one so much larger, where the bullfrogs reigned, massive and sure of their place on the largest pad. I knew mental fear, but swore too that when I came back again to Montreal I would be taller in mind, as tall as any other man of science. So the sailing ship *Lake Erie*, then only two years at sea, bore me away from my own humble pier, and Mount Royal receded to no more than a hill, then a smudge. Anna stood a few feet ahead of the remainder of the family at my moment of departure, and waved the longest.

The weather was with us while we remained in the river, passing the familiar marks of my receding youth. Captain Sclater's intention was to go north of Newfoundland, through the Straits of Belle Isle, and I was hoping to mimic his course in my cabin with charts of my own and navigational instruments I had bought for the purpose. I saw myself as a man moving through unmapped territories, and I wished to be prepared.

I shared a cabin on the *Lake Erie* with a young man destined to remain a friend, one John Rimmer. I cannot say we became so on the instant; the first impression I present gives pause, and takes, as it were, "sizing up." But with proximity, involuntary or otherwise, there often comes amicability, and in a ship's cabin there is proximity to spare. Our companionship was quickly put to the test when a storm rose in the Gulf, and engulfed us for three days. I was in for only two of those days, but Rimmer was much more seasick than I, perhaps because he gave in to it too much. The cabin filled with several inches of water during the blow, and Rimmer, whose trunk was fortunately tin, stayed abed except when he staggered out in nightwear and boots to try and catch some air that wasn't his own. When the ship changed tack, the water ran across the floor in a horrible way. The steward bailed away all the time but we could not keep the cabin dry and anything but very light reading was unpalatable.

The gale defeated our intention to go through the Straits of Belle Isle and, as we turned to head below Newfoundland, the cabin stove, which we later kept lit constantly till the morning before we got to Glasgow, broke away and the chimney fell down. As well, my apples spoiled; they were so extremely ripe that once they began to go they all went off together. We had fresh beef for about two weeks and then fell back on canned beef and chickens, preserved milk for the tea and coffee, and real milk for the porridge. Needless to say I learned very little navigation, counter to my intentions. To amuse ourselves gastronomically Rimmer and I concocted famous suppers after raids on the steward's pantry when its guardian had retired for the night; Welsh rabbits with cheese and biscuits fashioned on the stove and apples with the core removed and the cavity filled with sugar before roasting.

I had but two days in Edinburgh before catching the train to London, yet I did not manage to escape the attention of my cousins

My sketch of the Lake Erie, *the ship I sailed on to England in 1869.*

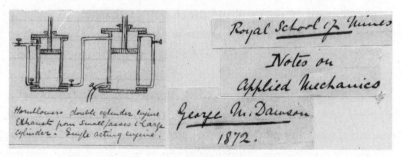

Lecture notes from the Royal School of Mines.

Christina and Ella, who maintained a particular concern for the well-being of my Presbyterian soul. As I departed, she presented me with a beautiful little Testament, with an India rubber strap to hold it closed, a new but quite effective idea I later incorporated into my field notebooks. Christina was both devout and a little bigoted, a combination less rare than might be supposed. She was anxious that, when I reached London, I attend the right God; the Scottish God, the same one who heard the prayers of Father, Mother, Grandfather, and all the Dawsons and Bells gone by. But God, at least a kilted one, and I had grown a little estranged sometime in those years spent indoors. To this day, when I think of it at all, I use, and I know Mother would be saddened to read this, the term Creator instead. Once in London I wrote a letter to Christina reassuring her I had found a suitable low Anglican church nearby, Trinity, and was giving it my attendance.

For the three years I attended the Royal School of Mines, I stayed with a Mrs. Guest at 20 Halsey Street in South Kensington. These premises had been found for me by a friend and longtime correspondent of Father's, a Mr. John Bigsby. Mr. Bigsby had been to Canada as a much younger man, and had published a two-volume memoir of his visit with the charming title *The Shoe and the Canoe*. I had read this book, and now met its author. He was a gentleman indeed, and most helpful during my time in London. Mrs. Guest, a widow, was then about thirty-eight but looked a decade beyond that; experience had weathered her. She was short but neither very fat nor very thin. The house was one of an identical row of fifty split into two sides of a plain street, and numbered sequentially, rather than the usual even to one side, odd to the other; thus, in my twentieth year, I lived between nineteen and twenty-one. My room, to save me too many stairs, was on the first floor at the back overlooking the immaculate pocket handkerchief of a garden. My room was woefully low on bookshelves when I arrived, the previous occupant being in banking. I purchased a second small table and established it by the window as my, as it were, Canada Post Office.

Already on my arrival Mrs. Guest handed me a sheaf of famil-
ial letters, some from Canada and one from my Scottish cousin Ella
wishing me God's guiding hand in my instructions and looking
forward, now I was on the continent, to more visits and boating
outings. According to her wishes, I read a little bit of the Bible
every night and got halfway through Matthew by Christmas.

At that small table beneath the rear window, with Anna's gift
of knitted bed socks on my feet and her photograph hung above, I
kept up with the quotidian events of my siblings and the ministra-
tions of my parents. William, then a young man of fifteen, had,
before I left, been showing signs of becoming cynical and mis-
anthropic, and I wrote to Anna to not let him relapse that way but
to try to cure him by a little poetry, or music, or a judicious
mixture of both; the amalgam had often worked for me. Rankine
and Eva, six and five respectively, were of the age when most of
their utterances were interrogative. I urged Anna to feed them all
sorts of romances and fairy stories. Though not a parent myself, I
have always thought this very necessary, for if children are always
matter of fact when young and have no exercise for their imaginations they lose that very useful power when they grow older, and
degenerate into dull, weary materialists.

Despite my admonishments to my brothers and sisters, the
weight and length of schoolwork often left me little time for reading
or listening, and I was unable to practise what I preached, always
hastily replying to previous letters that were in danger of turning
stale, and often composing unimaginative gossip when not in the
best of humours. I should perhaps have invested in some good
baking powder to prevent my letters from being so flat. In writing,
you have the conversation all to yourself, which is very tiresome. I
much prefer indeed someone who will continue talking in a most
oratorial manner, with only the slight encouragement of "quite so"
and other such platitudes to keep them going. Over the years, I have
found that ideas and those sorts of things cool down when they
travel thousands of miles across oceans and continents. I have no

doubt that if we could each have a personal branch of the glorious Atlantic Cable laid on, we would all get along in that respect much better, and ideas would themselves travel further to the mutual betterment of all.

The lounge at 20 Halsey had a fireplace nearest the road, which could barely hold at bay London's wintery damp, and a piano at the rear which Mrs. Guest did not play on. When seated in the lounge reading by the fire, which I often was, Mrs. Guest had the gift of talking or remaining silent as she sensed you to wish. Another lodger was a Dr. Davies, a displaced Glaswegian working in London as a shipping agent, a man of stalwart self-confidence who, on my first day there, having established my pedigree, took me under his financial wing and advised me to put my £70 posthaste in the Scottish bank on Kensington High Street. He returned from his offices the next day in a cab accompanied by a small oak bookshelf that he claimed was surplus to his requirements at his bureau, an endearing act that confirmed my lifelong belief that it is kindness, not love, that makes the world to go around. Love merely makes it oscillate peculiarly on its axis.

I had no time for idle perambulation in the district, having arrived on a Saturday with my first class on the Monday morning. I rehearsed the walk to the Royal School on the Sunday, so as to have no trouble arriving in time the following forenoon. The better part of it, I was delighted to see, took me through the high trees and elegant foliage of Green Park and past one side of Buckingham Palace, which I thought to be rather a lump of a building, grand but somehow undernourished for an edifice that symbolized the centre of an Empire. The park gates allowed me onto Piccadilly at the entrance to Green Park underground station and I then set a course towards Jermyn Street, turning down towards it when I arrived opposite the gateway to Burlington House, which held within it the newly occupied offices of the Geological Society and the Royal Academy of Arts. In the course of my tenure at the School of Mines I had occasion to frequently pass through both doorways. Montreal, which could boast Paris as its grandparent, felt young when I came to London; the air itself felt saturated with history, and the fog seemed almost composed of it.

The prevailing spirit of the neighbourhood around me was very much that of the Prince Consort, Albert. He was, one might say, the neighbourhood ghost. I was but twelve at the time of his death, but recall the McGill students having the day off in mourning, and reading reports of the Queen's deep grief in the *Gazette*. During the Great Exhibition of 1851, the Prince himself had opened the Jermyn Street building wherein I was now to receive instruction. The School was a stone palladium conceived by an architect much favoured of the colonnade, high windows and other Grecian references. It was my pleasure through the three years I spent there to escape from the Hades of the basement laboratories to the highest floor, there to gaze out over London as the light dimmed, and the Thames became transformed from lead into silver – provided the fog had failed to show up. The fog! More than once I happened to be out in it and it was quite curious to see, or rather not to see, everything. You could barely make out the lamps on the other side of the street, and one could not make out the people at all. The cabs were mere shadows as they passed down the middle of the road. It made your throat sore for about six inches up and down.

My education was now in the hands of a collection of minds each of which rivalled that of my first instructor, my father. He knew them all by reputation of course and commended them, although I know that spiritually Father was adverse to Professor Huxley's notorious theories on evolution. Professor Huxley, who was to teach me Natural History, had only a few years before my admittance published a slim volume popularizing the theories of his close friend Charles Darwin, advancing his own global researches into the origins of Man. It was his belief that Darwin, through the hypothesis of mutating, refining species, had essentially rewritten history. For this he was known as "Darwin's Bull-dog." Father held, with his full heart and soul, to his faith that History, with Man within it at its apex, was a story authored by God alone, and that there was no need of adding a branch to our family tree for Mr. Ape to hang from. I have always maintained that an open mind is a scientific tool, and kept mine handy.

My other professors, whose public light did not perhaps burn as bright as Huxley's, were nevertheless admirable, determined to elevate me despite my own lowly estimate of my powers. They were men of a serious nature: Guthrie on Physics, the aptly named Goodeye on Applied Mechanics, Smyth on Mining et al., but not without humour. On the first day Professor Frankland, the chemistry master, showed us a beautiful experiment. He set on the table a large glass vessel which contained a dead cat covered with a layer of charcoal. It had been so, he informed us, for three years, and we could not help laughing when he bent over it and began sniffing to assure us that no smell was perceptible. Then what is that strange odour? the class wag asked. "The rising Thames" was the reply.

Although my main hours of instruction were passed in Jermyn Street, I was anxious to explore London, the same London that had decorated the pages from Mr. Dickens that Father had read to us at dinner. Here was a great city at my beck and call, an inexhaustible laboratory of wonders and moments; I only wish that I had been equally indefatigable then and able to plunder its riches more than I did. My curiosity, stoked in those years of confinement, was an animal released, but I did not possess a feral energy, and would return to Halsey Street only just able to mount the stairs. Father had provided me with a list of people to whom he had forwarded introductions, so I had social obligations to maintain as well as educational, but I found these, coming as they often did at the end of the day's studies, an extra strain. Thus I was obliged to rest up at home prior to an invitation to dinner in the evening with Father's geological companion Sir Charles Lyell, the patron of my father's famous study of Acadian geology, so I was anxious to make an impression. But it was a good distance by the underground and then a half mile to walk to their residence, and I was afraid of tiring myself too much for the next day's mechanical drawing, the one course I found needed the greatest application, so I rescheduled. I could have used the dreaded chair, a confounded wheeled contraption that had been sent over by separate lading from Montreal to assist me in getting about. Father, ever the anxious parent, still had me pegged as recovering, whereas I saw myself, thanks to Dr. Brown, as beyond all that now, lacking only stamina which a steady diet of walking would soon replenish. Anna, at first, made me testy with the over-solicitousness of her letters, but it was out of love, and I asked her to forgive me and then we talked no more of it.

But those taxing social calls upon my energies were balanced by London's unfailing ability to provide on a whim some chance, refreshing happening. One day, for example, I was an hour late for my drawing class at Jermyn Street because I had waited to see the Queen go in state to open the Holborn Viaduct and Blackfriars Bridge. She passed me on her way from the railway station, where she had arrived from Windsor. She looked then quite blooming, the severity that characterizes her now, thirty years later, not yet in her features. In apposition to that regal sighting, the very next day I came on a ragged little girl, with a pretty good voice, going up the middle of the street singing hymns and eagerly picking up the coppers which some people threw out of the windows. On another occasion I went to the Rag Fair. It was a halfpenny to go in, and once in there was nothing worth seeing, only a dirty-looking little market with a lot of dirty women selling filthy old boots and shoes. Most of the footwear was distorted and hard, full of holes and almost impossible to get your foot into. I would have preferred to go barefoot.

In contrast to that ragged sight were the pictures in the National Gallery in Trafalgar Square. There were a great many just then on display by Mr. Turner. Some of the Turners I liked very much, but others were too Turneresque and, not being artistic, I fell into the vulgar thought of admiring his worst. One of the very prettiest was *The Fighting Tamerlaïne being Towed to her Last Berth*. In that one, unlike others, one could really distinguish where the water ended and sky began. I tried to take in as much of London's art as possible, perhaps hoping for some osmosis of talent to occur. I saw and admired Raphael's original cartoons at the South Kensington Museum, immense pictures so well known as engravings that it was doubly interesting to see the originals.

On a sort of pilgrimage one afternoon when I had finished early in the laboratory, not long after my visit to the National Gallery, I visited the Coal Exchange on Lower Thames Street, with the organized riot of Billingsgate market on the opposite side. Naturally, it had been opened by Prince Albert. The building was in the shape of a rotunda with three distinct galleries, each sixty feet in diameter and crowned by a dome. The floor consisted of 4,000 pieces of inlaid wood, and represented the face of a mariner compass. In the centre of the compass was the City coat of arms, and the dagger blade in the arms. A beadle was explaining to a gentleman, no doubt for the millionth time, that it was made from a piece of a mulberry tree planted by Peter the Great when he worked as a shipwright in the Deptford dockyards. The walls of the interior were decorated with views of the Wallsend, Percy, and other celebrated collieries, as well as some of the principal ports from whence coal was shipped. Inside the dome were paintings of specimens of the flowers and fossil plants found in the coal measures, and I made some small sketches, and noticed another young man doing the same, just as I had seen art students doing in the National Gallery. On the galleries of the exchange there were a few cases containing specimens of coral and fossil plants found in different parts of the world. A plaque on the wall announced that, in excavating for the foundation of the present building, the remains of an old Roman bath were brought to light, which had now been enclosed, and could be seen upon application to one of the beadles, which pleasure I left for another day.

All too soon the timetable of lessons and the twice-daily scurry along any one of a selection of routes between Halsey and Jermyn

Streets, became lock-stepped. I could either go along Pall Mall or through the park, then along Piccadilly to the plain brick church of St. James where the poet William Blake, certainly a man who could not be called down to earth, was baptized. Or I could go under the Admiralty Arch and straight up to the school doors. I wrote to Anna saying things had now got into such regular rhythm that I might almost write the news for the next week a week in advance. My little weekend trips out became all the dearer for their adding spice to my plain workaday puddings. The Geological Society held regular meetings, and I attended as many as would allow. The rooms there were all hung round with huge maps of newly explored parts of the world, and it seemed another map went up every time I called in. I recall Lord Houghton giving a lecture on the Suez Canal, which had lately been in his charge. A steamer which had been sent along the canal to clear the way for the Empress Eugénie, the wife of Napoleon III, got so stuck so as to prevent any passage. Houghton, as viceroy, was awakened with the intelligence late at night and immediately went with three hundred men and managed by six in the morning, two hours before the Empress was due to pass through, to get her off. He said that had he not been able to pull her off he should certainly have blown her up.

Winter came on in London, not as it did in Montreal with a change of bedding, a thick blanket of snow, but simply by becoming miserable, weepy, and overcast, half-frozen puddles in the street and the ashen leaves nearly all off the trees. I don't think one can truly say there is a winter in England at all, only an unnecessarily protracted autumn and spring. It was altogether in keeping with the season that one of its highlights in mid-November was the Peabody funeral. Mr. Peabody, an American lifelong bachelor of considerable wealth, settled in London and climbed up among its first rank. He was a rare bird, rare even among his species, a man who had built up a great wealth in his time by fair means, among them, of course, the railways, and yet had retained a sense of compassion. Mr. Dickens himself had applauded the vast sum the City of London had accepted from Mr. Peabody to erect tenements of affordable rent for the working poor. Later in my life I had occasion to use the facilities of the Yale Museum of Natural Science, also a Peabody bequest. Would that other men of substance, some of whose gilded doorsteps I have crossed, could acquit themselves before judgment day with such a record.

That first Christmas away from home promised to be a flat one, also in need of baking powder. On the day before Christmas, the first of the holidays, I made an excursion downriver to the Tower. It was one of those places scattered throughout England where you are shunted through by a guardian who explains the historical objects. Some of the inscriptions on the walls of the prisons in the Conqueror's Tower were very curious. One, a complicated diagram for casting horoscopes cut into the very stone, was signed by its sculptor, a man put in prison for witchcraft (no doubt he was simply a scientist ahead of his time). He had made it throughout the month of May, three hundred years before my birth.

Christmas Day itself, I visited a Methodist hall in the evening, and observed the flat uniformity of the congregation. The speaker had an uncanny resemblance to a speaker I had heard in Edinburgh, Mr. Darby; his head was bald in the same place, and his beard of the same cut. My mind drifted on this train of thought to my cousin Ella. Ah, the foolish, impossible dreams of youth, and their lingering power to interfere with our adult decisions.

On Boxing Day, I went south of the river to the Crystal Palace down at Sydenham Park with Mrs. Guest, who had provided a fine Christmas dinner the evening before. I only went to see the crowd and had a very good chance of doing so as there was nearly forty thousand people there, most of them slowly promenading down the Great Walk and then out into the surrounding grounds where questionably accurate life-size replicas of dinosaurs promenaded and copies of great statues stood, as though an assemblage of historical figures had been frozen by some glacial event. Even before we arrived I could hear the great organ in the Centre Transept, the world's largest according to the programme for that day's recital, booming out some tune of Empire into the throng. Despite the wonders within, including the geological displays, I was happier in the open air, off to the side of the throng rather than in amongst it. Observation from a distance has always been my preferred vantage point.

As the New Year progressed, news came from home that Mother and Father would be coming over in the Spring, on the earliest boat the ice would allow. Father had arranged a series of talks and visits, including one with his old mentor Sir Charles Lyell, but I suspect some of the reason for the visit was to check up on my health. While Father normally saw to my well-being above the neck, and Mother coddled my remaining parts, both were no doubt residually concerned. (I realize as I write this that Father probably had "spies" among my professors, and was well informed as to my state, mental and physical.) Over the weeks remaining before his arrival Father and I corresponded vigorously, and he willingly took up the role of consulting tutor as my studies went deeper. In between his lines of writing I felt the pressure, already, to decide on my future involvement with the natural sciences. Even then, the magnetic influence of the west, of the newly conjoined regions of Canada, extended that year by the sale of Rupert's Land from the Hudson's Company to the Confederation, was upon me. It was as though the Pacific were a lodestone, and I a small magnet inclined towards it.

Spring came earlier to England than to Montreal, although late March 1870 had a surprise in store. It was snowing a little when I started out for Covent Garden in search of a platinum crucible for laboratory work. By the time I got to the Underground at Moorgate Station it was coming down in small snowballs, sticking to me all over and everyone was running into me — as usual — with snowy umbrellas. The snow lasted a day, and I felt briefly at home, but then England reasserted itself. I saluted the new season a week later with a visit to Kew Gardens with a fellow student, Mr. Fisson. We had intended to wait for a fine day to make the trip, but the sky was constantly encumbered with great cold clouds. I remarked to Fisson, as we moved beneath the rain, as we had every day for a month, that I would a hundred times sooner live in any part of Canada than here. The English climate did not agree with me (as opposed to the Scottish, where being under my ancestral meteorology suited me better). He concurred, knowing nothing of Canada, but he reminded me of the cultural opportunities so near at hand, which was true. Throughout the year we had watched the new Albert Hall of Arts and Sciences as it rose, towering above the neighbouring houses. It had been built by shareholders, each getting according to his investment a number of seats, and constructed on the most scientific principles with regard to sound. It was due to be opened that summer in coincidence with the International Exhibition.

To get to Kew Gardens we had to pass beside Kew Green, and there were hundreds and hundreds of people enjoying themselves in a rougher way than was allowed in the gardens themselves. They were waltzing to cracked fiddles and wheezy accordions, playing at Kiss in the Ring, eating periwinkles, shrimps, and oranges ad lib. The gardens themselves allowed only propriety and order, not even smoking being permitted. The palm house was magnificent though Fisson, being rather corpulent, nearly melted when I insisted we go up the winding stairs to the gallery. I especially admired the bamboos, their foliage so light and graceful. On the boat in the way back to London, we observed the swans setting themselves to sleep on the mud banks which the receding tide had left. Fourteen years' transportation, according to Frisson, a native Londoner, was the punishment if one should injure the precious birds, more years no doubt than an equal injury to a boot black.

I am not one to relate my dreams; dreams are without plot or logic, and in them anything can happen. Therefore as story they hold no tension or anticipation of what might happen next for the listener, and are boring. However I will intrude here to say that on returning from Kew, I slept soundly and dreamed, to my surprise, I was in Murray Bay again. As I was looking around with a dreamer's painterly eye I said to myself, "Well, I never expected it, but since I am here I will take the opportunity of going back to that favoured hill where by climbing a couple of spruce trees one gets such a splendid view." And I did just that. On waking, the pull to return to Canada was strong, like a tugging arm, but it was no doubt merely nostalgia for the nimbleness with which I could ascend a tree trunk in a dream.

It was not long after this dream that London and the rest of the country, and then readers around the world, learnt in the daily headlines that Mr. Charles Dickens had died, on June 9th, shortly after six in the evening, after a day of unconscious struggle. He had apparently written at his desk the day before, working on the next number, the sixth, of *The Mystery of Edwin Drood*, the first number of which had come out in April and which I had seen in the book-store windows in its habitual green cover. The Queen expressed her sorrow in a telegram from Balmoral, and the *Times* called the next day for a burial at Westminster Abbey, which event took place within a few days. Mr. Dickens was fifty-eight years of age, and he had been a constant in my life and his wonderful works have remained so. He came as close as Niagara Falls on the United States side in the late winter of 1868, just two years previous, while I was in Montreal at my studies. Ill health and equally ill weather had forced the cancellation of his appearances on Canadian soil.

Then, with my first set of exams over, and the rather mediocre results in my hand to show them, Mother and Father, after stops in Londonderry and Liverpool, arrived, and Canada had come to me, with the last of the snow only just gone from its shoulders. Father brought news from home barely a month old, delivered face to face, and I drank it up. As usual it seemed that whenever a fellow left home all the people there immediately died, got married, were born, and so on as if they were afraid to do so until you left.

Father also related the fate of the surveyors, kindred spirits to us geologists, who had gone out west that summer to Red River (even as I was leaving for London), there to lay down the guidelines of future settlement. When the crews crossed into the lands the Métis considered theirs, there was confrontation and the somewhat exciting stages of rebellion ensued, with a governor's forces turned back by the rebels. The rebel leader of the Métis, Mr. Louis Riel, then declared unilateral governance, after the murder of a Canadian prisoner taken when the settlers rose up against the Métis at Upper Fort Garry. The government, Father said, was in the process of raising a force to quell the high spirits of both sides, and I urged Father to persuade fifteen-year-old William to join the Red River expedition, as it would be a fine way to spend his summer holidays and he would see so much that is worth seeing out in the west. Mother hushed me right away, and Father's eyes bespoke a need for a change of subject.

While in London Father, like Mr. Carroll's White Rabbit, made his rounds. There were presentations at the Royal Society and such, a joint visit to the House of Lords where, after being ushered from usher to usher, we spoke with Lord Grenville, and the next day an afternoon playing croquet in the garden of fellow Scot Alexander Macmillan, the great publisher whose edition of *Alice's Adventure's in Wonderland* I had read, and which I commented on to him as we played the game with mallets instead of pink flamingos. In betwixt studies and sorties I sorted the large chest of fossils Father had brought over to illustrate his talks. I fear collecting, sorting, and labelling fossils may be a Dawson family trait, certainly I have always had a flair for taxonomy, and Father being far busier than I, I was glad of the chore, and of handling those ghostly impressions of earlier Nova Scotians.

Father and Mother left for Scotland ahead of me, and the moment the second set of exams were complete, and my fears as to their results dispelled by the prospect of a Scottish summer, I joined them in Burntisland, across the Firth. There, I was reunited with my dear cousins, and in particular, with Ella, who, to my evident joy (Mother commented in a letter on my mood to Anna, who of course relayed the comment to me) stayed with us, and to whom I was supposed to give lessons in drawing from nature, not my strongest subject at the School. I seemed as a young man to be improving backwards in my artistic talents, but it was a necessary skill in my career. As in previous years, we boated every chance we got. Once Ella, myself, and cousin Marie went for a row as far as a place called Starley Burn, and then rowed back at great leisure, singing away, the water as calm as a plate. There were several other boatloads floating at about half a mile apart, and when one began a song the rest would join in and you could hear them quite clearly across the water. It was a scene Mr. Carroll would have been happy to be a part of, and I like to think that it fixed itself as deep in Ella's memory as it did in mine.

Vacations run on an accelerated clock, always over before they should be, and soon Father left for Liverpool to catch the *Prussian*, and a fortnight later Mother went across on the *Nestorian*. I travelled on into historical Scotland in early September, the excursions and sights being well set near the top of the list all travellers make, sights familiar to the rest of my family but not yet to me. The steamer *Rob Roy* carried me the length of Loch Lomond, into the famous sightseeing region of Scott's poem, *Lady of the Lake*, the only two lines of which I can remember being "*Crags, knolls, and mounds, confusedly hurl'd, The fragments of an earlier world.*" Touring Scotland demanded a visit to Stirling Castle, where I thought the new Wallace monument very handsome but rather clumsy. It rained as I stood on the castle battlements on Ladies' View. There, cut into the stone, were the initials of two queens, Marie, who had etched M.R. 1566, and three centuries later, but close by, her majesty had written V.R. 1840. Somehow, those four initials cast a greater sense of the past for me than much else of a grander nature I saw in the years I was in London. Two uncommon young women had paused in their prominent lives to, as any common child might, leave a mark that would survive them. It was as though they were putting their signatures to history itself. As Victoria herself had done directly after signing the stone, I returned to London. There I took up my second year at the School of Mines.

As a student, I was happier in the doing rather than the absorbing; more occupied in the metallurgical laboratory under old Percy's tutelage than hard seated in the library. The laboratory was decidedly manual work but I liked it especially as it indulged to the full the taste I always possessed for melting lead, gold, silver (which we harvested from the change in our pockets, and later sold in bulk form to regain our loses), copper (my favourite), and other metals. Lighting your own furnace of a morning, stoking it all day, breaking up coke to a suitable size, and shovelling it in wearing blue spectacles to preserve the eyes, this was labour I enjoyed.

Emerging from the depths of the laboratory at weekends, I would head out in search of wide open spaces to clear my brain. The larger churches served well in inclement weather, although the Dean at Westminster, where, if I was early enough, I would manage once and a while to get a place inside the rails, was a platitudinous old fellow who spoke loud but not very distinctly. In fact his words seemed to echo in his mouth before they got out. I preferred St. Paul's, despite the trade winds that had set up within the vast chamber, and I rarely escaped there without a sniffle coming on.

The grandest of places for expanded thought, however, remained the Crystal Palace. I often went up the great tower, where the water tank for the fountains is placed, and which afforded a pigeon's eye view of the park. More often than not all sorts of amusements were going on in the grounds. One rather curious contrivance was a sort of circular velocipede. A ring of iron rails had been laid down, and on it ran a circular carriage, composed of numerous segments, each of which had a pair of driving wheels. The people paid their pence and then mounted up, and at a given signal a man standing in the middle began to play an organ, and everybody commenced working at their treadles, so that in a short time the carriage was going round at great speed.

By way of further relief from the heat of the laboratory, and in preparation for the mineralogy examination, set for the last day of March and which I was afraid of, there being such a terrible mass of minerals to learn up and as much pure memory required, I spent hours with some of the other fellows in the British Museum. We arrived by ten o'clock to digest their splendid collection which occupied four long rooms. They were arranged chemically, so to find the ores of any metal necessitated looking in perhaps a dozen different cases, forcing lots of walking, and the others were kind enough to perform some advance searching for me, which I commented was "gneiss" of them.

These intense studies were interrupted with a visit on a Saturday evening by Mr. D.W. Kemp. My cousin Ella had married Mr. Kemp a little while previous, and he had been called quite unexpectedly up to London from Edinburgh on business, so he had come to call on his cousin-in-law. Mrs. Guest, who had come to expect the unexpected in relation to my relatives, gave us the front room and after a hasty tea we arranged to meet at Farrington Street station at ten the next morning. I must confess here to both a liking of Mr. Kemp and a lingering adolescent jealousy at the fact of his marriage, or rather to whom he was married. Ella, as with Anna, is a steadfast confidant, a soul to whom a deeper layer of thought can be conveyed, and such converse produces a bond.

On the very first day of April, thinking I was entitled to some dissipation after the mineralogy exam, I started at the early hours for Mortlake to see the Oxford and Cambridge boat race. I thought I would be there at the finish and I planned my route accordingly. A boat had not sunk for a dozen years or thereabouts, and I was betting both would make it to the end. At Mortlake, though it was still early, the place was alive with people passing towards the river on foot and in carriages. The banks were densely covered with the throng, but I managed to get onto a barge on which a great many were carried along the course. The race depended on the tide, so the starting time was always slightly uncertain.

There was a bend just opposite where I was stationed, so between watching the crowd and listening to the music the time passed quickly enough. After half an hour, there was a murmuring sound heard down the river which became louder and louder till the boats appeared and the sound became a regular roar. Both crews went past in beautiful style with Cambridge ahead, and Oxford appeared to be in not quite such good form as the other boat, throwing up the water a little with their oars, and so Cambridge won by about two boat lengths. The instant the boats were past, hundreds of skiffs shot out from the banks and among the barges, and the water was covered with them bobbing about in the swell raised by the umpire's steamboat and the team steamers. As all these were covered with flags and bearing the dark and light blue, it was a very pretty sight.

The days of the other examinations came and went close on the heels of Easter, another of the holy days I spent in London in the Jermyn Street library, which remained open whenever exams were imminent. I was glad of the time alone and the need to leave my nose in the books; study helped to reduce the length of the do-nothing holidays, when the others returned home to their families. The solemnity of the library contrasted with the uproar abroad in the streets, brought on by the match-tax which Mr. Robert Lowe, Gladstone's Chancellor of the Exchequer, had attempted to bring in. It created quite a stir. Everyone thought it strange and foolish to tax such useful articles as matches so highly, the tax, at a half-penny a box, amounting to one hundred and fifty per cent on their value. All the match manufacturers, who were centred in the East End, were very indignant, and gave their employees, almost all of them women, a day off to allow them to get up a demonstration. They collected in a great crowd near the Houses of Parliament. Some of them were noisy and uproarious and were arrested in Trafalgar Square, and on the Embankment. All the comic papers of course made great fun of Mr. Lowe and his match-box budget, and finally the match tax was snuffed.

By the first week of July the results of the year for 1870–71 were put up, and I was very agreeably surprised by my standings when I went in, receiving congratulations on all sides. I had placed first in Mechanical Drawing, Paleontology, which I had feared even getting through, Mineralogy, and Geology. The latter position – I was one mark short of a hundred and the next man got ninety-eight – entitled me to the first Director's medal, which I had no idea was dependent on the second year's work. The medal has Sir R. Murchison's head on one side and a trophy of fossils and hammers on the other, the whole thing being surrounded by a wreath of graptolites, the tentacles of a coral creature particular to the Silurian age, the period Murchison himself had first unearthed in Wales. Mr. Murchison was at that time the victim of a paralytic affliction, and would be dead before I left the School, so receiving an honour vouchsafed with his name was poignant. With his medal came a twenty-five pound prize of books, the books to be chosen as one liked as long as they were scientific. As I had the greatest number of marks for the year I also came into a scholarship granted by the Prince of Wales, as Duke of Cornwall, worth sixty pounds, divided between two years, dependent on regular attendance and passing all upcoming exams with credit.

With these results, and a new hat size, I set off north to take up membership with a survey team attached to the British Geological Society and then at work in the Lake District. Mr. Ward, a man I developed a fine respect for and who taught me much, was the team leader. The Lake District boasted an English prettiness not found in Canada, where as I have said the spectacu-lar presides. The valleys of the District, running up among the mountains as they turn and bend, offer hundreds of pictures for the brush or the shutter. One was constantly coming upon artists on the roadside, or perched on the top of rocks like a breed of sheep. One day we were climbing the stony bed of a brook in a gully, overshadowed by trees, enduring a gentle rain that reminded me of the Grand Russian at Murray Bay. Turning the corner we saw an indefatigable artist using a rock for a table and patiently painting away in front of a waterfall, under the shelter of a ponderous sheet of gingham.

These fleets of valleys all had fields and farms traversed by narrow winding lanes embowered in trees and lined by great bushy hedges. The fells consisted of swampy bogs full of wiry grass and little pools. While up there, I seldom met any living thing but sheep, dumbly unaware of the beauty about them. I examined the course of a trap dyke one day near Borrowdale and saw the famous Plumhays Mine, or rather the place where it had been, as the site now consisted of several heaps of rubbish cast on a hill slope. A grove of trees said to be the oldest in Britain stood nearby. Seathwaite, near the mine, was and no doubt still is, said to be the wettest place in Britain. Considering the number of times I paused to ring out my hat I had no trouble believing it.

One beautiful moment, which I am certain would take first prize in any photographic contest, came the day I climbed up a brook called unpoetically Sour Milk Gill, into the coombe in which it takes its rise, walled in on every side by an amphitheatre of mountains with long slopes of debris at their feet. At the bottom of the coombe a stream wound through, and in every pool trout were rushing to get under stones as they caught sight of me. Climbing the sides of the coombe put us at the summit of a high ridge, two and a half thousand feet above the shining Solway Firth, and the Scottish Hills on its far shore forming the very horizon. Westward in the long valley lay Buttermere and Crummock Water, shining like scissors. The sun was low, colouring the mountains full of deep indigo shadows and purple highlights. One might have looked all day.

All too soon my summer survey was over, and I left Mr. Ward, with whom a friendship had been forged, for the company of my Scottish cousins the Bells, spending a few days first in Edinburgh. It was Walter Scott's Centenary, and the hotels were lit up on Princes Street which was perfectly packed with country people and flags. Grandpapa had taught me several of Scott's poems by heart when I visited in Pictou, and I saw some I recognized posted in windows and heard them recited on street corners. It was a rougher crowd in Edinburgh that year than I was used to, and several times, on my way to a bookstore or to the offices of the Geological Section of the British Association to say hello, I was taken in arm by some merry fellow and advanced up the street. Resistance, particularly in my case, was futile, and besides the ride cost nothing. On the Saturday, the Geological Section of the British Association adjourned to Arthur's Seat to hear a Professor Greekie explain the structure, in the midst of a voice-stealing gale, and I was among the windswept herd. When we retreated the grass was slippery, and coming down many surprised themselves with their own velocity.

I was able to purloin a few days from the calendar to spend time on the beloved Forth of Firth with my Bell cousins before returning to the School of Mines. The urgency of study was never further from me as when I was there, and the days took as long as they needed to unfold, as on the day Ella and Louise and I went for a walk along the seashore till we came to a castle, an ivy clad young ruin, if there can be such a thing. As the sun slid down the latter half of its arc we borrowed an old boat from the castle dock and pointed it east, out to sea. Rowing is a singular physical skill, performed seated and accomplished with grace as much as force, which I enjoyed and as we bugged our way forward I shouted out some lines of Scott's from *Lady of the Lake*. "His noble hand had grasped an oar: Yet with main strength his strokes he drew, And o'er the lake the shallop flew."

———

AS THE TRAIN pulled into London, the October chills had seized the city, and I was glad to be back before Mrs. Guest's fireplace, there to catch up with the city's news, and that of young Lyell and my fellow laboratory trolls. My final year at the School lay before me, and the pressure of study, of not sliding down the slippery grass, and of not tarnishing my medals, kept me tied to a desk. The hours dragged by and I was quite looking forward to Christmas, as a time when I might be able to do a little reading as well as go about a little in the city. Anna had again indicated which segments of the Bible I should read this year, and I soon got through the Acts, quickly tired of the New Testament, and went back to the Old for a change.

Late in November we read that the Prince of Wales was pre-vented from paying a visit to some Maharajah by a feverish attack, and it was the talk of the classroom. It soon appeared that the malady was typhoid. The illness progressed so quickly that within days the Queen and Princess Alice hurried to Sandringham Palace where he lay. A slight rally was followed by so serious a relapse that for some days the family despaired of the Prince's life. While he was in this critical state bulletins were issued three or four times a day. They were posted everywhere, in many shop windows, at the police stations, telegraph offices, often at the public houses, and little crowds were constantly collecting round them. At Marlborough House when news was first posted, quite large crowds gathered to wait for its arrival and then somebody read it out. Everybody was hourly expecting to hear of his death, and they said so much popular sympathy had hardly been known before, and all classes seemed to share in it. Under the skillful treatment of Sir William Jenner and others, however, the crisis was surmounted by mid-December, and by Christmas Day the danger was regarded as past.

As in the year before, it was Anna's letters in the New Year that were an antidote to the homesickness of missing Christmas with the family, and I wrote and told her that her letters were the next best thing. There was much noise and talk about Spiritualism and psychic forces at that time in London, and a certain Mr. Crooks had entered into an investigation of them which I was following, and of which I informed Anna, a confirmed sceptic. He latterly came to the conclusion that there was something in it, and in fact became a convert and wrote of his experiences in the *Quarterly*

Journal of Science. Of course everyone laughed at him, and Dr. Carpenter from the School of Mines took it upon himself to offer a more complete refutation in the next *Quarterly Review.* Dr. Carpenter was very personal about Mr. Crooks, writing without signature, though everyone knew he was the author. His article had the reverse effect he intended, advancing Crooks' case. Crooks rebutted the Doctor with a little pamphlet which was bound up in the subsequent *Journal of Science,* in which he handled Dr. Carpenter quite unmercifully. No doubt the psychic forces themselves profited from the whole affair as well. Naturally, I mentioned none of this when I dined at the invitation of Mrs. Carpenter shortly after.

From time to time Montrealers from our circle would arrive in town, and Mrs. and Miss Phillips did so in mid-January, taking lodgings at No. 5 Halsey Street, from whence they walked over for tea. I found Miss P. to be a very pleasant sort of person, active, tall, thin, and talkative, while Mrs. P. was quite the reverse, not very short, but certainly very stout and slow and extremely short-sighted. But they carried on them the air of home, and that was refreshing. The next arrival on my doorstep was a huge parcel of toffee and cocoa-nut tablets from my Scottish cousin Ella. It was sunshine in my mouth.

London made no effort to refute its reputation for damp, and I began a letter to Anna by mentioning the astonishing fact that there had been *two* consecutive days without rain, and that the pavement was actually slightly dry in places! One evening when the rain had resumed I attended a meeting of the Royal Microscopical Society, through a fellow student, Parker, whose father was the president. At the soiree there were no ladies and no refreshments, or if there were they too were microscopical. The Society had decided to save money, and Parker said that if ladies and refreshments were introduced it would cost forty pounds more. There were, I must say, some splendid microscopes and all sorts of new dodges and devices.

Gradually, in the laboratory, we worked our way through wet copper and got well on with the dry assays. I was anxious for the labs to end as I was falling behind and needed to work up my reading, although I do remember that Father had sent a set of essays on modern science for Christmas and I was enjoying them. I was prevented from finishing them by the arrival of Mr. Ward from the Lake District at Jermyn Street; he was anxious to look over some volcanic rocks from Wales and compare them with some from Cumberland. We could have gone on late into the night, but Mr. Ward had to return to his lodging. It only reinforced my regret that living as I did in lodgings I could not show hospitality to friends like Ward when they were in town.

The papers of February 14th were filled with grand rejoicing at the recovery of the Prince and the Queen's decision to go in half-state to St. Paul's to offer thanks. Her route was to be decorated and in the evening there would be illuminations. The papers the next day told of the price already being asked for seats at windows along the route, the better ones going for anything from a pound to seven, and one window in St. Paul's churchyard was going for three hundred. The next day was Anna's birthday, so I wrote and told her how the Queen had instructed Londoners one and all to celebrate my sister's twenty-first birthday.

Although I had not yet graduated, my mind refused to avoid thinking of the future and the decision I faced whether to stay in England or return to Canada. Certainly at that time I did not like at all the idea of remaining in London. I hated the climate and saw no chance of finding anything to do there I could enjoy. To defuse my thoughts I considered all this speculation premature, and stuck to my work. Applied mechanics was my *bête noir*, and the Natural History, under Professor Lyell, was mostly concerned with evolutionary theory which was, to use the phrase that was popular at the time, "up a tree." Mining also seemed a most unsatisfactory subject, so large and intangible, and I was at a great disadvantage as I did not know anything about it in a practical way as many of the other men did. Looking back, I see now that I was experiencing the normal long night of doubt that all students feel as the final examinations approach.

On my way to the bank on an omnibus a few days after my career ponderings, I was treated to a ringside seat to the preparations for the Prince's Thanksgiving. Nearly all the shop windows were cleared out with seats to let, and every nook and gateway had tiers of seats built up. From Charing Cross to St. Paul's all the lampposts were painted in blue and gold and a Venetian mast erected beside each for banners. Opposite Temple Bar, the largest stand of all, built to hold seven thousand people and draped with flags and illuminated at night, was as impressive a sight as the great triumphal arch erected at the foot of Ludgate Hill.

I did not venture out on the day of the Thanksgiving itself, when at least four or five million people were estimated to be swarming about in the streets, but a young lady friend of Mrs. Guest's came over the same night for tea, and spoke of it. She had sat with friends in a great crowd near St. Paul's, and a woman died just beside this young miss which caused her to faint several times in succession. With difficulty she got out to a side street to catch her breath. Another woman was so frightened in the crowd that, thinking she could not herself escape, she threw her baby to some people and implored them to save it. As it was being passed along from one to another the baby fell and was killed. Altogether about fifty accidents were reported in the paper, although only five or six were immediately fatal. Thus was celebrated the recovery of the Prince of Wales.

—

WITH SPRING IN THE AIR at the end of March, Nature took a step back and as I looked wistfully out of the laboratory window, where I was assaying silver, it began to snow heavily. Two inches came down and stayed on the ground, and it was quite doleful to see the young leaves on all the trees crusted over and to hear that much fruit would be lost in the South. There was talk of cancelling the boat race, but it went ahead, with Cambridge winning again. I did not go to the regatta that year, but the Underground was packed to bursting on the day itself. When it snowed again the next day I was transported back to Montreal, where the city would still be in its cloak of white. I was aware through Anna's letters that the proposed park on the mountain behind McGill was finally to become a reality, and that Mr. Olmstead of New York's grand Central Park was to be its designer, and I imagined how I would go about the task myself, so that its winter face would be attractive. (I happened to know that Mr. Olmstead would not face too large a task when it came to timber cutting on the mountain, as several delinquent families whose names I shall not mention had over the years helped themselves to firewood, a shady fact that the park's surveyors had turned up.)

Easter came and went, and I had to decline a fine offer from Mr. Ward to spend the holidays with them at Keswick in the Lake District. I knew I could not go the moment he asked, as time was too short and the distance too great, two reasons I hoped would soon evaporate. My suppressed appetite for exploration was revived, however, despite exams on the near horizon, by attendance with Dr. Bigsby at a very good meeting of the Geographical Society. The proceedings began with a report on Dr. Livingstone, saying nothing very definite as to either his safety or position. The journalist Stanley was still in search of him. The rest of the meeting was devoted to the Society's encouragement of the Government to fit out another polar expedition, using a route previously declined by the Admiralty that would take a team as far up Smith Sound as possible. They would spend the winter there, and in the Spring set out by dog sledges to the north of Greenland for the pole itself. Everyone was of the opinion at the meeting (despite Dr. Carpenter, who treated us to one of his long harangues and sat down among ardent signs of dissatisfaction) that no other nation should be allowed to carry off the prize of first to the pole, and we had to show them how to win. (The expedition, I must report, despite a great deal more talk, never did set out, and an American attempt the following year met with disaster.)

As the Mining exams came rushing up, I had a brief unexpected visitor for just two days, in the shape of Mr. Harrington, an employee of the Geological Survey in Canada and a graduate of McGill well known to Father. He had brought with him some maple syrup on Anna's instruction, and I rationed myself on it in the weeks thereafter until the very last drop. It tasted of summer on the St. Lawrence. Anna and I were then in the midst of a transatlantic discussion on the subject of "riches" as there was talk of my going to work for the Geological Survey of Britain. She had mentioned in a letter that she thought "little money" was preferable to hard grinding toil for riches, to which I replied that while there was some degree of hard grinding toil involved in the life of a geologist – for example, going up and down mountains on a hot day – in the matter of riches I didn't see the applicability to the Survey. One might find gold or coal, but one's job was to report on it, not capitalize on it. That was in the nature of other men. The point was moot anyway, as any geology then left in Britain was of so minute a character and of such local interest. More importantly, I wanted to be back in Canada. There was plenty of geology still to be done there.

To clear my head of mining techniques and mineral classifications I took a walk all around Battersea Park, and saw several street preachings going on. The first man was a temperance lecturer with a pretty large audience. He was relating his experiences and telling funny stories. Next there was a great discussion going on between a man who called himself a "Humanitarian" and another man of more orthodox opinions. Then there was a man in a little pulpit with some text in very large letters painted on the front, discussing away at the top of his voice to a very small and scattered audience. I had seen this man often before, and he was always in a great perspiration, without a hat, and he had hardly any front teeth. They had no doubt been blown away in moments of special vehemence.

Counting down to the forge of examination, I placed my face in the books and left it there, coming up for relief for brief moments; lunch at the Huxleys' one Sunday followed by a trip to the new Albert Hall to hear the organ play sacred music; a visit to a paper-making exhibition where a man sat at a machine composing type for the newspapers; his hands moved with the greatest casual dexterity I have ever witnessed; to a Methodist church to hear a stupid sermon from a loud vulgar man who dropped all his H's; to Westminster Abbey to hear Dean Stanley, for once, deliver a good speech – I walked around the Cloisters afterwards where they were repairing the masonry; and to the College of Surgeons for an hour or so a day to get permeated with bones so that I might recognize any that might be presented in the Natural History exam. I had now fallen into a despair with regard to my subjects, thrown so far behind by my emphasis on laboratory work, and yet I was not half as anxious about things as they all seemed at home. It seemed impossible that I would pass with any credit. Then, at the end of June, on two successive Saturdays, the examination room at Jermyn Street filled with silence as I dipped my pen and scratched away at the testing papers.

As it turned out, all my gloomy anticipations of the exams were groundless and in early July I heard that I had got through in all I had intended – even the dreaded Applied Mechanics. Also, I blush to admit, I took the Forbes Medal in Natural History, which Professor Huxley said I deserved, and would have had the medal in Mining as well but there were regulations disallowing a student from having more than one. As a bonus to all this most welcome news, I had found employment in Canada to begin as soon as I could return there. A Mr. Giles of the Albion Mines Company, on a visit to the school, had contracted me to assay some deposits of iron ore near Pictou, an ideal location to begin my life of work. The contract was for a few weeks only, to be followed by a report. I was due

to meet Mr. Giles in Liverpool (England) and accompany him to
Pictou to seek out a suitable site for a smelting works. Mr. Giles
had agreed to pay my sea ticket and a fee of twenty pounds and,
as I told Father in my last letter to him from London, it seemed
better not to throw away the chance to "work my passage."

In the time remaining before I returned to Canada – I was going
home! – I decided to pack up my London affairs as swiftly as possible and take a week out of the city to visit some iron works in the
Middlesborough area to see how the ore was worked and smelted.
The packing was awfully hard work, every day something new
turned up, as well as business I had in the City and all over London,
but at last I arranged to have picked up and booked for passage to
Canada four boxes as cargo on the *S.S. Emperor*, sailing from Liverpool
on July 18th. The baggage would go on to Montreal while I remained
in Nova Scotia. One box contained the cursed chair designed for my
posture that I had hardly dented, another my books and two boxes
of what I called my Philosophical Apparatus, the tools of my trade.
On the final day in London I took a train out to Notting Hill on the
Hammersmith line and there met an old school friend of Anna's,
Nina, who was in town. We had tea together and she showed me a
very recent portrait photograph of my sister that Anna had given
her for me to see. She had grown more lovely, and the slight smile in
the photograph seemed to me to say "See you soon."

On the train going up North – dear Mrs. Guest had seen me
off at the station, with promises from me to return again and again
– I met, by chance alone, another student called Charleton from
the School who lived in Middlesborough, in fact the gentleman who
had taken the Mining Medal, and we toured together, visiting the
Upper Leatham mine and studying the ore that cropped out along
a hill thick with fossils.

Middlesborough was in effect a great big workshop for me, the
place where the iron ore from the Cleveland district met the coal
from Newcastle and several hundred blast-furnaces and rolling mills
manufactured iron, and the sky at night was quite lurid with the

glare as though great conflagrations and battles were taking place in all directions. From the bright night sky of the Midlands I took a nine o'clock train to the bustling port of Liverpool and met Mr. Giles, and together we boarded the *Caspian*, sailing towards Halifax on July 16th.

I arrived back in Canada on July 26th, and from the dock at Halifax, where a postal order from Father was waiting with some set-up money for Pictou, I sent the following message through the wires of the Montreal Telegraph Company:

"Arrived this morning fine passage have your note all well"

The job for Mr. Giles was completed in a matter of weeks, and so I returned to Montreal and sat once again at the foot of Mont Royal, wondering what the world had next in store for me. The aspirations of a Father for a son, particularly the eldest son, the one who has marinated in the parental thoughts the longest, often cleave close to the path the Father himself has taken. I witnessed this phenomenon time and again in my friends, obvious examples being readily to hand in the Huxleys in London, and in Montreal in O'Hara's stumble away from medicine into banking. Father himself had been raised in Grandpapa's amateur enthusiasm for education and natural science, and I had long known in my bones that in the science of wonder was where I belonged. It fitted me. What I should be was settled in my youth, but where I would perform it was not so easily assigned.

The School of Mines had made plain its wish that I become a teacher, that I turn and face the class, so to speak, but I was no convert to London. The East had granted me the knowledge, but I dearly wished to practice it in the West, and Sir William Logan's Geological Survey, headquartered in Montreal was, I sincerely believed, my true ticket. If the chance came not at the first knock, I would knock again, firmly. Father knew of my desires, but he had faith in the bird in the hand, in the decided over the possible.

Meanwhile, I had perforce to work, to pay my way in the world, and so the day after the last day of Christmas, a Sunday, I left Montreal for Quebec to take up my position as a lecturer at Morrin College, another educational institution founded by a Scot, a Scot who had also been Quebec's first elected mayor. The College had, under Father's guidance, become affiliated with McGill and it was not unusual for men from there to deliver a lecture series to the young women of the college and the town's folk. I arrived by train at Point Levis almost on time and took the steamer *Arctic* comfortably across the river. There was a thin skin of ice on the St. Lawrence which would have frozen more so but for the steamers continuing to cut it up. I had some little difficulty in finding the quarters my superior Dr. Cook had arranged, eventually discovering the lodging house was on rue Henchy, not Hendry, as I had written down. It was connected with the Henchy Hotel, and sat opposite St. Andrew's church, then (and still, I would imagine), the oldest Presbyterian church in Canada. The house, when I reached it, was not at all comfortable, as even the scrappy façade foretold, and it was noisy and crowded – thereby meeting none of my essential needs. The drawing room, which would have been so pleasant to write in, turned out to be both the only parlour and the smoking room, liable to constant interruptions. My bedroom was the last one unoccupied, small and warmed by an unglassed space over the door to the hall, not having a stove or any preparation for one. The only idea of bedroom lights was a tallow candle. The table, the most important item in any room for me, was very good but rough. I determined to find some other accommodation, not least for the reason that I could not dream of inviting Anna there.

I had hardly arrived when Dr. Cook appeared and carried me off to dinner, on the heels of which Mr. Weir asked me to take tea and we went to St. Andrew's; it was so old for a Canadian church that I fancy I heard a choir leaking up from the vault. Weir, another McGill alumni who had taken advantage of the affiliation with Morrin College, taught there and had a class of young ladies on his own account. The McGill connection was a bell that would ring again and again throughout my life, and I doubt if there is any part of the continent I have been to where a McGill alumni did not pop up before the sun set. Weir had been there since the College opened almost a decade earlier, and he told me it had previously been a gaol, a ghostly legacy, he said, which seemed truer and truer the more he stayed. Actually I believe he was enjoying his sentence immensely.

The next night I gave my first lecture, and it passed off moderately well. About fifty tickets were sold and about forty to forty-five appeared. In the weeks to come attendance was rather fluctuating, but that was to be expected. When men are not really students, having a definite aim before them, they do not mind losing a night or two of chemistry. As it was, I read the inaugural lecture rather fast, and got a bit confused towards the end. It was the first time, I realized when I got back to my rough, cold room, that for two hours I had been the locus of attention in a congregation of strangers, wherein I learnt two things. Firstly, that I would never be entirely comfortable standing at the centre of things, preferring myself to be edgy, as it were, and that despite my discomfort I might as well get used to it, if my hopes for myself did indeed go according to plan. But I resolved to strive to keep my public appearances to a minimum.

Fairly soon after arriving I found new rooms, in the pleasant house of one Mrs. Escudore, with a nice sort of people in it, and felt much better. Dr. Cook had initially timetabled the public chemistry lecture series at Morrin for Tuesdays and Fridays at eight in the evening, then switched them to Mondays and Fridays which the populace seemed to prefer. As he told me this on the day of a lecture, I had to get an experiment prepared in a hurry. That night the result of the hurry was that the apparatus went wrong and I nearly ended the hydrogen lecture without any hydrogen to speak of. However, with the help of providence and a bit of Indian rubber tube, I managed to wriggle through. Thus, trusting in my powers of improvisation, I settled in for a Quebec winter, grounded behind the frozen walls. In fact, it was, for Quebec, quite a mild season, and this delayed the formation of the ice bridge across the St. Lawrence, whose progress I noted with some attention. More than once a thaw would result in a horse going through, and the bridge would close till it had hardened again. On the day of a lecture, I always wrote my scheduled texts out twice; this consumed a lot of paper but also happily occupied a great deal of time.

On non-lecturing days I finished my reports on the Nova Scotia iron deposits and maintained the family correspondence. Anna was herself taking lectures that seemed to have no natural break and at the same time found herself bound up in matters of the heart. She had decided to rebuff a suitor, a gentleman she referred to as H in her letters, who had proceeded hastily in his suit, an act that had upset her and she had only just got her mind back to the, as she called it, serenity her faith allowed her. I told her that if a rash youth without sufficient cause proceeds to extremities, he must be ready for any consequence, and that she should judge for herself the liking or not liking of anyone, and if she had even the slightest doubt as to the nature or amount of her affection she should dismiss them. H, in the dumps after his rebuff, had threatened to request banishment to British Columbia from Dr. Selwyn, his boss (and hopefully one day mine) at the Geological Survey. Privately I still had hope for H, who had taken it hard, and I wished for him that, after the initial shock, life would be found not to have lost all its balm. There would be, I wrote to Anna, a next time, never fear.

There are a handful of times in a life when news arrives of a vital nature, news that will outline the course of things to come. I returned to my room from a lecture to find a letter at my door, unopened and forwarded on by Father. The lecture, being the tenth, had put me halfway through the series, and the end of my spell in Quebec was now closer than the beginning. I still coveted a position with the Geological Survey that would transport me across the country into *terra* (relatively) *incognita*. I sat before the rough table with the ominous letter atop my stack of lecture notes and opened the future. An order in Council, I read, had appointed me to the position of Naturalist, Geologist, and Botanist on the British North American Boundary Commission, and my salary was to be two thousand dollars per annum. Father had mentioned this possibility to me, but I had ears only for the Survey, and I had not thought him serious. Now he had surprised me with it. My services, it seemed, were required somewhere other than my own wishes would have taken me.

The letter put me in a chronic state of misery. I now considered any British Columbian appointment lost, and the mere thought of anyone else going to survey that splendid country alongside the Pacific put me in the blues, deeper even than I had been at the worst of my illness, and for ten days I was too cross to write silly, gossipy letters to anyone. During that time, when I scolded even Anna for siding with Father, I had just gone to sleep when a sudden shock awoke me. I thought it might be a small earthquake. I looked at the time and found it just half-past twelve. I wondered at the quantity of light coming in at the window, as the moon was well set. Shortly afterwards, I opened my eyes again and saw a fire must be taking place quite near. I got up and dressed and soon found the courthouse in flames and a great part of the roof already broken in. It turned out there had been an explosion of gas shortly after the beginning of the fire which had rendered it fierce. Very little was saved and the burning of so many documents and registers caused great trouble in legal circles. It was a very cold night, the thermometer being about twenty degrees below zero.

I must say I hoped for a similar fire to somehow destroy my appointment, and sent several lists of specific objections to the people at home which were answered by hopeful, annoying generalities. The Commission was compliant at responding to my more important protestations, but there seemed no way to retreat. Eventually Father sent one of his terse telegrams, "Consider boundary decided," and I knew he had been bothered by my response a great deal. I did not wish to upset him any further with my selfishness. He had done what he considered best, and I hoped it would prove so. I could, I figured, at least put up with the Commission for a year or so, and Father wrote to say that Dr. Selwyn had agreed to hold a place for me at the Survey, and that British Columbia would be my first assignment, and so I was somewhat appeased.

So, caught somewhere between a smile and a frown, I resigned myself to lecturing but another month, and then returning to Montreal where I would have to assemble myself as a travelling man. Though I was only partially westward bound, it could be said (and I did say to myself, many times) that at least I was to assist in the definition of the southern border of the country, of defining the twelve-hundred-mile demarcation between two progressive neighbours who but two generations earlier had fought a war. That was certainly better than tromping around lead mines, or lecturing.

In the weeks remaining I did some pertinent reading, including a very pleasant chatty book on the North-West Territories called *The Great Lone Land*, about an officer named Butler who had been attached in a kind of a way to the Red River Expedition. I also saw some of the sights of Quebec, although on a visit to St. Matthew's Church, which was very pretty, the effect was spoilt by a very twaddly sermon. Dr. Douglas and I journeyed out to Montmorency to see the frozen falls, an equal attraction in winter as in summer, due to the cone of ice that rises up at the base. The cone was said to be very high that winter, but when I saw it for the first time it appeared rather lopsided and leant towards the falls in such a way that one fancied a great piece of the back must soon fall in.

By mid-March I was almost done, and made a final round of visits to the families who had shown me hospitality, the Douglases, the Cassels, the Thompsons, and the Wotherspoons, whose eldest daughter was Nina, Anna's friend, and whose acquaintance I had remade after seeing her that time in London. I found her very jolly, in fact rather too much so, lacking repose. Her brother Frank had come to my lectures, where he had sat on the back bench and sloped off rapidly at the close. Anna, despite my several entreaties, had not been able to visit me, a sign perhaps that in her heart and head she had become busy. After delivering my final lecture on almighty oxygen on a Monday night, I got away on the Tuesday evening, with just a handful of weeks to prepare for the North American Boundary Commission.

THE AGE OF THE LINE

—

THE OFFICIAL CONCERN of the Boundary Commission in the years 1872 to 1874 was the lower, central portion of British North America, where the floor of Canada meets the roof of the United States. The Prairies were familiar to me from books and maps, but now I would come to know their face, or at least a line upon them.

Geographically speaking, British North America sits between the bookends of the 53rd great circle in the east and the 141st in the west, a matter of some eighty-eight degrees of latitude at the 49th parallel. There being forty-four and a half statute miles to the degree at that latitude, it thus requires a line 3,916 miles in length to stretch from the city of St. John's in Newfoundland to Mount St. Elias on the borders of British Columbia. This four thousand mile span is more than twice that of the ocean which separates the said St. John's from the nearest European port. If I can render that mathematical portrait accessible to the imagination, it would take a man walking twenty miles a day two hundred days to traverse British North America, should he wish to do so; a stage coach travelling day and night without ceasing at the rate of ten miles an hour would cover the distance in seventeen days, and were there such a train as crossed the country on an unending rail moving at twenty miles an hour, one would be aboard eight full days, during which time one would see through the window a great work of natural art.

It is the 97th meridian that bisects our northern continent, and the Commission, as I shall refer to it henceforth, had its starting line two meridians east of this bisect in the Lake of the Woods, a plain yet apt description. Within the Lake of the Woods the borders of the United States and Canada meet, at the irregular tip of the state of Minnesota and the ruler-like eastern side of the province of Manitoba. This point is known as the North-West Angle.

On the map, the point where the neighbours meet is a scrappy one, and the culprit for this untidiness is political history. At the conclusion of the American Revolutionary War, at the Treaty of Paris in 1783, there was general, theoretical agreement that the border between the (temporarily) peaceful neighbours was desirous of definition. The area of most potential confusion, it was apparent, would be at the aqueous, western end of the Great Lakes, where the border, as it were, got back on dry land, like a boat coming into shore.

After a considerable number of proposals and counter-proposals, the British ministry suggested that the boundary line from Lake Superior west follow "the usual water communication to Lake of the Woods, thence through the said lake to the most northwestern part thereof, and from thence on a due west course to the river Mississippi." This read well, except for the fact that the Mississippi River does not lie west of the Lake of the Woods; it lies about 140 miles south of it! The negotiators had made the mistake of relying on "Mitchell's Map of North America," published in London in 1775 which confidently showed the Mississippi River being exactly where it was not. Fortunately, the neighbours postponed the solution of this problem by warring again from 1812 to 1814, and when the dust settled yet another treaty was being negotiated and the question of where to peg the boundary revisited. In 1817, a boundary Commission dispatched scientists, surveyors, astronomers, and others representing both governments to the eastern juncture of Nova Scotia and Maine. Their faces to the setting sun, the party inched caterpillar-like across the landscape, over land and lake, until by 1823, with diligence, they were near the North-West Angle, whereupon a fresh set of deliberations broke out. The Commission dispatched another specialized party to find quite where in the Lake of the Woods the Angle was, and hence from there find the exact start of the straight, uncomplicated line, that would run clear along the 49th parallel to the Pacific. In fact, the man whom the Commission asked to locate the North-West Angle was David Thompson, the man the Indians called "He who looks at stars," and with the aid of his son Samuel Thompson he did just this.

Three decades later, in the September of 1872, some two-hundred and fifty astronomers, blacksmiths, cooks, engineers, medics for the work animals and the working humans, naturalists, surveyors, topographers, wheelwrights, and woodworkers, gathered at the small, isolated town of Pembina two miles south of the parallel. When their American counterparts, flanked by the United States cavalry, arrived, the five hundred members of the North American Boundary Commission were united in common cause. Their first task was to corroborate Thompson's work. Assisted by Métis guides and after considerable sodden struggle they found the hole where his pole had rotted away in the interval. The pole was replaced, and a line due south gave them the first land point of the line that, sixty miles farther south, would turn ninety degrees and grow westward for twelve hundred miles, its progress to be marked by posts or indicated by stone monuments.

Two brief months later, the United States party returned to their warm hearths and homes, but a goodly portion of the British and Canadian assembly wintered over at Fort Dufferin, which lies just North of the 49th parallel, the mirror image in a sense of Pembina. While those hardy souls were at their labours in the snow-bound Red River country, I was across the Atlantic in surroundings that could not have allowed for greater contrast, below ground in the laboratory of the School of Mines, or in my rooms at Halsey Street, my face fixed on an open text book. It was not written on

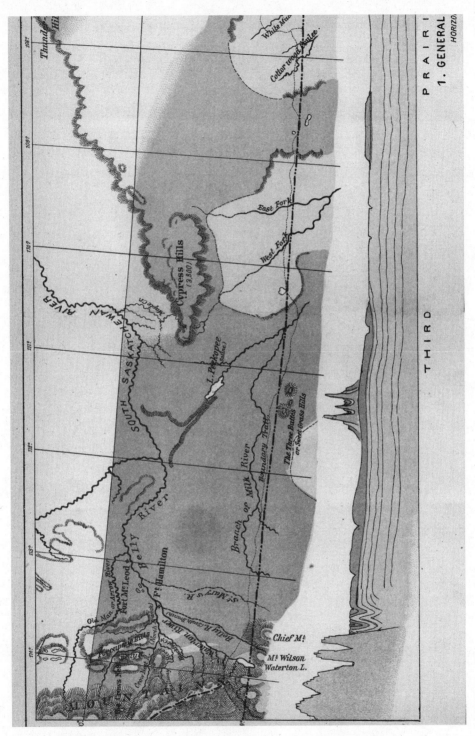

The route taken along the 49th parallel by the Boundary Commission, 1873–74.

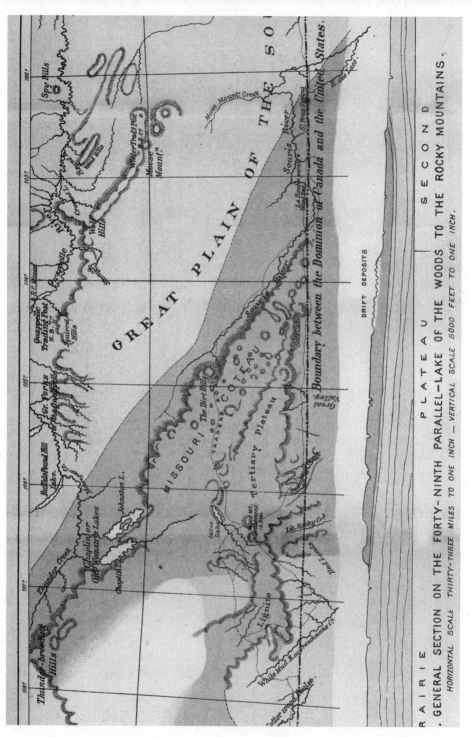

The route taken along the 49th parallel by the Boundary Commission, 1873–74.

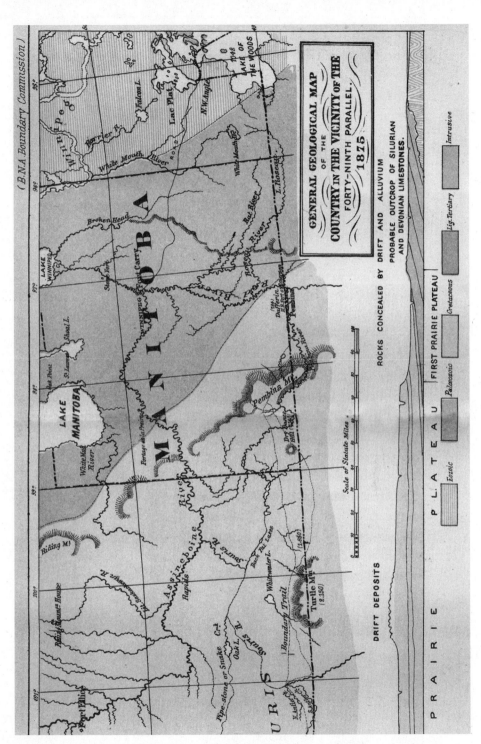

GENERAL GEOLOGICAL MAP
OF THE
COUNTRY IN THE VICINITY OF THE
FORTY-NINTH PARALLEL.
1875

ROCKS CONCEALED BY DRIFT AND ALLUVIUM

PROBABLE OUTCROP OF SILURIAN
AND DEVONIAN LIMESTONES.

DRIFT DEPOSITS

Scale of Statute Miles

PRAIRIE   PLATEAU   FIRST PRAIRIE PLATEAU

Eozoic   Palæozoic   Cretaceous   Lig.-Tertiary   Intrusive

The route taken along the 49th parallel by the Boundary Commission, 1873–74.

any page I studied that within the year I would be standing side by side with those self-same men.

My orders from the Commission were that I was to present myself at Fort Dufferin as soon as springtime passage along the Lake Superior and up the Red River would allow. At the beginning of May 1873, after several intense weeks of equipping myself mentally and physically for the task, I travelled first and with relative ease by train from Montreal to the port of Collingwood on Georgian Bay, where all of the Great Lakes lay before me. (The news agent on the dock had my father's recently published book *The Story of the Earth and Man* for sale, proof of his increasing popularity among those readers who, like him, were unable to accept Mr. Darwin's original theories. Father had built his refutation of Darwin around three fallacious gaps in reasoning, as he called them, that he felt simply could not be reconciled with our Christian understanding of time.)

Though it was mid-May, the ice had not yet released its grip on the shore, and the paddle steamer was delayed in getting away. All day Sunday we had stared at a great deal of ice packed along the southwest shore of Georgian Bay and extending several miles from it. The ice being honeycombed, it did not give much trouble once we were away, at one in the morning, though it was a little dangerous to the paddles. With me as my rail-side companions were a gentleman named Ashe, who would become a firm friend in the months ahead, and a young fellow called King, fellow members of the Commission. The Captain did not judge it wise to try the possibly ice-bound inside passage, so we steamed right out into Lake Huron and made straight for the Sault River, where we could pass through the American Canal into Lake Superior. We caused quite a sensation when we put in at the Sault village on the Canadian side, ours being the first laker boat of the season they had seen. We passed an hour or two there and then steamed across to the counterpart village on the American side and lay in all night to take on coal. I took the time to examine the American Canal, a fine piece of engineering which was in the process of being widened. The notion of a canal on the Canadian side had, typically, flared and died more than once, but the opening of the American passage a generation earlier had permanently snuffed the idea. Two companies of their soldiers were stationed at the fort and we watched them go through a drill, all upright and uniform in motion, as we passed through the canal at six in the morning.

The journey to Thunder Bay was icy and noisy. The ice was of every gradation, from large cakes twenty feet long, solid and blue as little icebergs, with small pieces and slush filling up the water between the icebergs, the whole making a peculiar tinkling noise as it ground together. The Captain had all the oars passed round to stave off the lumps and so we went bumping and grinding along without injury to plates or paddles, but to the obvious discomfort of many of the passengers as evinced by the decimated numbers at table that evening. Finally we pushed and crushed through several miles of half-rotten field ice into Thunder Bay, where we docked at a habitation of some two hundred or so buildings and shanties, and a fine new wharf, on which the inhabitants appeared and celebrated our arrival with immense cheering. There we got rid of a hundred or so travelling men together with overseers, clerks, postmasters, and so on, and an immense quantity of freight which had been loading us down nearly to the rails.

I was glad to see the back of the travelling men. They had been a considerable drawback to the pleasure of the voyage, choking up every part of the boat, even sleeping on top of the luggage at night. They were partly French, partly Scotch, plus some Indians and they were very contented and merry, cultivating the boat with songs now in Gallic, then in French and in each case with a tremendous chorus. After the last of them had vacated, I went ashore to view the landing, which was ringed behind by a semicircle of huge stumps and tall burnt spruce woods. The chief imports to the town seemed to be, besides the ordinary necessities of life, whiskey and tobacco, and I was told that for the last month or so there had not been much in the place to eat but pork and beans. I drew the conclusion that the normal state of the majority of the townspeople was to be half-seas over, as every second building was a saloon.

The following day a steamer assault was made on Duluth but there was impenetrable ice about for thirty-five miles out into the lake, the ten or so miles at the front being the previous night's formation. This latter we passed through in good time but then we hit solid floe, and turned back to Prince Arthur's Landing, docking this time without any sort of cheering. We existed the next few days in a state of constant suspense awaiting the arrival of the boat from Duluth, and passed some of the time with excursions in the environs, invariably involving swamp of the worst description, which pretty much used up my entire suit of clothes including my hat. These excursions yielded not much and then, in wondrous irony, the day before leaving I found a very neat Jasper arrowhead right in the street.

> Hat. Roof of the forge
> and working house of thought
> Shield from sol's fierce ray
> Thou summer rag at best
> And prey to winter wind.
> I have thee here.

It was on the brave *Algoma*, a paddle steamer, that we crossed Superior, despite the paddle floats reducing their size by casting off large pieces in the jarring and shaking against the ice, but with Duluth about ten miles away we got in an extra firm place, unable to advance or retreat and the captain lit down the steam in the engines. Two men tried to gain the shore with two planks, standing on one and pushing forward the other and so on alternately. A quarter mile from the boat they were obliged to return. It rained all day, softening the ice and when the *Manitoba* from a rival company went past in good style the Captain's ire was roused. Later, we passed her, making Duluth at dark, just as a fog set in.

The next day before transferring to the train, I walked the town and found it to be a happy combination of solid rock and bottom-less swamp, everything exceedingly new, and two handsome stone blocks going up.

The customs people came down and examined our baggage, but my transit obtained in Montreal worked wonders and I was aboard in no time. However the rail journey was even slower than the boat. The train's departure was delayed by news of a land-slide, then once away we encountered, twenty miles out, a train coming the other way. Then two trains appeared behind us and there was quite a mix-up involving a long retreat to a siding. Once away again we entered a region of dreary tamarack swamp and blueberry barren, then pulled into Brainerd, where the locals were happy to show us a tree in the square where two Indians were hung the previous September for murder. On again for Moorhead, and of course there was no sleeping car so it was precious little good sleep that any of us obtained. The latter part of the trip, viewed through bleary eyes, was over a prairie as boundless to all appearance as the sea, and as flat as you can suppose, not a swelling of any kind to be seen, not even on the horizon.

Several adventures further on I was on a crowded boat sailing up the Red River North from Fargo. The sagacious American com-ponent of the Boundary Commission had telegraphed ahead and taken up all forty of the sleeping berths. By dint of sheer proxim-ity I made the acquaintance of many of them, my future travelling companions over the summer. And so, we arrived en masse at Fort Dufferin, our marshalling point and principal supply depot on the west bank of the Red River, three miles north of the international boundary. The scene was of movement in all directions, with small hillocks of equipment standing patiently beside the largest number of Red River carts I had witnessed, although a mere two would have been sufficient for that statement to ring true.

Towards the end of June I got to make my first real sortie as a Commissioner. Several of us made a brief run of just thirteen miles to examine a limestone outcrop which resulted mostly in allowing the horses to get the carts stuck in streams and having to unload and haul the waggons out with ropes. But I was not too distracted teaching horses where on the compass "forward" lay to notice that the alluvial prairie around the Red River was of a uniform fertility that could not be exaggerated, the soil a dark mould to a depth of four feet, mingled with much vegetable matter. The soil was high quality and lay ready for the plough. In Spring, the Red being a northern river, it can be in flood from the melt at one end while the ice at its mouth is still quite firm. Thus constipated, extensive ice jams are apt to form and even a small elevation of the water above the banks serves to overflow a great area of the country. The silting up of the mouth also no doubt has something to do with the recurrence of great floods at regular intervals. Repeated flooding, however, has made the soil extremely fertile, so the rising waters are a blessing in the long term and a curse in the short. The summer season there is one of excessive heat, and one of the Commissioners told me that a temperature, on May 8th, was raised by a strong south wind to 100°.

With two carts, and two teamsters named Spearman and Duckworth, I was next instructed to trek to the North-West Angle myself that I might there make a survey of the Lake of the Woods. The night before we left, the mosquitoes were the very worst, it still being 83° when I went to bed. They filled the house and kept up a humming like a hive of bees. I lit a tremendous smudge in my room, temporarily stupefying them, but they soon recovered and began straining themselves through the net according to size. One man, a nervous unstable sort of fellow at the limit of exasperation, crept under the bed of another seeking protection and the pair of them passed the night executing the insects.

We went via Fort Garry, then a collection of log shacks clustered around McKenny's general store, which shortly after my visit became the city of Winnipeg, and being halfway between the oceans now carries the sobriquet the "Bull's Eye of the Dominion." The whole distance to the Angle and the Reference Monument was about 175 miles, and I had calculated on paper at Fort Dufferin it would take us ten days, which indeed it did. There one could stand facing south, one foot in Canada, the other in the United States and yet the Canadian border at the 49th parallel was still sixty miles below. The Reference Monument was tucked on the north shore of the North-West Angle Inlet, a narrow arm of water running westward from the junction of the two major lakes in the Lake of the Woods. The Reference itself consisted of a plain squared post, standing at a man's height in a log crib filled with rocks and I had my picture taken (a rare event) standing to the right of the post bearing a rifle, well aware that almost half a century earlier David Thompson, a man whose maps I had studied and whose exciting pages I had read in my sick room, had graced the self-same location. The western end of the Inlet enjoined the eastern terminus of the road coming down from Winnipeg, in connection with which there was a Government station for immigrants, a Hudson's Bay Post, several trader's houses and, usually, a large camp of Indians.

I sent the carts and teamsters and my horse back, and hired two medium sized canoes and two Indians to paddle with me around the Lake of the Woods, since I had been told that I was free to go where I liked, an order I had awaited from my days of involuntary confinement that had ended but a decade earlier. I elected at the last moment to reduce the expedition to one "three fathom" bark canoe across to Rat Portage, and two men with me in it. My companions of the thwarts were Berg, a half, or to be quite correct, one-eighth breed – he had been around the lake before – and an Indian who unfortunately could not speak much English.

The Lake of the Woods, I discovered, in the days that followed, is over seventy miles in extreme length, and has a very extended, frayed coastline. The water supply of the lake is in the southern portion derived chiefly from the Rainy River, a magnificent stream whose mouth has been, from time immemorial, a favourite camping place of the natives. At Rainy River there was another Government

Post, known as Hungry Hall, between which and the North-West Angle a steamer had started plying regularly, forming a new link in the through route from Lake Superior to Manitoba.

The northern part of the lake was studded with innumerable islands, some of several miles in length, others of very small size, few of which were then marked on any map. The shores of that part of the lake were rocky and bold, the water deep and clear, hence its common name of Clear Water Lake. It communicated by several narrow passages through a maze of islands with the southern portion, which, like some siblings I could mention, was related but totally different in character. There, islands were comparatively rare, the water shallow and somewhat turbid, and the lake formed a broad sea-like expanse easily thrown into violent agitation by the winds, rendering our canoe navigation somewhat precarious. The shores were low and swampy, often bordered by humble sand-hills, with great reedy Muskegs behind them (Muskeg is a Chippewa word that I found suited these wide grassy swamps, sounding like the noise a moccasin made being pulled out). I preferred to call this region Lake of the Sand Hills. A third great division which lay between these two lakes on the eastern side, White Fish Lake, had never, as far as I could learn before arriving there, been properly examined. A smaller lake, west of Clear Water, named Lac Plat, then the great wild rice ground of the Indians, was easy of access by water or portage.

This circumnavigation took a week, the last four days spent dodging along behind islands and in the lee of coasts as the malicious weather went in search of canoes to capsize. At one camp, in a dripping wood stuffed with spongy moss and rotten, saturated leaves, not the essence of comfort, we traded some flour and a cup of tea with an Indian for a huge dry sturgeon. A few days later, when I had returned to the Angle after an extensive portage, the same Indian came in great alarm to report the breaking out of some infectious disease at his camp on the lake, near where we had met him. A woman had taken ill first, broken out in spots and died.

Thinking the disease infectious they had burned her completely up. Then, her three children took the disease and were covered in spots. Very probably, though I did not wish to find out, it was the measles, which is very fatal to them.

My assessment as to the capabilities of the Lake of the Woods Region for settlement and agriculture, which opinion was part of my Commission brief, was that only a very small portion of the country immediately surrounding the Lake was at all suitable for agricultural settlement, and the southern and western margins were utterly useless, and a more forbidding and desolate a region could scarcely be imagined. Around the North-West Angle, the Indians grew some patches of maize, and all the ordinary vegetables and cereals could doubtless flourish, as I indicated in my notes, were there sufficient inducement for their cultivation. In the shallow waters of the lake a large species of rush, Roseau grass, abounded. It was used by the Indians for making mats. The wild or Indian rice thrived best in sheltered lagoons. I thought scarcely sufficient attention had been paid to this native grain, as it seemed to afford a prospect of utilizing great regions of swamp. The grain, though dark in colour, was palatable, and the straw was then coming into use in the manufacture of paper.

The journey back to Fort Dufferin from the Angle, where I met up again with Spearman and Berg, began with a tow south behind a steamer to Flag Island, in the north of Lake of The Sand Hills. Next, we coasted south across Buffalo Bay with our canoe heavy laden with samples and specimens I had collected to the mouth of the Reed River, which turned and twisted in a remarkable way. The next day we reached the river's source and, despite my anticipation of difficulty, quickly found the beginning of a portage, a sort of track through the reeds. All jumped out and soon a tug of war began, the other two tied by ropes to the thwarts of the canoe and pulling manfully while I pushed behind in a pair of long "beef" moccasins, but they would not do as at each step I had to lift a foot and a quart of water. Taking them off

Standing with a rifle at the North-West Angle monument, 1873.

The North American Boundary Commission on the move, 1873.

I tied a pair of stockings around my ankles with string and in this rig got along capitally.

We were in regular muskeg covered with wiry grass and moss, small groves of tamarack here and there, and the water every now and then became waist deep. In some places there appeared to be bottomless swamp muck, while in others the bottom moved when stepped on for ten feet around and a patch that appeared like dry ground would sink under your weight giving out copious streams of sulphurated hydrogen. As well as us, there were young pike poking about. At dinner time we chose a tussock of grass raised above the rest, made a fire of dead tamarack sticks and boiled the kettle for tea standing all the time knee deep in water.

Then we went on again, on and on. The going was like walking through very deep snow, but more uncomfortable. That night it got dark before a camp could be found and so we were obliged to sleep in a poplar grove, where the soil was rather squashy and there was no place for a tent. The next few days were occupied cutting windfalls across the river, breaking up beaver dams and making portages around impassable jams. Then we had no choice but to go across a great treeless swamp where we had to carry wood in the canoe to cook. We made our beds on a mud bank due to the repeated lack of site for a tent. Woken by a storm we crept under the canoe. It took several hours the next day to find a place with plenty of wood and, with millions of ducks for conversational companions, we made a big fire and got things, for a few precious moments, dry. The next two days were occupied in getting the canoe down twenty miles of almost continuous rapid, full of boulders. One day we paddled twenty-eight miles of loops and turns, which took us on our way only nine miles west. And so finally we arrived back at our Dufferin headquarters, considerably exercised, and happily dressed for a dinner of more than one course, which we ate seated on dry land in dry clothes.

—

IT WAS ALREADY near the end of August when we got back to Fort Dufferin, and my mail had accumulated while I was in the muskeg. Before I left Montreal, Anna, concerned for my well-being as always, had supplied me with a new style of mosquito oil, that was supposed to be efficacious, and she wondered if it were so. I replied that it was good in so far as if you smeared yourself with it no mosquito would light on you for about half an hour, and at the end of this time it lost its effect and you had to repeat the dose from a small bottle carried in the pocket. The remedy was, therefore, at best worse than the disease and its frequent application was destructive of comfort and clothes.

> There is a sharpness in the prairie air
> There is a haunting presence everywhere
> Of a myriad whetted strings
> As gay the light mosquito oars along.

I was now able to put faces to the men whose names I had been given as the constituents of my party for the journey westward. Under the heading "Naturalists" I appeared first on the roster as the requisite officer of that branch of study, and although I was entitled to two teamsters, the man designated as such, Mr. Stuart, claimed he did not want a second. A Mr. Nilson was to be have been my servant, but he was substituted temporarily by Mr. Spearman, Mr. McDonald was our vital cook, and the aforementioned Mr. Duckworth was our ensign. For shelter we had two bell tents, and for transport a whitewater waggon and a buckboard, and in the equine department, in order of rank, a riding horse, three draught horses, two pack horses and two saddles.

So there was I, at the age of twenty-five, in charge of these good men and horses, whom I would be leading across the great prairie. To provide them with a mental image as best I saw it, I asked them to imagine us crossing a bookshelf with good solid bookends but no books in between, the eastern bookend being a rocky plateau of the ancient granite that forms the bedrock of the Dominion. The western bookend was nothing less than the Rocky Mountains, rising abruptly from the elevated plain, presenting almost perpendicular walls of rock.

The interior region of the continent, the shelf itself, is not in reality perfectly flat but slopes gradually eastward (at the average dropping rate, as I calculated, of roughly my own height per mile for seven hundred and fifty miles) from the base of the Rocky Mountains to the foot of the Laurentian Highlands, an inclination not guaranteed to attract special attention as one rolls across it. Thus the bookshelf has, we could say, a pencil under the westward end, and a rounded pebble would tumble down it west to east. However, within that supposed flat shelf two remarkable step-like rises occur, making three prairie "steppes" in all. I have no hesitation in calling these steppes among the great primary features of the country, impressed as they were on the landscape by the action of a once proud and dominant sea and of former great lakes whose far shores were beyond all human sight.

The first or lowest prairie level, and the narrowest at one hundred miles, is that of which the southern part lies along the Red River, and which northward embraces Lake Winnipeg and associated lakes, and the flat land surrounding them. A great part of this prairie level is wooded more or less densely, and much of the low-lying land near the lakes appears to be swampy and liable to flood. To the west it is limited by the more or less abrupt edge of the second prairie level, forming an escarpment at the 49th parallel (which I shall refer to henceforth as "the Line"), known as Pembina Mountain.

The second steppe is bounded to the west by the Missouri Coteau and is two hundred and fifty miles in breadth at the Line. The rivers that dwell here have acted on the region for a much longer time than on the first steppe, and are now found flowing with uniform currents in wide ditch-like valleys excavated in the soft material of the plains, depressed up to three hundred feet below the general surface. In these valleys, the comparatively insignificant streams wander from side to side, in tortuous channels, which they leave only at times of flood. The surface of this prairie steppe is also more diversified than the last, being broken into gentle swells and undulations.

The greater part of the third and highest prairie steppe appeared to be almost entirely devoid of forest. Its breadth at the Line was four hundred and sixty miles. This portion of the great plains broke first free into sunlight in the Tertiary period (the age of mammals and modern plants) after millions of years spent submerged under the melted glacial waters. The immense denudation of the prairie, by river and rain, is evidenced by the size and depth of the great ravines and gullies which have been cut and are still busy extending themselves among the soft sandstones and clays.

The relentless action of geological time, a time in which a million years is no more than one small piece of punctuation in an entire novel, has provided a thick mantle or carpet of sands and clays that covers almost the entire surface of the plains. A geologist such as I could travel, with increasing frustration, a hundred miles out there without once being able to observe a section of the underlying older rocks. We are thus grateful, unlike future passengers on the trans-continental trains will be as they head west, for the great uniformity and simplicity of structure of the subterranean prairies, which renders much easier the very difficult task of unravelling the geology of so vast a region. Simplicity on this scale is rare in nature, and yet it is imbued with its own beauty. This is not to say that the interior region of the continent is completely without irregularities and exceptions in detail, the scars of previous local events, the consequences of which shall become apparent in the pages to come.

—

IN THE LATTER stages of the Summer and Autumn of 1873, my employment with the Commission saw me to following on behind the waggon train, which was itself following the astrological imperative of an agreed though imaginary line on a very real and sometimes difficult terrain. Whereas the main party was obliged to proceed as though laying rail, I was able to drift a bit more, somewhat like the dust that rose in large plumes behind the carts. As well, the main party had a sufficient head start on me, gained while I was on the Lake of the Woods, that I was perhaps somewhat cursory in my first transverse of the steppes, treading in their cart tracks. It was in the following year, 1874, since there was no need of repetition on the Lake, that I moved at a considered pace that allowed greater attention to detail, and I shall give a fuller account of that shortly. For now, a brief summation of the Line as I saw it in 1873.

Twelve days of intense carting from Dufferin brought me to the Depot Camp on the Souris River. Another fifty-seven miles west of there, at a place bearing the ominous title of Wood End, beyond which there was no wood for a fabulous distance, I caught up with a portion of the main party which was already on its return journey. As we discussed the Line thus travelled, I gathered together the rough tracings and maps they were able to provide and planned my route on to the termination of that summer's astronomical work. It was the task of the Astronomy Party, by dint of sun sightings and calculation to pinpoint the exact location of the Line. Their work by then had taken them and the main party close to four hundred miles west of Fort Dufferin. By the time I returned to Wood End a week or so later, a week infested with quite horrible weather, almost constant snow storms abetted by high winds, I had journeyed within a mile or two of the end of that year's work, a distance of 387 miles from mile zero at the Fort.

Journeying out and back from Wood End, I was in the land of the buffalo. Indian hunters I met told me about them as well as they could, given our mutually foreign tongues. One band of Indians I encountered had killed about 800 buffalo in three days, generally with steel pointed arrows which sticking in the flesh stopped the animal very effectively and were a great saving of ammunition.

Even those Indians possessing good rifles were armed also with bow and arrow for the chase.

Every hole containing water was poached up by the thirsty beasts and they had created well worn paths in every direction. Buffalo are very fond of rolling over and over in the dust and the whole plain was dotted with their wallowing spots, the sod broken in a circular patch and the area filled with dry powdery dust from constant use. A buffalo wallowing in one of them raises such a cloud as to altogether obscure himself, and it has a most singular effect when he suddenly stands up and becomes revealed. The appearance of the animal was altogether nightmarish and weird; it looked like a survivor of a bygone age or a revivified Tertiary monster. The head is densely matted with black hair, among which short horns stand up, and sports a long beard. The hinder quarters and hind legs seem to dwindle rapidly away, as though so much bulk had gone into the front end that the rear arrived too late. The animals I saw were beginning to show a short thick growth of fur, a good winter coat already looking immensely thick and strong.

The animals stalked slowly along in lines one after another, or fed in little herds. Often they lay down in groups in precisely the attitude assumed by a cow. When disturbed, they broke into a strange lumbering run, but withal made good time, and twirling their little pig-like tails could give a horse a good chase as it sought to get abreast of them. Their bellow has a hoarse hollow metallic sound and strikes a peculiarly eerie effect when heard coming across the prairie after dark.

While I was in Wood End, for a day and a night we were engaged fighting a prairie fire which threatened to burn up the depot. Several days earlier, it transpired, while I was still out of the Depot, some men from one of the final surveying parties about eighty miles West had made a fire for cooking and a gust of wind carried it among the grass and in a minute they had to run for it and leave their hard-earned wood pile to its fate. We were camped near the place at the time, so we were kept in a state of anxiety all night. The wind fortunately began to take the fire eastward and left us safe. It seemed to be travelling at a rate of twenty miles a day and it made itself evident to the South long after departing. As it travelled away, we made our way into Wood End. Then towards evening the wind changed to the southwest and the reflection in the sky became very bright. A guard was put on, and by the time I turned in, about twelve o'clock, the smell of smoke was quite palpable. In less than half an hour I was called up and found volumes of smoke drifting past through which the moon looked quite red. The wind was transporting lots of ashes as well as smoke, and the whole southern sky was in a glare.

The camp, fortunately, was on a peninsular around which a moat-like stream wound on all sides but one. It seemed likely that, though the brook was fringed with bushes and small trees filled with dead leaves, the fire would not cross it in dangerous volume. Dr. Burgess, the Commission physician, was the only officer in camp at the time so we consulted in harmony as to the best plan of defense. All attention was given to the narrow neck of the peninsular which was grassy and had a fringe of bushes on each side. The men set to work and cut out a clear space in the bushes and drenched a broad track with water from the creek. A number of old oat sacks and such were tied to sticks to form "beaties" and a row of buckets filled with water placed along the line to wet them in. The fire very soon appeared over the crest of the valley and beating it out first in one direction and then in another occupied us until about half-past three. I turned in for the second time at about four, all immediate danger seeming to be past. Then between seven and eight another alarm was raised, the fire having crossed the stream and coming down now from the North side. All hands turned out again and worked the greater part of Sunday morning getting this too put out. We took breakfast around eleven and no one seemed disposed for any physical activity the rest of the day.

—

MY RETURN AFTER that along the end of the line, in the company of a Colonel with the somewhat ironic name of Forest, given that he was perhaps the only forest within several hundred miles, was spent in a carapace of wet clothes, there not being enough wood to burn and therefore small chance of drying them. Forest's men were not in the best of stomachs; they were short of rations and had been living for some time on nothing more than bread and tea. In Wood End I was informed that twelve head of oxen which had been driven out there for beef had surreptitiously lost themselves and no trace of them had been found, so the men in Wood End were only getting one pound a day of beef instead of two. Fortunately the day I left a trader passed through the Depot from Pembina and I secured from him enough pemmican to feed my own small party. We intended to dine sumptuously on such duck as volunteered itself on the way back.

But as it transpired, for the last week on the way in to Dufferin we had a pretty rough time of it. Nearly all the prairie along the line was burnt, and for a picture of desolation I don't think burnt prairie partially covered with snow can be surpassed. There was no grass for the horses, and what with very little hay and oats many of the steadfast animals were played out. Several carts and animals expired and were left behind. We were on the move all day and every day and had we been camped in one place with plenty of wood and a stove in the tent we might have been moderating comfortable. But we were not and often were obliged to make camp when benighted. At the end of a day crossing terrain such as that, one's chief thought was to get warm and get something to eat, then wrap up in your blanket and go to sleep. Beef and bread and ink being frozen was not conducive to comfort and getting up in the morning before daybreak with the thermometer far below the freezing point was, in understatement, unpleasant.

However, all ended well, and the whole of the men, myself included, got back to Fort Dufferin by the end of October without accident of any kind. The Fort had grown into quite a little town

while we were out on the plains, stables had been erected and stores
and all was bustle and preparation for the winter. The straggling
parties coming in over the last week would have given good opportunity to some caricaturist who was fond of drawing motley groups;
men with torn clothes, others with gaping boots, some with blanket
suits and some with none at all, others wearing Macintoshes below
coats and head pieces that had seen a summer's wear, some stopping
for lunch with a chunk of bread, thawing it slice by slice by the fire.
The winter had come on quite unexpectedly and communication by
water was stopped by the freezing in of the boats. The tri-weekly
stage was the only remaining chance but so many of the Fort's
guests were seeking exit by means of Fort Garry and other points
north that I had great difficulty in getting away, what with having
to arrange for several heavy boxes filled with prairie wonders awaiting catalogue preceding me. But manage it I did, and I was home by
early December.

———

It is noonday here and toiling
And the floods of life are strong
And the dusty highways teeming
With the busy moving
But the west is in its morning
And the shadows still retreat
While the dawn in its adorning
Follows fast with shining feet

At the beginning of April my Commission boots, stored
pointing West, were directed out the door again, eager as I was to
rejoin the Boundary Commission and trek our way once more
towards the foothills of the Rocky Mountains. The trains were on
time all the way through to St. Paul, Minnesota, a good start, and
along the way we had one day in Chicago, and managed to see a

little of the place, though it did not appear to have any special points of interest. We walked about the streets and looked at the shops. Those which had been rebuilt were very handsome, although the libraries and museums that had been burnt up in the fire of 1871 were unreplaced. The huge fire, which we were told had been subsequently traced to a barn, had cut a swath over three square miles in size before it expired, leaving one hundred thousand people homeless, and most tragic of all, causing three hundred people to lose their lives.

The journey by stage from Morehead to Georgetown, sixteen miles north, was not so smooth in any sense of the word you care to take. We went off the road and took to the prairie sod and drove miles and miles round the end of flooded coulees and through half frozen swamps. The driver, we then discovered, had not been on the road for ten years, and so was unaware of a vital bridge over a stream just three quarters of a mile south. As it began to grow dark, he began to be doubtful and steered toward a light on the river edge and there enquired as to the best way to proceed. Aware now of the bridge the driver got the coach got completely stuck on the way to it and we walked to Georgetown through the most frightful mud. We required still to cross the Red River and go on to Fort Garry, but the ice was too rotten and so we went across partly in a little boat and partly by walking on the ice, and found another stage which was very old and required two hours from the driver to tinker it up into shape for the ride. At the next station we expected to get dinner but found none, and were obliged to go to the next stage at Goose River, and there we made dinner and supper combined. Actually in expedition fare breakfast, dinner, and supper are much the same except in name. They generally comprise pork fried in remarkable fat, potatoes, and if you are very lucky, eggs, and for dessert the remains of the eggs of two or three seasons stuck between the iron prongs of your fork.

After a curt rest we were on the road again, pushing against a gale of wind and a storm of sleet and snow. The driver tried to light the lanterns but found one utterly smashed and the other with one pane out and not wind tight. We very soon lost the road in the dark and once more wandered about the prairie. Someone managed to stop up the broken side of the lantern with canvas and light the candle inside the stage and at last we made Frog Point. Off we went the next morning at eight o'clock. Three miles out the fore stage got into a water hole and, the wheels promptly pulling out of their seating, the driver flew off the box after the horses! The stage had to be unloaded entirely, and after a good deal of lifting and prying we got the wheels put right again and went on. The very next coulee was filled with a great drift of snow, so the stage had to be unloaded again and drawn over the snow by hand on blankets and buffalo robes spread out for the purpose. We arrived at Grand Forks as though already dead and had dinner. We started out next morning about six and the driver, it became obvious, had been imbibing rather freely and in a very liquid bog the wheels on one side went down to the hubs. The coach was on the point of turning over when we all scrambled out up to our ankles in water, with the driver now hopelessly drunk. We recovered the coach and soon a light became discernable in the distance. The revived driver whipped up the horses and we rushed along until the station was reached. In the morning, the red-eyed driver excused himself, saying that he did not respect the man who would not get drunk on such a road. A replacement was bribed into action and only one bad hole was met with during the next day, where the fore horses fell and then the others on them and the stage nearly on top of all. However, no serious injury occurred and we reached Fort Dufferin by midnight.

In the light of day, I found Dufferin much as I had left it at the end of the previous year, with the addition of one or two outbuild-ings. I was one of the last into the Fort, arriving at the tail end of April, with the boats still running irregularly. Captain Donald Cameron of the Royal Artillery was already there, as usual quar-relling with everybody. He had managed to turn off all the teamsters who had been with us the previous year by reducing their rations. They sent in a petition and some compromise was reached. Otherwise, Fort life could well have been monotonous, had I not still work to do on my maps and reports and refreshing my team on last year's progress. The U.S. officers had left us some information in the form of a track map as to where we would be heading for the first part. In his notes one officer said that several times they had had to sit up all night fighting the buffalo to keep them from going into the pools on which the camp depended for water. I deduced from this that we should not want for fresh meat, but that the country must be remarkably dry.

We were divided into parties for the second summer, an Astronomic Number One and Number Two and a Reserve; a Survey Team, and Natural History party, which was mine. The Headquarters party consisted of Captain Ward and Captain Cameron when he deigned to take the field. My team for the second leg was constituted of one servant, Nilson, who was an active and civil sort of lad; Stuart, the teamster, an old hand on the plains who gave out to know all about Indians, in contrast to Cook Macdonald, who said he had never cooked in his life before, but no doubt would learn. We would be conveying ourselves as before in a white water waggon, a Red River cart, a buckboard, with three horses and a pony and two pack saddles to do the work. I cut myself out two horses, Jerry and Sampson, and they served me well. In addition to the previous year, the buckboard was fitted at the rear with an odometer, thirteen feet in diameter, with a metering device incorporated in it that counted the number of revolutions made in forward progress. Simple mathematics produced a figure for the ground covered in any given day. Sapper Duckworth was also there from the previous year, and I soon had him hard at work shooting and skinning birds. The general plan of the Commissariat, which had to organize the feeding of so many moving men, was as follows. About fifty teams of oxen were to accompany the main parties to Woody Mountain. The rations of each party were packed in separate waggons and Depot men accompanied them and the rations dealt out every three days.

Camp life, with my party all ready to go, was a matter of hurry up and do nothing for several weeks as we awaited the *off*. I generally always found something to do, even if it was just pressing flowers. We took late breakfasts, generally about nine o'clock, an opportunity for tardiness seized with both hands, as later the chance would not come again. Those who claimed to have things to do went off and did them, while the others sat around the stove in the upper hall (our drawing room) and smoked. About four we went for a walk or shoot, or looked at the river or some other excitement, and after dinner adjourned to the drawing room again for chess, or talk, or reading, then a whiskey toddy and smoking occupied the remainder of the evening. The lax routine seemed to spur the Commissioner into action, as nearly every day some order was fulminating forth from him.

There were a lot of furs then in the Fort that had come from the Indians at Forth Mountain, a good many mink and some badger, bear, deer, and wolf and fox, and several of us went over to the store one afternoon and picked out a few. Then the gentleman at the Commissary raised the price per skin from $2.50 to $3.75, the Montreal market price for prime skins, and accordingly we to a man returned all our skins to the store. I will admit to keeping a first-rate skin shirt and a pair of trousers to match, which I still have and which remain a fine fit.

As I had arrived in camp earlier than the year before, I was able to chart Spring's natural arrival on the Red River Prairie. It unfolded, my notes tell me, thus. April 15th: Ponds beginning to open. Ducks observed, and several of the small birds of passage. April 24th: Ploughing commenced, ground still partly frozen. April 25th: First frog heard. April 26th: Many ducks, geese, and cranes, flying northward. April 27th: Quite a concert of small birds in the thickets for the first time. Buds of the earlier willows and poplars bursting. April 29th: Frogs noisy. May 1st: Grass beginning to look a little green in swampy hollows.

It was three weeks before we put the fort gates behind us, on
May 20th. We hoped to join the main waggon train at about Turtle
Mountain and had fourteen days provisions and oats packed for the
trip. We soon discovered in nightly camp that the mosquitoes
intended to be even more troublesome than they had been at the
Fort. I attempted to ward them off using the spell of poetry, combined with powerful clouds of smudge.

> Oh smudge Oh glorious smudge!
> let me entrench in thy sweet noxious cloud
> And nose and eyes all smarting with thy stench,
> there curse the winged crowd.

We reached our camping place at the western slope of Pembina
Mountain on May 22nd. The country passed over on the trail was
undulating prairie with many old buffalo roads running in a north-
westerly direction and occasional small swamps which were willow
fringed and vividly green with strong young grass. The sappers for
a while were on one of these trails, chaining and putting up pickets
along the Line. Clearly the territory had been completely burned
over last fall or early that spring. Many of the boulders thus exposed
were of limestone and metamorphic rocks and showed strong glaciation. I gathered some pebbles outside the entrances to badger sets
promiscuously strewn there by their digging, feeling somewhat like
a child collecting marbles, and recorded their separate numbers
thus; yellow chert dark rocks, probably Huronian – 4; soft reddish
decomposing rock – 1; grey pebble, probably part of a nodule from
Cretaceous shale – 1, and so on.

As well as the geological samples, and remaining true to my des-
ignation as both geologist and botanist, I collected some plants by
the way; Marsh Blue Violet and Bird's foot Violet, Nodding Wake-
robin, and I found several other flowers new to me in the thickets
at the mountain base. The Saskatoon berry was just blooming, as
was the ubiquitous while common choke cherry and the wild cherry,

wild plum, and wild gooseberry were just about to bloom, and the banks of the coulees were festooned with wild strawberries in blossom. The dry and warm season that year seemed to be forcing things on very rapidly. The trail generally on this stretch was a very rudimentary one, and I learnt to appreciate the full value of Red River carts, as much of the riding was done through bushes taller than the horses.

Just before crossing the Pembina River we passed through St. Joseph, a Métis settlement of a few houses in the usual Red River frame style, and a small building used as a Roman Catholic church. It was not without difficulty that we forded the river there, the water coming up to the floors of the waggons, and the current was very strong. There was, we discovered, a quite discernible mark, an edge, where the true great plains may be said to begin, at a fork in the trail on the west bank of the Pembina River. East of this line stood a clump of willows and poplars, and to its West lay the great open undulating grassy prairie.

On the morning of the last day of May, the Astronomical party placed the last Manitoban picket, at the southwest corner of the province. A milestone of sorts, but my eye was distracted by a duck's nest near the Line on the dry open prairie, with no water or marsh nearby as far as could be seen. The bird, unimpressed, flew off as we rolled toward it and I could not tell what species it was. The nest was merely a hole, taken advantage of by the duck, a circle of blackish down with a space in the centre where lay nine eggs. At almost the same time a very large white crane rose slowly and unconcernedly and gradually soared to a great height against the wind, taking no notice of a rifle bullet fired at him. That night at about three o'clock, a very violent thunder storm, sufficient to wake me where other tempests had not, passed over and some of its flashes fell very close to the tents. I noticed as I stood outside the tent in one instance after the passage of a flash that its course was marked for an instant by a row of luminous spots like beads strung in the air along an invisible string.

The next feature of note was Turtle Mountain, where we went on about four miles West of the old Depot to the first stream with good water and camped. This provided the mosquitoes with ample opportunity to dine with or rather on us. The crocuses were now going to seed in some places, and the whole prairie was covered with their brownish grey woolly heads. An Indian camp lay nearby and we had soon some fine-looking Sioux as visitors. There was also a half-breed train of Red River carts camped near us going East having come from Woody Mountain where they had wintered; they had done this in either 27 days or 19 days of actual travel, I see from my somewhat confused notes on the subject. They were carrying furs and robes for trade and I spoke to the head man who was exceedingly polite, constantly using the word "pardon."

The approach from there to the Souris River was made over gently undulating prairie of fine appearance. Another party of Sioux travelling from Turtle Mt. to the Souris passed us, their goods packed on the back of a small pony with a travaille dragging behind. Several of their dogs with similar triangular drags behind also carried a part of the stuff. Plainly visible on the ground were stone circles indicating the position of old Indian lodges. No such circles had been observed East of this. We caught up to the Commission ox train shortly after lunch and on arriving at the Souris itself found that all the parties had just camped. The river was so high as to be unfordable and preparations were underway to build a bridge. Teamsters Rowe and Burgess attempted twice to take a rope across by means of two box water carts lashed together, but they did not succeed and Mr. Rowe finally had to swim over with a rope.

The next morning all available hands were put to work at bridge building. Some parties were cutting wood while other men were engaged fitting together and hewing stuff. While all this was afoot, I went across the river by boat with Burgess and two men and we dug into one of so-called "Mandan Houses," a collection of mounds the greater part of which were situated on the tongue of land between the river and South Antler Creek. One of these was chosen for excavation, a mound with a diameter of a little over fifty feet and a height above general prairie level of about six feet. The ground around the mound showed traces of having been already dug into for the materials within. Inside we found the remains of three skeletons. One was probably adult but it was much broken up and not much of it was visible. Another was that of an infant while the third was nearly perfect and appeared to have been buried in a sitting or crouched position. The skull was short and broad and sloping in front and the bones were very small though the teeth were undoubtedly adult. Very probably it was a woman. Sticks of wood with which a sort of covering had been built up over the bodies were still visible though they were rotten and crumbling. Overall, the interment did not bear the aspect of very great antiquity. One of the men also found near the skeletons a flat smoothed piece of deer skin, which was used perhaps as a scraper.

Just the next day, while the bridge building was going on actively we had a visit from some Sioux Indians, including one who was said to be chief over a hundred lodges. Mr. Rowe, by the aid of an interpreter, asked them about the old mound and it turned out they belonged to the Sioux themselves and that they still buried their deceased in them. They mentioned some of the interred by name, including the woman and child of the day previous. To me, this was a strange departure from the habits usually ascribed to the Plains Indians in the scant literature on the subject, and I was pleased to be able to add my part.

The bridge was finished by mid-morning of the next day. It was 164 feet long, slung on five timber cribs and fastened with treenails, with long and strong logs laid on each side from crib to crib. Small logs were roughly fitted across for a roadway then covered with a facing of straw and earth. By mid-afternoon one hundred waggons had crossed and all were over except for a party sent back to hunt up four lost, or perhaps stolen, horses. Before we crossed we filled up the mound we'd opened, so that passing Indians' prejudices might not be offended. The botany party moved westward thereafter at a prairie snail's pace, which suited me for there was much to collect and catalogue. One particularly slow day I spent much time at a rather good spot for land snails, which I knew would please my brother William, who was also interested in them and no doubt at that moment doing likewise in Cape Breton where he had taken a holiday. We stopped to water the animals at St. Peter's Spring, which was surrounded with many new flowers, among others a magnificent Evening Primrose with a delicious fragrance. The Wolf willows were now in full bloom and scenting the surface of the prairie wherever little groves of it occurred.

Since the Souris River crossed the Line three times, bending back on itself after a brief run in Canada parallel to the line, then dipping into the United States only to loop back up to Canada as though anxious to return, we were in hope that its second fording would be easier than the first. The old ford from the year before was visible when we came upon it but the water was rather deep and the approaches very bad, being steep and soft, making it almost impassable for an ox train. We could see buffalo bones embedded in the banks. An attempt was made to cross by easing the waggons down one side with ropes and men, and doubling up on the other side to pull it out. Then, it was happily revealed that a lower ford, one employed by the U.S. party previously, was much better, so the remainder of the party went round to it, and the ox train crossed there.

Camp broke early the next day, at six in the morning, and Mr. Ashe and I by agreement the night before set out quickly with Nilson to the nearby River des Lacs (the River of Lakes) and there climbed the self-explanatory "Hill of the Murdered Scout" to get in some shooting. We left the horses on the bank and walked some way disturbing great numbers of ducks and some geese, which flew up and down over the water. Those shot above the water proved impossible to get, the lake being deep and the bottom soft. Ashe at length managed to bag two flying over the land, and in the course of locating them I found a well-preserved and cleaned pelican's skull. We camped that night on the western bank of the Souris.

When we were on the verge of leaving camp the next day, a messenger rode in to say that Lieutenant Rowe had been hurt. I drove on quickly with Ward to the scene and found him about a mile West of camp. His horse had stepped into a badger hole while in full career and thrown him very heavily. Fortunately Dr. Burgess was almost on the spot at the time. A tent was put up on the spot and Rowe's party halted. He was in swoon at first but gradually became sensible. Burgess did not think it a very serious fall, Rowe being generally shaken and bruised and his face cut, but he feared to move Rowe for some time in case of inflammation affecting the brain.

The Depot at Wood End was a day's waggon ride ahead of the scene of Rowe's accident, and so we moved on to there. It was very different in June from when I had seen it last Autumn. The Valley was full of trees and beautifully green, contrasting finely with the bare yellowish and reddish clay banks. A gang of men was already there, and had been occupied cutting wood for almost a fortnight, there being no wood westward on the "Traders Road," as the trail ahead was known, for over two hundred miles. In the morning I waited behind to hear news of Rowe, conveyed by a scout sent down for the purpose. He returned after breakfast with the report that my friend was a little better if anything, but he had been worse hurt than at first imagined. Burgess would not move him for a day or two yet, and Mr. Ward elected to stay behind with him and his party who were furnished with ten days provisions.

The rest of us travelled on by the Traders Road, crossing the Souris the third time by an easy ford, soon after leaving camp. We found on the river bank a recent grave with a little wooden cross set up over it and an inscription in French stating that a Monsieur So-and-So had left Wood Mountain, in company with persons named, at such a date and that several other traders coming along a few days after had found his body by the side of the stream, and buried him. He had evidently been drowned while trying to cross the swollen creek.

After the final fording much of the road ran over dry clay-bottomed swamps, often showing patches of alkaline efflorescence. Now the temperatures were high as we moved ever to the west, and during the highest heat of the day we would halt about two hours, and amuse ourselves lying under the shade of the waggon fighting the mosquitoes if the heat was oppressive, or lying in the lee of the waggon if colder, reading or more likely sleeping. Lunch consisted of bread (baked by the cooks one day utilizing some dead willows we stumbled upon; the taste was much improved) and cheese, or an imperfectly smoked bacon and tea and perhaps stewed dried apples, with supper being a bacon repeat, all this enlivened by the occasional duck. This, of course, if one could eat it, for I barely could, I had a toothache which came on just after leaving the Souris behind. As the ache departed it left a swollen face which rapidly increased until one eye was nearly bunged up and it was so difficult to chew that I had to subsist on soft food. It came to a head at last with a good-sized gumboil, and then happily passed away.

We were now up on the third great prairie plateau, the Missouri Coteau, having graduated onto it in mid-June. The country was much broken into deep basin-like swamps and alkaline lakes without outflow and high ridges and hills. We skirted a very prominent butte to the left which seemed to run Southward a long way and at its base were many circles of old lodges. While examining a seam of impure lignite two feet thick, I found an Indian silver ornament which had evidently been beaten out from some coin. (The more common name for the fiery fuel lignite, which is used in steam power manufacture, and which may strike the reader with greater familiarity is "brown coal," being soft and lying somewhere between coal proper and peat. It can on occasion combust in the natural from within.)

Occasionally we came across dead buffalo with the skin still hanging about them which must have been killed in the last season. Near a large saline lake, the shores of which were already white in broad patches, the local whirlwinds raised the dust in pillar-like clouds with curious effect. Great numbers of young grasshoppers not yet able to fly covered the country and rapidly destroyed what little grass there was. One evening, while writing letters and indulging thoughts of home, a sudden squall with thunder and very heavy wind and rain broke against the tent, lasting only a few moments but then hailstones of great size fell with force against the walls. I felt then I did not want to be anywhere else, that the west was my calling, and would remain so. I had arrived, so to speak, where I was meant to be.

On the day we arrived at the Woody Mountain Settlement and Depot, just before noon on June 22nd, a few miles North of the Line, we witnessed roses and bluebells in flower for first time. The road approaching it had been very hilly and tortuous. The settlement consisted of a few log shanties in a valley which has a small stream, wooded along its banks with fair-sized poplars. Only two or three families were there, the others being "out on the plains." Fortunately, some oats were delivered to the settlement by a contractor in Montana, the first in several days. Watching the oat train come in was something to behold, something Mr. Dickens could not have dreamed of. It was a most extraordinary sight composed of a huge Missouri freighting waggons, like Noah's arks with canvas covers. Two and in some cases three of these were fastened together like the cars in a train and furnished with powerful lever brakes. Eight or nine yoke of oxen were attached to each set of waggons, stretching the caravan out to enormous length and all hitched in unison to a strong iron chain. Only the leading oxen and wheelers were required to be broken cattle, the rank and file being filled up with young animals.

It certainly felt as it the settlement had seen its palmy days; both the buffalo and the Indians had already moved on too far west and were unlikely to return. Most of the settler families still there were speaking openly of spending next winter at Cypress Hills to the West. As opposed to the unsettled settlers, there were quite a few wild oxen happily grazing in the surroundings. They had escaped from American forts to the south and now lived on the plains, wintering out and getting quite fat. One of our party killed one by riding it down and shooting it like a buffalo. Yet again, a heavy thunder storm in the night with accompanying gales of wind prostrated several tents.

For the first time in weeks I was able to send mail to Anna and Mother, as a portion of the waggon train which brought up our supplies from Dufferin was set to return to the Fort. I estimated that a letter, if all went well, would get to Dufferin in about thirty days (at the end of July) and reach the family about the first week of August. I wrote that there was nothing in particular to write about.

The next leg of the trail saw us coming down off the mountain and forging south till we reached the Line again, whence we struck west for the White Mud River, also called Rivière Blanche or Frenchman's Creek. We reached the river with many names without a deal of incident, excepting that one of our Red River cart wheels which had been patched up showed signs of giving way altogether and it required frequent stoppages for wedging and tying it up with rope. All around us were red-topped hills, the colouration being caused by clays baked by the combustion of lignite to the hue and consistency of brick. The Prickly Pear cactus with its large, disc-shaped leaves was in flower abundantly, the flower large and pale yellow and turning orange on falling. My horse Jerry started three Sage Cocks, large birds with the general habits of prairie chickens, and there were many ducks with flocks of young ducklings on the stream. Elk must have been very abundant there at one time as we saw a great many antlers lying about in different parts of the valley, as well as traces of the recent slaughter of buffalo and a great many jackass rabbits. I was informed by one isolated settler on the White River that upward of one hundred and fifty families of half-breeds of that region were congregated at Big Camp, north of the Cypress Hills, where they were engaged in hunting buffalo. The half-breeds had a natural tendency to club together for protection, and as it were formed a tribe of themselves.

The valley of the White Mud was very deceptive, though it looked steep-sided and very broad from the bank, it gave no idea of its real character at first sighting. We constantly encountered clay banks so sheer and so encumbered by masses of boulders from drift that they were almost impossible to ride down and often a horse or rider or both were entertained by rapid repeated visions of the sky. There were lateral gorges and ravines running in all directions through the shales and clays rendering great circuits necessary. In addition the temperature made no effort to drop below 90° in the shade, which was no joke.

Geologically speaking, the character, if I may express it thus, of the cross-sections in this region pointed in my mind to the conclusion that the rock under our wheels, my old friend lignite, was dying away about this point. We were atop the thin edge of a vast wedge of it. The beds below this lignite, the sandy clays, were now taking the opportunity to rise up to the surface, to be baked in the heat of the sun.

It was within these clays that I dug free a panoply of bones, what I guessed to be the fossilized vestiges of turtles and of some large vertebrate which I believed, due to their suggestion of once belonging to a creature of considerable size, were dinosaur bones. This was a find of considerable pleasure for me, since not two years earlier I had sat in Professor Huxley's natural history class while he lectured us on one of the greatest scientific discoveries of the era, the small dinosaur fossil found in 1861 that established the ancient link between reptiles and birds, and which for him was the "missing link" that carried Darwin's theory of natural selection from the possible to the certain. A little brushing of one of the White Mud specimens revealed a part of a jaw with grooved teeth which must have been mighty masticators when the terrible reptile fed. The remains of those ancient vertebrates I knew from the lectures were closely connected with ironstone, which indeed is an oxidized iron, and are often converted over time into that substance, which likes to overlay clay. This alchemic conversion from bone to stone has the effect of traversing the former bones in all directions with lines of fracture which is precisely what had happened here, so that I picked up several bags of fragments, of jigsaw pieces, some of which were actually lying loose as though they had tumbled from a giant's pocket, and which hopefully were capable of identification by an expert.

(The fragments were later dispatched for examination by Edward Drinker Cope in Hadenfield, New Jersey. Mr. Cope was a man of independent wealth who had dedicated his money and considerable energy to advancing the science of paleontology, and he had gained a continental reputation as a "fossil hunter." Cope's published analysis of my boxes of bones involved a great deal of Latin which I will spare from reproduction here, but he was confident that, "while in but few instances are the fragments so characteristic as to admit of specific diagnosis" the fossils did "leave no doubt as to the animals to which they belonged" namely "Dinosauria, tortoises and gar-fishes" a gar-fish being pike-like in nature but with a mouth resembling a musical instrument, a short flute perhaps. Rankine, when I showed him this trio of creatures I had made acquaintance with, remarked that it would be a most foul-tasting stew that used those ingredients.)

As I sat by the campfire that night on the night of the second of July, translating the odometer readings, with Jerry looking over my shoulder to make sure I got it right, Mr. Stuart called my attention to a curious star. I looked at it with the telescope and saw that it was a comet approaching the sun. The brightness of the nucleus was remarkable, being equal to a star of 3rd magnitude and the light quite concentrated. From our perspective it seemed to be on a suicide run at the moon.

The treeless-ness of the landscape we were in had the effect of making everything acutely visible, almost regardless of distance, and as we travelled any event in the landscape caught and held the eye. I turned my head, some few miles east of the White Mud, and saw a number of young foxes playing round a hole, and several old ones at some distance, and then at the crossing of the next creek came on the same band of wild cattle we'd met with a few days before. On sighting them Mr. McDonald quickly mounted while Nilson hastily unyoked Jerry from the buckboard. Duckworth and I crept up behind some hills while the others went to head them off. McDonald and Nilson shot at them several times, and wounded some slightly. After a run of about half a mile, during which they did not come near our hiding spot, they became moderately tame, and Duckworth and McDonald drove them along the road without difficulty. The oxen were herded into camp easily enough but the difficulty then was to tie them up and secure them. They finally became quite furious and one, having been tied up, broke away and knocked Mr. Duckworth down, fortunately without hurting him. Then they all dispersed and disappeared in the twilight. The men scattered in pursuit and finally shot two not very far from camp.

At this stage of the trek, about four hundred miles from Dufferin, my Red River cart broke beyond repair in the midst of moving my heavy stuff – the several boxes of geological samples, or "Dawson's Rocks" as they had become known – from one camp to the next. I had the cart's remnants brought into camp, and discussed the situation with the Captain, who finally decided it was best for Nilson and me to go all the way back to Woody Mountain for a new cart as all my stuff could not be crowded into the other waggons. I got there, my spirit rendered as wobbly as my cart wheels by the detour, and was informed by a habitant that two old carts remained near the half-breed houses, which they had probably thought in too poor a condition to take on to the Cypress Hills. Thinking that something might be better than nothing, I took the best, an old stager, mended up with poplar, the axle and much of the wheels being also of that wood. Parts of the cart were also scientifically bound with shaganappi. I was occupied sometime getting it put in a little better repair and arranging other little matters.

Red River Country carts, I have since decided, are little use in that part of the country to anybody but the half-breeds. Given the stony and rough character of the roads, breaks are frequent, and when the wheels are broken there is no hard wood to hand to repair them. The sand and grit also rapidly wears away the axles unless iron bushes are used and then a poplar axle has to be substituted at the risk of breakdown at any moment. The extreme dryness of the air causes them to split and crack in all directions, especially the hubs, and when this happens the spokes work loose and nothing will save the wheel. By keeping the wheel always wet this may be avoided but water too is scarce. With the half-breeds time is no object and cheapness is everything. They put on light loads and travel in large trains so that if one cart breaks down the load may be distributed and the fragments retained for future repairs.

On the return off the mountain in the rickety cart we travelled till nearly dark, and had still not found water at proper camping time just some in pools with a strong saline taste and a repulsive yellowy colour. Next morning the sunlight revealed that if we had come but a mile further we would have got good water, and then the irony was compounded when we found that the tent had fallen out of the waggon and I had to send Nilson back for it in the buckboard about four miles. The grasshoppers for the last few days had been very numerous, well able to fly and they could be seen passing along in the direction of the wind in that part of the sky nearest the sun, at great heights. When they rose from the ground and flew back with the wind in one's face they inflicted painful blows, especially when they happened to light in one's eye. Their appearance in passing before the sun was more like drifting snowflakes than anything else.

Halted for a day by the Commission's slow advance ahead, I occupied it writing up notes, pressing some plants and wrapping up fossils. Captain Campbell, one of the higher ranking United States Commissioners, rode in with reports of thousands of buffalo a day's march West of us. Also not quite as many Indians. The latter, it appeared, were trying to head off the buffalo which were moving Northwards, and drive them down towards their hunting grounds on the Missouri. A large party of them had come down on Mr. Ashe's party, who were obliged to give them flour, matches, and other comestibles to some considerable amount. They might have gone through the provisions to a still greater extent but for the timely appearance of Campbell's train.

We left the Depot with the sunrise, and Campbell's squad and mine combined made us a party of ten waggons, one cart (just), one buckboard, and fifteen men. During the day's march the grass-hoppers were again innumerable, hovering in dense clouds over all swamps and green places. The trail beside them passed over the gently undulating prairie, which however became more markedly undulating westward and then terminated against the foot of an area of elevated country, extending as far again as we had yet gone from Woody Mountain, some fifty miles. Great numbers of buffalo recently killed were strewn about the country and in some places still polluted the air with the stench of their decay. In tandem with the buffalo were frequent half-breed and Indian camping places marked by circles of lodges, decorated with heaps of broken bones, about the size of road metal, which had been boiled to remove the fat for pemmican-making. Piles of dung chips were also frequent and abundant and made a good fire, especially with a little wood to start it, never mind the smell. We depended entirely by then on the chips for our cooking, being nearly a hundred miles West of any sort of wood.

I now made an effort to rejoin the train which was far ahead, and at one point met one of the scouts with a cart coming back from the East Fork Depot with supplies. He said he had seen three Indians close at hand who had run after him but had not done him any harm. As the scout receded eastward we drove on, and soon saw two horsemen at a distance who, on catching sight of us, set off at full gallop in a direction guaranteed to intercept us and became concealed behind the hills. We thought it best to put our rifles in a conspicuous place that they might see we were armed. They came suddenly out onto the road just as we caught sight of the our train and turned out to be two wild looking half-breeds with rifles slung over their backs. They asked about the valley of Woody Mountain and I gave them all the information I could, which since I had just come from there twice, was in fair proportion.

About the 534-mile point, to be precise, we came suddenly to the Western edge of the patch of coteau-like country we had been on for several days and nights, and now we at last distinctly beheld the Three Buttes, though they must have been a hundred miles distant, known to the half-breeds even on the Missouri as the Sweet-grass Hills or Montagnes de l'herbe santé. We could also make out the Little Rocky Mountains subtending a large angle to southwest, about 60 miles distant and looking very ridgy and rough and, in addition to all this highness, the Cypress Hills to the North.

Soon after entering that land of visible hills, a lone Indian on horseback approached with great caution and, when not repulsed, followed us to the next camp and watched the operation of our style of camping with great interest. He was a very young fellow who said he was a Da-co-tah. He stayed long enough to have something to eat and then went away. His pony clearly had a very sore back.

The Big Camp of the half-breeds we had heard about back at Woody Mountain was just about a half a mile from our camp and on the same lake. I visited it in the evening. There must have been at least two hundred tepees, most of skin but some of canvas. The carts were arranged in a great circle enclosing a place for the secure keeping of the horses and into which they were all driven at night. Each family had its own tent or group of tents and a camp fire arranged around the outer edge of the circle. It being Sunday all were in best clothes and no work of any sort was going on. They had a priest in the party who held service on Sunday and no doubt conducted all marriage ceremonies and all of that. He also taught the children to read and write and helped to settle any points in dispute. The half-breeds said that they had about 2,000 horses and ponies and it certainly appeared not improbable. They spoke French and some of them Indian. Most understood a little English and all were anxious to know about the Red River troubles and the Métis chief Louis Riel's assault on Lower Fort Garry, where the new North-West Mounted Police were being trained. (The troubles three years earlier had been not entirely settled by the Wolesey Expedition, and they would smolder and ignite rather in a lignite fashion a dozen years later with the second rebellion of Mr. Riel, which ended in his hanging.)

The Métis spent their summers hunting on the plains, making pemmican during that season and stacking up buffalo robes when they were prime in the Autumn. They were mostly well armed with repeating and breach loading rifles. In the winter some did still resort at Woody Mountain and such places where there was timber and they already had shanties built, but most of them wintered on the White Mud River well into U.S. territory. They guarded their camp with great care, having two or three lines of scouts out. The Indians naturally did not like the half-breeds to come out hunting like a separate tribe, though they do not object to trading. The Métis council had just that day decided to go North back to the Cypress Hills, scouts having reported plenty of buffalo in that direction. They had only just come from the hills a week or two earlier and were recently engaged in an Indian fight, taking sides with the Sioux against the Blackfeet and driving the latter off, killing eight or nine of them. It would appear however that the Sioux did the hardest part of the fighting.

When we departed camp, and found the trail of the Métis cart train, I was at a loss to account for the fact that instead of following one behind the other as we did and making a well beaten track for the carts following behind they left ten or twelve parallel tracks over the width of a few hundred yards. I learnt later that this was a precaution against Indian attack. So many hundred carts would offer but a weak line, if attacked head on, but travelling abreast and surprised they could draw up in a solid phalanx and put the women and children in the centre in comparative safety.

The Captain let it be known that he needed to get some interpreters and men who knew the country. He soon had some applicants, but they were all very independent and imbued with the idea of high pay. Only one man among them thoroughly understood the Blackfoot language, and he was finally engaged at the exorbitant rate of five dollars a day with some others acting as guides at lesser sums. On the other hand the Métis valued the commonest ponies at forty to fifty dollars and for Coureur horses or buffalo runners they demanded all sorts of fancy prices, up to two hundred.

The nearest to the Milk River on the Line we could approach with teams was on the east side of a great dry coulee. A small stream originating from a spring ran at the bottom, but the water was harshly saline and tasted so even when camouflaged in the strongest possible tea. During the march to the Milk we passed by where the half-breeds had been running buffalo a few days before. The hillsides and valleys were strewn with carcasses. Those in best condition had been completely stripped, while the poorer ones and old bulls had had only the tit bits removed.

The valley of the Milk River was exceedingly curious and picturesque. The banks of the gorge were at least one hundred and fifty feet high where the Line crossed it and the flat bottom between the banks was about half a mile wide, and in the middle of our path across there was a curious Indian grave, a nearly cylindrical concretion hewed from sandstone which had been buried obliquely in the ground and painted with vermilion. Other stones surrounded this and on the ground were many offerings or gifts which had been left and apparently recently renewed; beads, a spoon, tobacco, buttons, and strips of various coloured Calico prints. In addition, a flat ornament composed of porcupine quills woven together and a number of eagle feathers.

I decided, by way of geological diversion, to follow the river for some miles on Jerry, and hoped to hammer out some suggestions of dinosaur fragments, for it was near here that other discoveries had been made, but the larder was bare. I rode back to camp at a good pace and, on arriving at the coulee near the tents, found a horse horribly mired in a mud hole. The mud had been softened by springs but was dried and caked on the surface, thus giving way like a pie crust under any weight. The horse was thankfully the right side up, and nothing but its head and a portion of its back were above ground. I got several men together and we managed to haul it out with a rope and by the aid of its own tail.

Once the horse was cleaned off, an American scout rode in bearing a heavy mail of papers and some letters which had come through from Fort Benton. Breathlessly, he related how he had left Benton with a horse running alongside his own to carry the mail. Once out in isolation and a good way from the Fort he was chased by Indians and took refuge in the "Bad Lands" for two days, then with care got back to Benton, started out again, and the second time got through safely. Some of the papers however were nearly worn out with the journey. It was a day fraught with incident, to be sure, and all taken in what had become, after five hundred miles, the accustomed stride. Yet while no two days of my journal are a matching pair, the days themselves were almost identical in the meteorological sense. The mornings were generally clear but soon small cumulous and cirro-cumulous clouds appeared as evaporation began. These clouds grew continually larger and more numerous, drifting with the prevailing wind and sooner or later in the afternoon thunder storms developed, many often being in view at once. These might go on and coalesce into larger storms but generally not. During the night all calmed down and equilibrium was established again.

The Three Buttes now appeared very large as we came on them, with bold and mountainous outlines. The hills around were dotted with buffalo and a small herd came nearly down into the camp in search of water, but then swerved and retired to another coulee. Several of us ran up on a hill to try and get a shot, but they were too far away before we got there. Out of luck ourselves we sat down and watched the others creeping up around three bulls that stood on a hillside about half a mile distant. Shooting began, and quite an exciting hunt took place. One large bull was soon wounded and fell behind, then shots fired at him in rapid succession from various quarters soon made him bleed at the mouth and nose. Trying to rush down a hill, he stumbled and fell dead and the knives came out. The sportsmen centred on him from all quarters and before long steaks were under preparation for supper. From the hill on which we sat one could view the whole thing through a glass, as though at the play house in Montreal.

I was in no doubt when I saw it of wanting to ascend the greatest of the Buttes which stood 6,600 feet above the distant sea, and so with Captain Cameron and another I left camp for the purpose, just as the cumulus cloud was assembling. Following the buffalo paths afforded us footholds on the steep slopes and as they were engineered on the principle of least resistance we made good time. The limit of equestrian progress (which for some time had consisted of leading the horses) was reached and we continued on foot, by which means with the due amount of panting perspiration we got up the last thousand feet or so, and the three of us were rewarded by a splendid view, the Cypress Hills to the North and the other buttes Westward, the Milk River stretching from East to West, visible by the scarped slopes of its valley, with coulees radiating in all directions from us as a centre. Great undulating plains lay below dotted here and there with lakes and ponds, and sprinkled over with buffalo singly and in herds. Spruce and pine formed a wood on the very peak, some being more than a foot thick but gnarled, and we were drenched in a delicious pine fragrance. Though we were probably the first Whites to ascend the peak, Indians had evidently been there frequently and had used the place as a watchtower or beacon. There were remains of fires and half-burned logs, also a rude circular shelter composed of logs piled together with some stones for a fireplace in the centre. Also a partially destroyed cairn of stones. One of the men had left a box of matches, a portion of the tip of a flint arrow head, and from below a stone I released a living mouse of the short-tailed variety which was quickly scooped up in one side of an opera glass and made a specimen of.

Coming down by a slightly different route we were rewarded with a vista of immense herds of buffalo scattered over the plain, and they were the major part of the day's activities. First Mr. Boswell rode after several and killed two, one an old bull, the other a calf. The latter he wounded, and drove across the road just in front of us, where I took a couple of flying shots at it, one of which I believe took effect. The calves ran almost quicker than the older animals and were very difficult to gain on. Then only a bit more down the trail a herd of about fifty buffalo rushed across the track in a solid phalanx about eighty yards in front of the buckboard. We put a few bullets into them and, though we could hear them strike, no animals fell out of the ranks. Near where we lunched, a herd of more than two hundred were, like us, feeding quietly.

The buffalo appeared again after lunch, and we were able to hunt after two bulls in tandem. I luckily struck one in the hip and shattered the femur. His companion did not desert him, and both went off at a slow pace, the wounded fellow on three legs. We followed in the buckboard and at last got pretty close. The sound bull at that point made off, leaving the wounded one. I had been afraid before this of his charging down on us, and so I then went in on foot and by a few bullets caused the beast to fall on his knees and shortly expire. He was a very big bull, fat and in good condition. One of the Scouts fortunately came up and joined us and we managed to dissect the old bull with our blunt knives, cutting out the tongue, slicing off the greater part of a hind quarter, extracting the liver and the suet from round the intestines, and loaded them all on the buckboard.

In the afternoon, I switched from botanist to geologist and took a walk up the brook in search of sections. I panned out a lot of gravel in the bed of a brook but could not get even the faintest colour of gold, although in recompense I found a small quantity of magnetic iron and some garnet dust in the residuum. Near the place where I panned was a shelter built of stones and roots, similar to that observed on the summit of the butte, likewise a little cairn of stones. Riding back to camp on Jerry I struggled through windfall and scree and then, getting onto the calmer grassy slopes I got along pretty fast to camp, stopping several times for water in the various convenient cold springs while a beautiful sun and purple light on hills lit the path for me.

Shortly thereafter, Mr. Ashe came into camp from survey work and reported that, in running a line, he had come across twenty-one dead Indians prostrate on the open plain. Conrad, our guide, said that they were no doubt Crows. He had heard of a party of about that strength leaving Benton last autumn on a horse-stealing expedition into Blackfoot country to the North. They had never returned. The Crows, Conrad explained, were connected with the lower Gros Ventres and spoke a similar language, while the Gros Ventres were connected in the same way with the Mandans. The Crows themselves were not a large tribe. The Peagins, Conrad was also certain, got the credit of having perpetrated the massacre of the Crows. They spoke Blackfoot and were a tribe of that nation. The Peagins, Gros Ventres, and Crows were once said to be the richest tribes on the Missouri but they now complained that they were the most helpless of people, much more so than they were a few years ago. Since they had kept pace with the times by getting breechloaders and repeaters, the Government could stop their supplies of ammunition the moment any trouble arose. In that short space of time they had lost to a great extent the aptitude of using the bow. Traditionally the buttes nearby and the line of the Milk River bound a sort of neutral ground between five tribes of Indians, and normally these tribes would never pass over neutral ground except in war parties. Evidentially, something had gone badly wrong with the arrangement.

We decided to send the photographers to the site of the massacre (I myself did not start taking photographs until I joined the
Geological Survey two years later) which was about ten miles off
on the open, undulating prairie. The bodies were scattered irregularly over a little area on the slope of a gentle hill and were in
quite a mummified state, the skin being tightly stretched over the
bones, the arm and leg bones projecting and heads nearly all broken
in. Other parts of the skeleton were only protruding where the
wolves and other scavengers had been depredating, and where
the scalps had been removed from the forehead to the back of the
neck. Studying the attitude of the corpses and their wounds and
the marked battle ground, the story of the fight was pretty plain.
The Crows, if such they were, had evidently been on foot and their
adversaries mounted. If they were mounted originally, their horses
must have first been stolen from them. They had been surrounded
by a greatly superior number of Peagins and made preparations for
a desperate resistance, digging shallow rifle pits, probably choos-
ing badger tosses to begin on, then piling stones and earth up
round the edges. There were about seven of these enfilades altogether, some larger and some smaller but all offering very poor
shelter at best. Their enemies had ridden around and around them
in Indian style, firing as they rode. The Crows must have inflicted
heavy loss on their adversaries from their positions, but had been
eventually all been killed. The bodies were lying all around the
edges of the pits, cut and slashed in all directions, often after death.
Some had as many as three bullet holes through the skull and one
body, on being turned over, showed five bullets variously flattened
and bent which had dropped out during decay. Nearly all lay on
their faces for the convenience of scalping, the scalps removed from
the forehead to the back of the neck. All had a great gash just below
the ribs, made by a knife for some purpose I couldn't divine.

It took more than a day for my mind to reduce this terrible
sight to a manageable level. Certainly, as the Rockies ahead climbed
higher in the sky, their beauty was an antidote to macabre inner

visions, and it was wonderfully refreshing after the monotony of the dry prairie to pass through so many beautiful little lakes and ponds, the majority of them perhaps formed originally by beavers, who were still clearly at work. The coulees were rimmed with sandstone about thirty feet thick, the upper layers of stratification weathered into all sorts of fantastic castellated shapes along the edges of the banks. The parts beneath these natural wild sculptures were very regularly stratified and perfectly horizontal, sometimes in very thin layers and showing worm tracks and other obscure markings, as though they were subterranean roads.

Then we crossed the famous Whoop Up Road, the main avenue of approach to the North of the suppliers and whisky traders coming from Fort Benton to their forts and posts on the Bow, the Belly, and other rivers. The road where we crossed it was deeply worn and wide, and showed evidence of recent and very heavy teaming being done over it. We met such a party of several freighting waggons drawn by mules and horses and heavily laden traders, six men and two women, heading North. They stated that they had been "cleaned out by Indians last season and one of their party killed," and evidently hoped for better luck this time. The illicit trade they represented was quite organized and many of the most prominent people in Benton had a hand in it. That is to say, they supplied the traders with whisky and took from them their buffalo robes. The burghers of Benton even accommodated the traders by going so far as to arrange for the liquor to be teamed out in waggons to various points on the Marias River, where the traders, many of whom were afraid to appear in Benton, were there to meet them. Besides the terrible injury inflicted on the Indians, the result of the trade was that a great proportion of the buffalo robes of the North West found their way into Benton instead of into Manitoba.

More of the life of these traders emerged when, with Boswell, Galway, and some others, I drove down in the buckboard to fish in the St. Mary's River about six miles South of the Whoop Up. I found a spot for the rod and had some very good fishing, getting a number of fine trout and some suckers. Returning on foot with the string of fish in hand, I missed the buckboard and waited alone some time on the bank of the river, opposite some whiskey traders' shanties. The traders had a herd of over a hundred ponies they had got from the Indians, and one of the traders came across the river to drive the horses to taller pasture, whereupon I had a long talk with him. He and his fellow traders were, he said, afraid of the U.S. troops that would doubtless soon be coming up with the astronomy parties, and thus intended moving off North of the Line the next day or the one after and burning their shanties. By ingrained strategy, they never traded two years on the same spot, always burning their shanties on leaving. They bought horses from the Indians for whisky in the summer, and then sold them back during the winter for robes, when the buffalo came up into the hills, making an enormous profit in both transactions. The man said they had traded 14,000 robes out of those shanties in the previous winter, which had been, for them, a terrible one to live through, three feet of snow falling on the level which stayed for three months from January and still snow was left in April. As many are wont to do when discussing the weather, my trader had a topper to this, to do with snow storms in August.

Evidently these people were a set of desperadoes, having no regard whatever for life. He proudly told me that eight Indians had been killed and five wounded "round these shanties during the last eighteen days." Not long ago some Indians made a plan to shoot him but they were discovered and three of them shot on the spot. Young Blood Indians stole away seventeen horses from them a few days ago, and they were taken in turn by Blackfeet and the latter brought fourteen of them back and got some blankets for their trouble. The Indians get drunk and then those of different tribes quarrel and kill each other constantly, the women very often raising the row by boasting about their relations with horses. My informant, known I believe as Castilian Joe, swore the U.S. authorities had a "dead clue" against him, for something he did "not know what though." I daresay he could have told me very well if he had pleased. He employed two Indian boys as herders and they were generally armed with "sixteen" shooting rifles for fear of Indian war parties. Joe went on to lament the good old times, when a robe was worth only a pint of whisky whereas often now he had to give a gallon and a half. Apparently anxious for my well-being, he warned me that it was not sage for a few men to travel alone in this country, though he did not mind travelling anywhere by himself, for if a party of Indians appeared he only allowed one to approach, and if they made signs of hostility he could put a bullet through him quicker than he could draw his pistol. Finally the buckboard came up in rescue, and ended the blood-soaked conversation.

It was not until mid-August that the end, the grail of the Boundary Commission's work lay within a day's march as the crane flew. The chief object of the expedition had always been to attain the Monument built on the watershed of the Waterton River by the former Boundary Commission. That Commission had come from the West to the East, from the Pacific Coast working inland, and had arrived at the site they sought in 1861. We had brought our Line to meet theirs, and by doing so we were braiding together the work of the three surveys to form an unbroken trace from Nova Scotia to the Pacific Ocean. But there was still ten miles to go, and it now became expedient to choose the most practicable route. The hills North of Waterton Lake were evidently composed of moraine matter, and showed rocky fragments of all shapes and sizes piled together, concealed under luxuriant vegetation and the close sod of foot hills. The glacier forming the moraine had evidently pushed North along Waterton Lake Valley and been fed by the numerous ravines and valleys opening into it on both sides. Where we were camped, there were the most impracticable intervening peaks we had encountered, piled between us and journey's end.

Captain Cameron with a few men attempted to get to it first. He tried the Kootanie Pass, but realized that he was bearing too much to the West. He went so far as to climb a peak to peruse the problem, about two miles from the Pass entrance, but he could see no sensible route. He then retreated back down to Waterton Lake; one of the streams flowing into the Lake was said to rise near the Monument but he could not reach the mouth of it except by raft, and was beaten in attempting to ascend the valley by a great number of substantial windfalls. Next, Captain Anderson attempted to break through to the Monument by a brook joining the main one just up the pass, which brook was also supposed to rise near the Monument.

While Anderson made his northward struggle, I ascertained from the Pacific Survey maps that the old boundary trail to the Monument branched from the Kootanie trail at a place called "The Forks" five miles on the British Columbian side of the watershed, and from there it ran down a branch valley. Thinking I would see as much of the country in that as any other way, I volunteered to go over with Duckworth and see what condition the old trail was in. We crossed a brook twice and then left the main stream, ran out of a valley to the left and began the ascent of the watershed ridge, which was very steep, encumbered with trees and rocks and exceedingly trying to the horses. The summit once attained was found to be a long rounded ridge of broken rock, with stunted trees and alpine plants, donating a most magnificent view in both directions. The old boundary trail was indeed there, branching off, and we followed it several hundred yards. Hardly a living creature had shown itself all day, the woods and hills being remarkably silent and lifeless apart from one parade of chickadees in the woods and a rather garrulous and harsh-voiced species of jay haunting the tops of the pines. The trail appeared to have been recently used and was well beaten, but we could not stay longer for fear of being benighted so we worked our way back again over the old obstacles and arrived at camp No. 1 just before dark, having been nearly twelve hours in the saddle or walking and leading the horse, and accomplishing a distance of about thirty miles by the worst possible kind of trail. Capt. Anderson however had failed in his exploration, not having been able to find a practicable track. The side hills, as he described them were exceedingly steep and generally impassible for pack animals, and windfall and forest filled the lower parts of the valleys; the only way to get along would be to keep above the timber.

At a quarter of eight the next morning the whole camp rolled out and travelled West by the Kootanie trail which was decorated with berries of various kinds, white flowering, and common raspberries, and blue berries, and amelanchier berries. This time the two Captains had posted axemen ahead, cutting impeding logs and making the passage much better. Nevertheless it was hard work driving and leading the pack animals with their cumbrous loads, all sorts of trouble befell them with the packs' lashings constantly coming undone, packs catching on logs and tearing off. Much heavy swearing was indulged in among the men.

After lunch a few went on foot to explore the old Boundary trail and after following it for some time found that the one used by the Indians turned off to the left up the shoulder of the hill and did not keep the proper direction and that this had been mistaken for the main trail. We retraced steps, and then discovered the true old Boundary trail, identifiable by the old cut logs and blazes in the undergrowth. No one had apparently used it in the last thirteen years and the aspect of the woods had no doubt in that time much changed, areas once covered with windfall through which there had been much heavy chopping just as we had done, now were graced with sturdy young growth. The Captains called camp and, exhausted, we made no argument. The Monument was situated only about a mile's hard going to the South.

Impatient to be there at last, after a two-season "chase," I left camp in the early morning with some of the men. We passed out of the woods and clambered up a very steep grassy slope, and with every few feet gained, some new valley or feature of landscape came into view. One hogback ridge we climbed separated two immensely deep valleys in each of which shone a little lake, formed

My odometer party out on the deep prairie, North-West Territories, 1874.

Waterton Lake, at the end of our border survey, 1874.

no doubt by the expiring energy of the glacier. The climb continued up along the knife edge and in one place I was obliged to climb
down a steep rocky face only a foot or two from the edge of a
precipice hundreds of feet deep overhanging the lake. At last I got
to a round-topped summit – and found that I must perforce go
down again some distance and climb round the flank of another
mountain to get to the Monument. However the hillside I had to
overcome looked so steep and rocky that I knew I could not pass
along it safely, so I returned to the top of the ridge again and clambered on over a collection of rocks. I came to a halt on a very bad
cliff, overlooking the Monument by no more than two hundred feet,
but essentially unreachable from there. I was not disappointed, and
felt quite contented with that proximity, and I sat down in a beautiful little meadow among the rocks evidently much frequented by
mountain sheep, three of which were seen making their way up a
distant ridge, while one or two adventurous men went on past me
to the Monument itself. Alpine plants were growing out of the
snow, which was still lying in large drifts. They seemed anxious to
be noticed.

In the valley to the East of the Monument sat a large lake and
another smaller in size. The water was evidently deep and from my
bird's eye view an intensive, opalescent indigo colour. There was
just a glimpse of Waterton Lake nearly due East, while Westward
ran range behind range of mountain as far as the eye could reach.
The high silence was only relieved by the sharp clear whistle of the
rock marmots answering each other from hill to hill. Back at camp,
as though ordered up, a very perfect double lunar rainbow became
visible as it rose to claim the vast sky. The colour of the inner
rainbow was very distinct and the whole luminescent arrangement
was placed in exact symmetry over one of the ranges of mountains,
looking like a gigantic frame.

—

ON THE RETURN to Dufferin, which commenced at the beginning of September, a more hasty journey of two months, we
travelled in one reasonably orderly party, twenty miles a day, the
waggons and carts always in a certain order, Astronomical Parties
at the front, ours and the scouts constituting the rear guard.
(Before setting out we lost two of the teamsters, Campbell and
Armstrong, who took their discharge to go prospecting in the
mountains with the famous prospector Barney Hughes, the old
miner who discovered the rich Virginia City diggings in Montana.
Hughes' remarkable story of his find, as Armstrong told me,
involved Indians that came down on Barney's party of thirteen and
took all their horses except two. The pedestrians then set out to
walk to some settlement and, halted one day at noon, Barney took
a pan and began washing in a little brook and soon struck gold, five
dollars worth every time he panned!)

Each night, after a day spent adding permanent metal "soup"
plates to each marker on the Line and checking their condition, all
the stock was drawn up so as to form a semicircular Kraal on the
edge of coulee or stream. Our tents outside, the animals inside for
protection. Two men stood watch the first half of each night,
relieved at midnight by two more who stayed on guard till four
o'clock. The camp was then called to awaken and the horses turned
out in hobbles and the teamster whose turn it was to herd the
horses took charge of them till it was time to drive them up for
their oats. I slept well under this regimen, apart from one protracted sleepless session when the coyotes howled all night around
a dead horse prostrated not far from camp. At six o'clock each
morning, without fail, we departed.

My notebooks (purchased in bulk from Dawson Brothers of St.
James Street, Montreal, a firm with which, while no relation to us,
Father and now I had outstanding professional relations) pertain-
ing to the eastward trek of the Commission back along the Line to
Dufferin are an equal catalogue of incident to the Westward half,
simply less in quantity of content, not quality. Without, as it were,

going over the same ground, I will offer at this juncture the Odyssean "highlights" as the editor of the *St. John's Telegraph* named them, in his three-part article on my time in the prairies published a year later.

On the very day we turned back I was presented, it being the only time this occurred, with a sample of coal from a point at the junction of Waterton and St. Mary Rivers. The unmistakable shiny blackness occurred in the banks of both streams, lying nearly flat, the seam on the Waterton River measuring about my height in thickness, a foot more on the St. Mary. The point of junction of these rivers was about fifty miles North of the Monument, so I had not the time to go, but the traders on the Whoop Up used the same coal for fires and in a smelting forge, and it was said to be of very good quality. The piece I was handling broke with a cubical fracture, releasing cut fragments with shining faces and looking like very good fuel, certainly capable of providing fine steam pressure in a railway boiler.

On the same St. Mary River a dead Indian was found, and it was the saddest grave I think I ever beheld. The body was in a little gully partly covered by earth. The wolves had dragged his bones about and also various things which were with him. He had not been properly buried according to Indian fashion, neither had he been scalped and robbed and killed by enemies. It appeared that he had been simply thrown into the hole just as he was, and with what he possessed at the time of his death. The skull was broken and seemed to have been gashed by an axe or some similar instrument. A large quantity of tobacco in a bag was found nearby, and a handkerchief full of red paint powder. A bag made of a fragment of carpet held a pair of child's moccasins and a little dressed skin pouch containing a charm, which had clearly not functioned well.

A gentleman by the name of Fish had been left in charge of our outward Depot at West Butte, and his heartfelt relief at our reappearance was indubitable. Almost alone, in our absence he had been bothered by Indians and obliged to let them do pretty much as they pleased. Peagins to the number of four hundred had camped near him with eight hundred horses. All our stores of sugar and tea had ended up in their camp and they had left not much of anything else at the Depot. They did not actually take the stores by force, but merely said they must have so-and-so, and so-and-so they did have. Fish did not attempt to deal with them in any mercantile way, but he did ruefully mention he could have got a moderately good pony for forty rounds of Spencer ammunition, which being worth only $1.20 could not be considered dear. Fish took me aside after generally telling this tale to inquire of a phenomenon he had witnessed regularly, and for which he sought explanation. There were several mineral springs in the area, and every now and then they produced a rush of bubbles which could be lighted and which burned for a few seconds with blue flame. I analyzed a sample (with my tongue) and was quickly assured that the springs must be nearly saturated with hydrogenated sulphur, which gave Fish the chance to perform the legerdemain of being able to ignite water. Also at West Butte, the U.S. party broke off for the Missouri and would be home in their own beds in Bismark after a twenty-day ride on flat boats. We had our last view of the Rocky Mountains at the Buttes, showing only as faint blue peaks above the horizon. The next day, they were gone.

Three of our party ventured ahead of us to reconnoiter the hunting possibilities, and by nightfall they had not returned. Thinking they may have struck beef, if not gold, we were concerned but not anxious. When we got near the Milk River we found a notice by the road saying that the lost men would be waiting at the selfsame river, having struck our trail again after wandering away from it in the wilderness for considerably less than forty years, but longer than they had cared to. We were much delighted by their safety, and hurrying on found the three men all right, though rather "played out." They had taken, they said, the trail south to Fort Benton in a mistake and on finding their error started North and succeeded in cutting the Commission trail but, being then much in want of water, were obliged to go to the Milk where they knew they could water themselves, leaving notice of their doings. Shortly afterwards they had killed a buffalo calf, and so were not suffering from hunger. They had been three days and nights lost, as I remarked in the land of the "Milk and Lonely."

On two separate but similar occasions I had quite a talk, all sitting in a circle and passing the peace pipe round, with two Indian Chiefs, one Assiniboine, the other Sioux. In both cases the sub-text was the future of the white and native races, and the difficult future ahead in which land formerly theirs alone would be shared. The Assiniboine chief, Red Stone, had several certificates of good character from Indian agents carefully stowed away in his turban. He and his people were moderately well-dressed in blankets and armed some with bows, some with old muskets, and one or two with Henry 14-shooters. While the Chief spoke I observed a friend of his who sat next to him fill and light the pipe, then take a whiff or two and before presenting the stem to the chief, turning the mouth piece for a moment upwards towards the sky. The pipes used were made of black slatey rock furnished with long wooden stems. Our talk ended as usual by demands for something to eat, which could hardly be complied with owing to the state of our rations. I managed to get a bow and some arrows from a "young brave" for a can of powder, some bullets, and a plug of tobacco. The bow was very neatly made and held originally together, with the arrows in a quiver made of dog skin with the hair left on.

The Chief Speaker for the Sioux was one White Cap. He said that the bad Americans had killed all their bravest and that he was not a chief, but was only speaking for the rest; that the bad Americans took their land and killed them; that this was not his own country but that they had been driven here by the Americans and in search of buffalo; that they found themselves here without any powder or bullets, and that they hoped that the British Colonel French would give them some ammunition, and also a little tea and flour, and sugar. Colonel French replied that the Great Mother, the

Queen, had black and white and red children and She loved them all alike; that She had heard that the Bad Americans were coming into her country and ill treating the Indians; that She had sent him out there to drive the whisky traders away and to take care of her red children; that they had not much provisions to spare, not having yet met with buffalo, but that he would give them some and a little ammunition.

White Cap answered that they were glad to hear all this and that they would be friendly with the English people always. The Indians also wished to know from us about the Line, and it was explained to them, and the method in which it was marked by piles of stones was shown. They appeared satisfied, and approached the main object of the interview by saying that having talked with the chief of the British they expected a little flour, and tea, and sugar. They got about half a bag of flour and some tea and sugar, and then all squatting in a circle proceeded to fill the peace pipe, which the chief man had brought with him, and pass it round. This pipe was a very neat one, being ornamented in a different way from the Assiniboine with inlaid lead or solder and made of genuine "red pipestone" from Dakota. Most of the pipes used by these Indians were common ones, actually got from the traders. They possessed a few stone ones, but all of those except this chief's pipe were made of black stone, which could be had for two dollars.

In a half-breed camp of thirty-seven tepees I conversed with an intelligent man, who said that the buffalo were being reduced so fast that in ten years he would most likely have to give up the buffalo business as a trade altogether. I replied that this seemed an impossible calculation, given that one day not too long before our conversation I had witnessed a stampede around our camp, with the buffalo passing our encircled Kraal for twenty-five minutes at an estimated speed of twenty miles an hour. But I had also seen the prairie littered with carcasses to the horizon and beyond, and I said that yes, I thought that in twelve years or so the Great Northern band of buffalo would be practically extinct, certainly so far as they could render support to the Indians.

A mail carrier who reached us in late September had numerous stories to relate of Indian horrors recently perpetrated. One example: Three men had been murdered on the Musselshell River lately, one of them burned at a stake. And the hired train which had brought our oats up on the way back had found, on the East Fork lower down than our depot, the body of a white man tied up to a tree, but the sight was so offensive that they did not care to approach it.

With Dufferin only a day's march away, a prairie fire sprang up behind us, near the line of march, probably set by the carelessness of some man with his pipe. A number of men were sent back to put it out, but were not able. It came down on us at lunch, and we were obliged to beat a long line of it out. Then, at long last, with the smell of grass smoke still in our clothes, on October 11th, with over fifteen hundred miles registered on the odometer, we rolled into the Fort, arriving at nine o'clock in the morning. The day was very cold and blustery with the sky clouded, but we were all smiles. Straightaway I got all our party's travelling things turned over, and then went into the Barracks to our old quarters and later took a stroll in the evening, a stroll without purpose or destination, a luxury.

The day after, such a beautiful Indian Summer day that one might have camped out, I drove down to the telegraph office and telegraphed home, a short message confirming my intact arrival, then drove down to the Hudson's Bay Post with Mr. Rowe to enquire about boats, on which I knew berths would be at a premium. The quantity of my baggage precluded a stage. Rowe was much recovered from his accident, but still rather shaky and weak about the head, where further complications were not considered improbable. Many flat boats were on their way to Garry with timber and all sorts of goods, but not as many passenger steamers. A possible imminent departure forced the speed of arranging and exchanging plants with Burgess and Millman, packing fossils, while

Duckworth was energetically engaged packing birds and re-cataloguing the specimens, and this rush of activity spilt into the next day, and the next. An inventory was made of all the stuff belonging to the department which had to go back into store. I have the list still, and it reads like a recipe of the ingredients needed for the essential botanical cum geological expedition:

20lbs cotton wool

30lbs shot

5lbs arsenical soap

1 box wads (gun)

5 boxes caps (100 in each)

1 small claw hammer

2 geological hammers

1 miner's pick

2 belt axes

1 soldering iron

2 traps (steel)

6 mousetraps

1lb alum

1lb saltpetre

3lbs corrosive sublimate

1 bullet mould

5 large preserve cans

1 bottle carbolic acid

8 papers press

2 boxes fish hooks

1 pocket knife

2 papers needles

16lbs cotton thread

20 quires plant paper

1 tin vasculum

3 fishing lines

1 Remington shotgun

1 cartridge case

28 brass shells

1 box blowpipe apparatus

2 sets egg drills and pipes.

The atmosphere meanwhile around the fort was chronically smoky and the sun was always setting as a round red ball, the haziness due principally to distant prairie fires. It was as though the great plains themselves were signalling the terminus of our expedition in the Indian fashion.

I was in the Fort another half-week before I caught the boat. I said goodbye to Mr. Rowe, who expressed his intention of calling up at the College in Montreal, and I hoped he would. The men of the Engineers went down to Halifax and the surveyors to offices somewhere in the Parliament buildings in Ottawa to work on their maps. A week after landing in Dufferin I wrote home with all this mundane news, and wondered how Rankine's stature would have changed after his success in the High School examinations; no doubt he would be looking wondrous wise for an eleven year old under a trencher when I saw him. I chided Eva, who had achieved double figures in age and who was thus now far too old to honour me with any sort of note of her whereabouts. Last thing before boarding the steamer I sent off the horses Jerry and Sampson, to Garry to sell. It was hard to see them go, particularly Sampson, who had developed the habit each night of wandering over to the camp fire and nuzzling my shoulder for a lump of sugar. If it was the sugar, I don't know, but his spirits never flagged, a virtue I found infectious, though I did not take my sugar in lumps.

> Songs and tales of by-past Summer
> How they basked at restful noon
> Of the stars whose silence speaketh
> Of the dew beneath the moon

On my return to Montreal I began again, after I had spent many hours with Anna exhausting my chest of stories of the West, and remarking several times on the cliff-like height of my brother and sister, and the onerous yet enriching task of writing my ultimate report on the botanical nature and geographical character of the lands we had surveyed between and contiguous to the Lake of the Woods and the Rocky Mountains. It was evident to me, on reflection, that I could amplify the opinion of Captain John Palliser as to the possibilities of settlement throughout the prairie. I had taken the opportunity in Montreal to give a prior reading to the Captain's engrossing *Solitary Rambles and Adventures of a Hunter in the Prairie*, published in 1853, in which he becomes a enthusiastic slayer of buffalo, and the later *The Papers of the Palliser Expedition*, wherein Palliser and Hector, Dr. Hind and Simon James Dawson conducted a survey similar to ours, smaller in scope and without the establishment of a boundary. Overall, Palliser's tone was pessimistic, doubting any great extent of settlement could ensue within the area that became known as "Palliser's Triangle," the roughly triangular region having the 49th parallel as its base, and the two inclined sides meeting at about the 100th meridian.

I was more optimistic. Manitoba and a great part of the northwest had before it, I believed, the future of a great agricultural country. After the fertile valley of the Red River was taken up, I posited, the progress of settlement would, in a warm flow of hardship and triumph, follow the valley of the Saskatchewan River to its head, then spread North and South along the eastern base of the Rocky Mountains. There were, however, certain adverse influences which would require early and close attention, if growth was to be as rapid and sound as it should. The great area covered by the coal and lignite-bearing formations insured a supply of fuel for all time to the settlers of the western portion of the plains, but only if, when the country was opened up, there were extensive agricultural communities depending on it. The great present object, it seemed clear then, of those interested in the northwest, should be to further agriculture. True, the severity of the winter season was one of the greatest disadvantages, but agriculturally the *intensity* of the cold was not so much a matter of importance as its duration, so where the length and heat of the summers were sufficient to mature all the ordinary crops the severity could, to a large extent, be disregarded. Besides, in the future, when the northwest was somewhat thickly settled, the long period when outdoor agricultural work was impossible would tend to foster the growth of mills and factories for the elaboration of the crude materials produced in the country itself; enter the fossil fuels.

Ranking them in reverse order of their need to be conquered, I listed the three most important natural deterrents to settlement as: the difficulty of attainment by the immigrant – the getting there; the grasshopper visitations; and the treelessness of vast areas of the plains. The first was imminently to be remedied, with the advance of the railway and some governmental enticement. But though wheat could easily be grown in immense quantity, the profit to the farmer must perforce be light, as long as the cost of transport formed so large a part of its total value at the eastern ports; again some intervention by the nation to assist with these costs should be put on the books.

To my mind, the greatest discouragement to future settlers, once settled, was the devastating western grasshopper, or locust, *Caloptenus spretus*, which possesses to a far higher degree the instinct and power of migration than its eastern cousins, making it a very suitable settler, unlike humanity, for the almost boundless plains it inhabits.

Locust will eat almost any plant in case of need, and the swarms are of an extent that can only be described as akin to a blizzard of snow. I had the misfortune to find myself afield when a swarm came into settle on a crop and begin digestion. I crouched in defense, head covered by hat and forearms, with only the back of my jacket as a rampart. When the battalions had passed beyond me, I straightened and removed my outer garment. The locust were amalgamated to a depth equal to the span of my hand.

These marauding locusts all came from the far west as a winged swarm, and where they happened to be when they reached maturity, that is where their eggs were deposited. In the ensuing Spring, the young come forth, and these young can cause more even more complete destruction of crops than their winged parents. However, they are not as imbued with as much vitality as the generation that brought them there; their progeny, in the third season, seem rarely to give much trouble.

When they do obtain their wings, they wait only in the forenoon for the advent of a favouring breeze, sailing in circles and crossing each other in flight. A slight breath of air induces them all to take to wing, causing a noise like that of distant surf. Swarm follows swarm, often for days together. I witnessed such a repeated invasion, and it had the peculiar consequence of almost destroying an oxen. The poor beast was yoked in such a way that as the swarm came in it was face-first to the advancement. It ingested such a quantity of hopper that it was in the midst of choking to death when I arrived on the scene. Fortunately, in one great spasm, the ox ejected a rotundity of virtually intact insects the size of a large rock, ensuring its survival.

When the swarm reaches the eastern limit of its path of flight, and the climate becomes less dry and warm, they fail. After the deposit of eggs they are much exhausted and soon die, after making a last short, fickle flight.

As a picture of their cycle of life on the plains emerged, so the question in my mind became: what can be done to prevent the ravages of these insects? It seemed inevitable that a very great area, comprising the chief breeding grounds of the locust, must always remain unsettled, or be occupied only as pasture grounds. The battle, I predicted, needed to be fought at all stages; in the egg, in the flightless stage, and when the hordes descended. Firstly, then, by a system of inspection in which many men need not be employed, the chief localities in which the eggs were deposited in autumn might be learned, and Fall ploughing, including the ploughing of roads and bare spots, would derange the egg tubes, burying them so deep in a layer of earth they do not come to life at all in the succeeding Spring. Then in the Spring, as soon as the young are hatched, they must be destroyed, aided by government bounties if need be. The war could be engaged by burning the prairie, rendering the country for a time so barren that the greater part of them would probably perish. Also the use of heavy rollers; driving the young insects together by converging circles and obliterating them with flat wooden shovels; driving them into straw which is then burnt, or into ditches and where large flocks of domestic fowls are kept they could materially assist by the simple defense of consumption.

Some alleviating acts of resistance are possible when fields are swarmed; by the use of smoke, which is allowed to drift across the fields from smothered fires or giant smudges preventing many of the insects from alighting. In attending to the grain, there was also a process called roping. A horse being fastened to each end of the rope, it is dragged to and fro across the field, brushing the insects from the stalks, causing them at last to fly off.

As for the absence of trees, one first had to understand that an area north of the 49th parallel of almost two hundred thousand square miles was close to treeless. But if in the course of time, a considerable fraction of it could be planted with trees, or brought under the plough, that seemed to offer a future prospect of amelioration, and it would bring about a remarkable, favourable change of climate. The supply of wood too for building fencing and fuel was a matter that required immediate, possibly legislative attention, likewise the prevention of prairie fires. Captain Palliser was wont to see the historical destruction of forest as almost invariably resulting from "wanton carelessness and mischief. The most trivial signal of one Indian to another has often lost hundreds of acres of forest trees, which might have brought wealth and comfort to the future settler . . . marring the fair face of nature for the future colonist." He was making partial cause the whole, I would have to say, but it was obvious that the evils of the absence of timber were too great for the settler to struggle against unaided. Here what was needed, I had little doubt, was planting carried out as a public work in the remote districts, while in the places where settlement was going on it might be brought about by legislative action; exemption from taxation for a certain number of trees set out, or even a direct bounty on planting. As well, the inclusion of Forestry as a branch of the Civil Service.

As I wrote of my days in the prairies, there was a sincere contrast between my view of Montreal under snow, the centuries-old buildings crowded together side by side, the look of permanence, and the treeless expanse of the western, unsettled prairie still strong in my mind. That there might one day be cities rising to rival Montreal out in the grasses, linked by railways, seemed more likely than not to me. My hope was that my report would make the forty-ninth parallel a geological baseline upon which future mineral investigations might be connected, and I am heart-warmed to note that this transpired in the subsequent years, the bound report published by Dawson Brothers selling out many times over.

—

MY TASK WELL UNDERWAY, there came the day I walked across the city to the Survey, which was then headquartered on St. Gabriel Street, in Peter McGill's former residence, facing the open space of the Champ de mars and directly across from the oldest Protestant Church in Montreal, St. Gabriel's.

There, in Mr. Selwyn's office he made the formal offer of a post, duly accepted and on July 1st, 1875 my heart's desire came true. I was appointed to the staff of the Geological Survey of Canada, and I would be working for the immediate future in the vast region of British Columbia. It was an auspicious week in which to begin a career with the Survey. Father had received the news just a week before, a little ahead of the papers, that Sir William Logan had died at the home of his sister in Wales, where he had retired but a few years earlier. Sir William had chosen his own moment of retirement, and had remarked to Father a few months before he affected it that an extension in scope to the Survey he had founded and partly financed was too big for him at his time of life. I wondered if I would be capable of the same self-insight when my time came, but as a young man of twenty-five I saw only exploration and discovery ahead, with retirement lying beyond a very far horizon.

Selwyn, who was already well known to Father, had been five years in the post, coming from a long stint as director of the survey in the colony of Victoria, Australia, via the Geological Survey in Great Britain. He was a man I could respect. He was born the son of a Reverend in Somerset, I believe, and had understandably developed his love of geology in Switzerland while being tutored there. He had an established reputation as a stratigrapher (a diviner of the separate stripes of rock that lie one upon the other in order of completion, rather similar to the chapters of a book, each layer a part of the story of the earth) and was an honorable, honest, and exacting scientist who would publish only when complete accuracy had been achieved and the chances of misinterpretation removed. None of these attributes appeared as anything but virtues to me, and I looked forward to our association.

THE AGE OF THE WEST

—

So IT WAS as a full-fledged field agent of the Survey that I sat in the train compartment leaving Montreal in July 1875, en route for San Francisco, where I arrived without delay or incident. On leaving San Francisco on the *Salvador* we passed through the Golden Gate Straight, named I believe not a generation earlier in reflection of the Golden Horn, which was the entrance to Byzantium. At once we were out in the Pacific Ocean, which though indeed moderately pacific yet favoured us with a long unpleasant swell. All hands were at once prostrated with sea sickness, certainly all the ladies. I managed pretty well, getting by with occasional unpleasant qualms.

The trip on the *Salvador* was in itself quite a voyage of discovery, as neither the ship nor any of its officers had ever been to Vancouver before, the line only just having received the contract for carrying the mails. The Captain was a big burly rough old goose who, thinking discretion might be the better part, bore away from the coast and after losing sight of the country near Frisco we never rightly saw it again till the day we reached Victoria. What with reading a little, walking about the deck a great deal, and sleeping when these resources failed, the time passed away. The crew of the steamer were chiefly Chinese, even to the boson, and so also were the waiters. They were remarkably hardy, neat, and extremely biddable, never grumbling and seeming to find a pleasure in everything.

There was a sort of Chinese flavour about the dishes we ate, reminding one in a distant way of opium.

One morning, I passed the time in the fruitless endeavour of fishing up some peculiar animals with which the surface of the briny was covered. They were of a jelly-fish nature, as long as my thumb and we sailed through them for two and a half days. We could seldom look overboard without seeing them and sometimes we came across them in large patches, nearly in continuous contact with each other. The Captain expressed his belief that there must be "fourteen million" of them. We set to work to catch them with a rope, one with an ordinary wooden pail at one end and at the other a small canvas bucket used for taking the temperature of the water. We used whichever of these we thought most hopeful but invariably went too fast, and when we had quite satisfied ourselves we could not do it we abandoned the apparatus. It was then seized on by a hopeful foreigner who within a few minutes had succeeded in losing the whole affair overboard. Soon afterwards the boy who washed up the deck cabins was to be seen anxiously enquiring in all directions for his bucket.

In Victoria I stayed in the St. George's Hotel, a small but remarkably comfortable house with a very good table. Victoria was a pretty place then, with a population about twice that of Pictou, diffusely built with moderately wide streets well laid out and nearly at right angles. Most of the streets had good plank walks and the shops and houses were not high and of a rather miscellaneous style of architecture. The shops had a way of throwing out a projecting veranda supported by light pillars stretching across the sidewalk. Business there took its time, getting up not too early and not absolutely rushing itself. However, I was assured that this was the dullest season of the year. There were some very pretty gardens and the rocks had a way of cropping up here, there, and everywhere. The trees had an English way of growing, seeming to go in more for horizontal, gnarly branches. Southward of the town the broken Olympia Mountains were in full view, at a distance the great snowy dome of Mount Baker arose. This was the only time I saw the peak, as at all other times clouds or smoke from burning woods never forsook it.

> To rest on fragrant cedar boughs
> Close by the Western ocean's rim
> While in the tops of giant pines
> The livelong night, the sea-wind's hymn
> And low upon the fretted shore
> The waves beat out the evermore.

I found Mr. James Richardson already there with full information about the best way of doing things and getting about. Richardson had been recruited by Mr. Logan into the Survey a full thirty years previous, making him almost a founder, and a man for whom I had considerable respect even as a boy. Before heading out on the survey proper, I arranged to go to Nanaimo with him, so that I could go over the ground and pick up the thread of his work with him at hand to explain anything right there and then. Our run started up at seven in the morning and the scenery was really very fine, passing up through the archipelago though the air was somewhat smoky. When we docked I went up to the hotel and had supper, but I found the arrangements so uncomfortable that I went back to the steamer for a bed. Nanaimo had probably a thousand inhabitants, built on a sloping hillside and straggling along to a considerable length. Saloons and billiard tables were abundant and the streets were extremely dusty. There was a Mechanics Institute, a couple of churches, and a daily paper but not so much as a sidewalk in any part of the town, and a bonded warehouse in the course of erection was the first stone building of any pretension in the place. In the vicinity there was little arable land though the whole country was clothed in fine timber.

The next day after breakfast, and after walking about the place with Richardson, during which time he recommended his

cook, who was called Reeves, as one man I should employ for my
initial enterprise with the Survey, I went to see the character of
the coal seams at the surface workings in the centre of the town.
The men employed in the mine were chiefly Chinese, and the
average output per man was two and a half tons a week. Indians
worked in the holds of the vessels trimming the coal, distributing
it evenly. In the mine office I saw two tree trunks on display
originally twelve feet around now compressed on the way to
becoming coal. They were reduced by the pressure of earth and
time to just over three inches across. Presumably the same
happens over time to human remains, I thought, and tried for a
moment to imagine the weight upon me. And what did we become
over the centuries; not coal. Chalk, perhaps?

After a brief return to Victoria I caught the steamer *Enterprise*
for New Westminster, passing four or five salmon tinning establishments at work on their second run, where again the Chinese seemed
to do the bulk of the work. Thence another steamer, of the Royal
City Line, for Yale, the head of steamboat navigation. Besides the
large pines that stood majestically on the mountainside, areas of
the woods on the lower ground along the river were covered with
poplar, and they had a great uniformity of growth, fringing the river
like a gigantic hedge. The river water was yet very high, higher that
year than ever known before, and on account of the overflow of so
much land the mosquitoes were still troublesome.

For some distance above Yale there were many Indian fish-
curing establishments. The Indians, or "Siwashes" as they are called
in Chinook, the trade language of the northwest coast Indians, of
which I had already memorized a smattering, were collected on the
banks of the river, laying up their winter stores. The stores
were salmon, caught in a sort of scoop net with the Indian angler
usually sitting on a little platform built out from the rocks. When
dry, the salmon were stored in caches in trees, in a little box-like
erection supported on poles at a considerable height above the
ground. To prevent squirrels and other small animals getting at

the store, a piece of tin was fixed round the trunk below, spreading downward and outward.

A few years earlier gold washing had been prevalent around Yale but now it was abandoned except as an occasional occupation by the Indians and a few Chinese. We pushed on towards Soda Creek, moving up onto a volcanic plateau that was said to be of too great an elevation for crops, but to make up for it the cattle ranch where we stopped for supper had the best butter we encountered on the road. When we reached Soda Creek, we met Mr. Glassey, an agent of the Canadian Pacific Railway, who assured me he had made all arrangements for my journey in compliance with the telegram he had received. However, he said, he had only one Indian and no guide, and we were also minus one horse. There was a man who said he could act as a guide but he was asking eighty dollars a month, which Mr. Glassey considered too much altogether. I now faced a choice, a Rubicon. The steamer left from the opposite side of the river the next morning at daylight, so the animals might be ferried over, another Indian hunted up and we could cross in a canoe, or I could wait till the steamer returned on Sunday, and in the meantime go alone up as far as the next settlement, Quesnelle, and see what could be had at the Depot there.

I settled for Quesnelle, and a wait of four days before breaking out westward. We steamed up against a strong current all day on the Wednesday, August 18th, and I filled a notebook with geological observation along the way, my eye drawn as always to the lignite deposits within the banks, on which topic I had produced a report. We arrived at Quesnelle at dusk, a little village of one row of houses facing a street which ran along the river. Like many of those mining towns, it had sprung up almost in a single Summer at the time of the Cariboo gold excitement, but had ever since been retrograding towards abject decay. In the evening I took a stroll down to the ferry with Dr. Jones, a dentist from Victoria who had been a fellow passenger on the way up. I really could not see what the people there lived on, if not on each other. The ferry, I recall, was a swinging one operated by the force of the current of the river, and I used it to cross over to examine some geographical sections there. When I got back to the river bank, at around one o'clock, I had to call out for half an hour to attract the ferryman's attention. I devoted the afternoon and evening to collecting insects and plants in beds opposite the hotel (bed here, I hasten to say, meaning the geological term, not that of the hotelier trade).

On return to Soda Creek, and knowing that once I began to steer my course I might not have the chance to write for some weeks, I took the opportunity to write a few lines to Mother. I had some points of interest to include, such as the somewhat odd fact that since arriving in British Columbia I had already come across three M.D.s from McGill and was able to talk with them of Father, who by then had been Principal for two full decades and was a known name nationally. I also mentioned that there had been news concerning Mr. Selwyn who was on the Parsnip River, a tributary of the Peace River. It seemed his Canvas boat was upset and some saddles lost and his cook nearly drowned. Selwyn either was or was not in the boat at the time, so the report said, and I had no doubt that the whole thing had been amplified by the general thirst for disaster that seemed to be always in the air.

The next day I took breakfast at four o'clock, crossed the Fraser in a canoe, packed and saddled the horses, and commenced my journey. We had only gone part of the way up the sloping trail that zigzagged to the top of a high bench when one of the horses missed its footing and went rolling and crashing down the bank among sapling spruces. We found the animal, which was not much hurt though it was not able to subsequently stand under its pack, one leg being lame. While this trouble was in progress, heavy rain came on and we were soon nearly wet through. But we walked on, through fine park-like country with belts of timber interspersed with large open patches of prairie covered with luxuriant grass, and when we got camp arranged we were very nearly dry again. There a Mr. Meldrum came over and visited, and though he had a fine ranch and many cattle in excellent condition, he complained like all farmers of the low prices produce brought and the high wages workers took.

Our next camp was at Riskie's Creek, where I interviewed Mr. Riskie, who was at that time under the weather but hospitable, and I got him to promise to send down a sample of his wheat for the United States Centennial Exhibition in Philadelphia, due to come off in May of the following year, and for which the Survey was already planning. The Survey eventually, and I know, because I was heavily involved in the catalogue production, shipped off to the Exhibit over a hundred boxes containing over sixty thousand pounds of specimens, a representative sample of Canadian resources. Now we moved on to our next camp, and passed several large cattle herds running about almost wild.

Onward we travelled from camp to camp, sometimes waking near the precipitous edge of a great valley, sometimes in the valley itself, sometimes surrounded by grass three feet high, or among deserted, still-sturdy wooden shanties built by the railway. At Alexis Creek, named after the chief of the Chilcotins whose territory we were traversing, we met up with Alexis himself and a large band of Indians. A crowd of them came round our camp and stayed till after supper. That very day they had caught the first salmon of the season, which they presented to us. In return, we gave them tobacco and pork, and after supper presented them with the remainder of our grouse stew and a cup of tea all round. This being Friday and they being good Catholics, they would not touch the grouse, but rather took it away to keep till the morning when it might legitimately be eaten.

Then we moved onto the Chilanco River, which occasionally formed into long weedy lagoons where we saw many ducks easily hunted, but we had no dog. The trail was often very bad, and the horses were tired on arriving in camp, and yet we would cross and recross the located line of the Canadian Pacific Railway several times a day, which manifested itself as a clear cut through the woods,

marked by posts from the original surveyor's chaining. It seemed
to me like an act of great faith to locate a railway through that wild
country. The month of September began as a very long and fatigu-
ing day, ending on a corner of a lake at an Indian camp, where the
men were all away. The women came out, one hideous old hag
among them and all of them ugly enough. They did tell us that the
camp of railway-surveying white men we were seeking, Mr.
Cambie's party, was *Si-yah*, meaning "far away." A little further on
we came across Charles Horetzky, the well-known photographer
with the railway surveys, at work. I paused to ask him some
questions concerning his trade, as I was anxious to begin using
photographs in the field myself. He seemed to have some difficulty
being polite or responsive, but he did explain that the descent to
Cambie's camp was still six hundred feet, so we camped out there
and then and followed the usual agenda for a night out under the
stars; a hearty supper, idle talk, and turn in.

Next day we descended and pitched out tents on the southeast
side of Tatlayoko Lake near to Mr. Cambie's more permanent set-
up, though he was out on the line. I remembered to change the
paper of the plants that I had in presses, and Henry Cambie came
into his camp late that night, too late for more than a cursory conversation. We resumed our talk at breakfast the next day, at around
five o'clock, and then on Cambie's advice I rode back to a place
known as Fossil Creek to collect specimens, which involved wading
in the water of the brook or climbing over and between tangled
masses of logs in its bed. The most abundant form of fossil I came
across was an oyster from the Cretaceous period, the period in
which the forests with their hard woods, the oaks and maples, the
sassafras and the sycamore as we know them now, appeared, as did
many species of bird, some of them flightless water-birds as large
as a man and some much smaller that were capable of flight. The
defining creature of the period is the mosasaur, a snake-like creature that was wholly marine in its habits, sometimes reaching a
length of eighty feet with teeth seven inches in length, but no part

of those eighty feet was evident at Fossil Creek. The next day being Sunday, a day that opened with rain but rendered up a fine evening, I read and wrote, while Mr. Cambie read prayers shortly after dark to such of the men as chose to attend.

I was now well acquainted, as one perforce becomes, with the staff of my small party, or as I was wont to call them, the "materiel." Reeves, the cook, was proving to be quite a character. He acted mainly as cook but was very useful generally and a good hand at getting up in the morning and calling out the camp, which saved me the trouble. A sophisticated Cockney, he was, I suppose, about fifty years old and he had once kept an eating house in London. Finding himself suffering from rheumatic gout, he took the advice of his physician and voyaged abroad to see his married sister on Vancouver Island. Finding it arduous having nothing to do all day, he engaged as cook on various surveying parties and was still, as he said, "seeing the country" with the intention of returning to England in a year or two. He was a most loquacious individual, full of all sorts of yarns and stories and a head loaded with many queer ideas. He was devoted to cookery, even under the most adverse circumstances, and made us better camp fare than I had ever tasted before.

The two Indians were from Lillooet, on the Fraser River, and they were brothers, one named Tommy and the other known as Jimmy, which names were no doubt as good as any others for the purpose of designating their respective owners. Jimmy, being the elder, seemed to consider it right and just that Tommy should do the hardest work. Like most Indians, their capacity for food was about double that of white men and capacity for work about one half. However of Indians in general one could certainly say they eat many things white men cannot, certainly not this white man. The woods in that part of the country consisted largely of a small species of pine, known as the lodgepole pine, and almost everywhere there was evidence of the natives having peeled great slabs of bark off these trees to get at the soft cambium layer beneath, a much enjoyed nutritional source but very difficult to swallow.

It was not many miles from where we were camped, on the Homathco River, that the Waddington party were massacred by Indians in 1864. The party, headed by Mr. Waddington, was engaged in cutting out a trail for pack trains, a speedier path to the gold of the Cariboo excitement. They were attacked one night, the tent ropes cut suddenly before they could get out or make any effective resistance, and all but two or three were killed. The succeeding summer volunteers scattered about throughout the country looking for the guilty parties. The Indians hardly dared to come down to the lakes to fish and were afraid to fire off a gun in the woods. Starvation at last reduced them, and I believe they gave up the most culpable, who were shortly afterwards tried and hung at Quesnelle.

With a little time on my hands for notes and correspondence, I wrote to Father, explaining my plan to return nearly on the same track and then head north by northeast for Blackwater, and of the magnificent section of fossil-bearing beds in the mountains I could see from the lakeside, but would require a week's mountain climbing to reach. I also enquired if anything had come of the Pictou iron ore business. This was in relation to the assaying and surveying work I had carried out for Mr. Giles, for which, three years later, I had still not been remunerated and which account Father was attempting to close on my behalf.

Throughout September we travelled on, and it wasn't until several days into October, when we had reached Blackwater Depot, that I was able to put pen to paper again and place some homeward mail on a steamer, although the notebooks filled rapidly en route. I took stock there of our progress; the horses I knew were getting weak, the brown horse especially, and their backs were very sore, and meanwhile Tommy had developed a sore leg which made him quite useless. The horses had skinned in places where the packs met them and the raw patches had begun to fester and discharge matter. One horse, the poor brown, stumbled and rolled on his saddle bags on arriving at camp, breaking among other things my only thermometer. Quite often the horses found only poor feed when foraging and showed a tendency to go astray and require retrieval several times in the night. One morning, two were gone altogether and only recovered several miles back on the trail after considerable detention. The undomesticated wildlife made an occasional appearance as well. In one ravine of many we passed along I noticed the cliffs were honeycombed with openings, and a species of hoary marmot inhabited them. They had dragged a great quantity of sticks and leaves to the mouth of their holes. We set fire to one of the largest of these piles, and smoke began to ooze out of the holes in various parts of the cliff. I caught a momentary glimpse of one of the animals, but most of them probably escaped by other holes above.

The hunting skills on that trip were better than in my early days on the trail; there were many prairie chickens available for target practice and one day I struck three on the wing but, owing to my light charges, I only got one of them. Another of my more accomplished misses was the day I saw three caribou and emptied my revolver at one without the slightest effect. I would not of course shoot anyone's mother; there was one sober, stupid, matronly looking grouse anxious for the safety of her brood who were just beginning to fly that I could never have attacked. The hunting of wildlife in those parts carried its own innate set of regulations. The Indians were particularly careful not to let the head of a beaver fall to the dogs, and neither were women allowed to eat this part of the animal. If this rule was infringed, then the hunter would have no more luck in the beaver department. They also said that it was dangerous to speak lightly of bears, or with disrespect. People doing so had shortly afterwards been torn to pieces by the animals. To show proper respect and avoid being bisected, the practice, universal in the region, was to hoist the skull of a slain bear on a pole. On another happier occasion, I bagged five spruce partridges and could have had more if I had thought it of any use. On that occasion, after killing the first two, an Indian attracted by the reports appeared, an old man rather bent with an old flint lock in his hand. He followed us for some miles till we came on his camp with several resident squaws and children. A little boy then followed us to *our* camp, a distance of about twelve miles, where he picketed out his horse and stayed the night. Along the trail I took note that the Indians of that district seemed to first bury their dead and then place over the spot a pile of logs, with a covering of bark. Over the whole arrangement a pole was set up with some rags attached and in some cases a tin pan or a hat. In one instance, a rusting musket was observed. In other places, we found evidence of life, not death; there were some basin-like hollows in the ground which were traces of the underground winter houses the natives built. Once we passed a camp of Indian women who said their husbands had all gone beaver hunting and left them no *muck-a-muck* (which was Chinook for "food") and I gave them a spruce partridge.

There was one species of animal, the fictional, which we did not manage to dine on. The most persistent and pervasive legend in the region was that of the "monster in the lake" variety. Although there was variance in detail and nomenclature from lake to lake, the monster took form in the shape of a gigantic fish of some kind that had the habit of swallowing any too daring explorer, canoe and all. In one lake, Francois, it was called Klug-us-cho, or "Big Snake" and was said to have a head a yard or more across, and lived in the mud at the bottom. When its belly was (or perhaps I should say is) full, it retires below and sleeps; however if hungry it rushes out, makes a great commotion and catches a passing, canoeing Indian in its gaping mouth, throws them in the air several times and, catching them as they descend head first, swallows them. Another lake, Cheslatta, had a similar monster called Pe-cho or the "Great Salmon Trout" which lived on fish, varied by an occasional Indian.

One evening, as we were following the railway survey line at this point, the major part of our mission being to locate coal deposits, the sine qua non of railway expansion, we heard shots and the sound of distant chopping, and so found Mr. Jennings' camp. Jennings, like Cambie, was in charge of one of the roving CP parties scouting possible routes for the rails. Mr. Jennings generously gave us two mules, plus an Indian packer named Joe and a guide named Fanny, thus enabling me to leave the sick horses with him (first obtaining a receipt, of course) and make it into Blackwater. While we were with him, one of Jennings' Indians named Charley walked down to the Clisbaco River with me and led me several miles up the valley to view rock exposures, a hard scramble through the woods all the way, where I found examples of three distinct junipers; the common, the Rocky mountain, and the creeping. Charley, as often happened with trail companions, told me a story to lubricate the mileage. Three generations ago, he said, some bad Siwash Indians came from the Salt Chuck. ("Chuck" was Chinook for water, so Salt Chuck was the sea.) They camped on a bluff and shot Charley's people with arrows as they passed along the valley, and no one knew how it was done. At last someone saw a fire on the bluff and a man was sent up to find how many of them there were. Then the other Indians surrounded the bluff and sent a *Klootchman* – a woman – to walk along in the valley below, attracting the attention of the Marauders. In the sudden onslaught, all the bad Indians were killed except one, the medicine man, who flew away from the bluff in the air, or as Charley put it, "All same wind Klattawa (travelling), all same chicken."

There was "snow snow, beautiful snow" as the old song says two inches deep on the ground as we entered Blackwater on Sunday, October 3rd, and geese from the far north were passing south overhead. The snow we considered merely a petulant out-burst and there was hope of an Indian Summer for a week or two. I found quite a mail awaiting me, the latest date on it being August 23rd, and I spent that night receiving a great deal of news and transmitting a little back. The item from home which clove nearest to my heart was the news from Anna that she had become engaged and that Bernard Harrington was the fortunate man, the same man who had visited me in London with the maple syrup. Bernard was then a lecturer in mining and chemistry at McGill, with four years tenure, as well as still being a consultant with the Survey. In her letter Anna, explaining her advancement, wondered if I had suspected anything, which I had not, especially as she had taken such pains to impress me with the attractions and solitary position of Mr. ___, a neighbour of the family in Métis. She also sought my advice on whether to occupy after the marriage a certain large house she had sighted, to which I replied that at that distance I had no way of giving a rational opinion, other than so large a house and one with such large rooms might prove rather a burden, and uncomfortably large for two people to inhabit. (I did not of course suspect then that Anna and Bernard would go on to have nine children.) I asked Anna to inform me as soon as she knew it of William's address for the winter. He had graduated from McGill while I was travelling and had gone over the sea to Paris, where he had enrolled in the École des Ponts et Chaussées (the School of Bridges and Highways), having handily passed the stiff examination that permitted foreign students to attend.

From Blackwater we were due to begin our slow return to Victoria, but not for a few days, so I had several days to myself, which I intended to use to the full. I did not mind the lack of forward motion, for there was something very pleasant in the autumn woods, the aspens turning yellow among the spruces and pines. However there were no maples to take on the really beautiful tints as they did in the hills around Montreal. Rather it was the scrub pines in that country I remember most, sometimes of fair growth and standing, often prostrate, often burnt black and prostrate with young pines coming up in dense thickets, all interspersed with the little paths they called trails, winding and twisting and seeking the path of least resistance or following the track by which the first Indian originally scrambled across the country. The simile I use to describe it now is that the country of the northwest much resembled a gigantic game of spillicans, the amusement whereby one tries to remove one stick from a pile without disturbing the rest. I was sure that when I got to Fort

George, if I began shaking the pile, sticks would be seen moving down at New Westminster!

It was actually ten days before I got out of Blackwater. In that time I progressed pretty rapidly in my knowledge of Chinook, and could understand it fairly well and speak a little. It was very easy to learn, there being no grammar at all and a few words going a long way. Mr. Jennings and I had in fact begun a vocabulary of the subject using the Indian, Charley, but we had great difficulty in getting the right answers from him and great trouble in spelling some of those obtained, with their queer nasal and guttural sounds. To advance my proficiency, I arranged at the start of the week to follow an Indian trail to some Indian houses and engaged a lad to assist in getting me there. The Indians were rather surprised to see us come into their camp. They had lately killed several beavers, the flesh spread out flat with the tail still attached and hung over sticks near the fire. It was a smoky, brown, oily, and repulsive-looking affair. The camp seemed to consist entirely of one very old man, very sick, coiled up under a rabbit skin blanket by a little fire. I half thought they had brought him there to be nearer the grave-yard when he died. Others appeared, a lame man, three old squaws, and some young women who evidently thought themselves attrac-tive and put on airs accordingly. Some of the women were tattooed, as was the case in nearly every group of Indians we had seen, the women more inclined however to pattern their faces than the men. The colour universally employed was blue. The young lad who had guided us in, now wrapped in a Rob-Roy tartan shawl which seemed to be quite the thing there, kept up on foot with the horses all the way back to the depot, where he made himself useful about the camp until I discharged him, prior to our departure.

Riding, writing, reading, fossil hunting, and walking in the rain were the orders of the days. I rode out on one occasion from ten through to half past five, and the contact of my nether garments with snags caused them to suffer considerable injury, which I had to repair before the next day, as we were leaving for Fort George in the morning. That same day a Mexican "cargador" or packer appeared, with the understated name Perfecto; he had travelled the route ahead of us before, and was to accompany us up to the Fort. It was on the second day of this leg that we turned off to ascend a prominent mountain which we got up most of the way on horseback. The Indians called it *Tsa-whus*, and it rose almost a thousand feet above the higher parts of the surrounding hilly plateau. A few steps before the summit I found a slightly overhanging surface of basalt which I observed to be distinctly shaped and polished by ice. This isolated, striated rock was to play a significant and unwitting part in the evolution and rethinking of my theory of glaciation. There was a compartment of my thinking ever active and set aside to deal with the problem of the interior glaciation of the continent, in particular how far it intruded down towards the United States and how thick and extensive a blanket on the land it was. Father's theories, which I could say fell a little short of mine, placed the ice's leading edge well north of there, and relied on detachable icebergs afloat in a melting sea as the cause of the observable striations and moraines. I was just starting to feel it necessary to leave a door ajar in my mind for the ice to flow in, as it were. Standing on that summit, my hand running along those striations and gazing south, I realized then that there appeared to be no escape from the conclusion that a glacier swept over the whole southeastern peninsula of Vancouver Island, and when I gave due consideration to the physical features of the country, such as the grooving in the rock and its very determinate direction, it became apparent that the entire Straight of Georgia between the island and the mainland must have been filled with a glacier. The ice's journey had been far and wide and it had left clues for all to see and interpret. The full implications of this have taken me a lifetime to resolve, and there are still doubts.

The next day we rode in to the Fort passing, just before arriving, two dead Indians, of whom only the bones remained. They had been dead some months, but only then partly buried, and no one knew how they died or who they were. Fort George was a

tumbled-down place, looking like active Hudson Bay Posts generally, surrounded by a number of Indian shanties, whose occupants
were nearly all absent hunting at the various small lakes and creeks
over the country. They were not due to return again till about
Christmas, disposing then of their furs and taking a short holiday,
before starting out for the rest of the winter.

I had expected to rendezvous in Fort George with Mr. Selwyn,
who was coming on from above as I entered from below. Though
the remainder of Mr. Selwyn's party was there, it appeared that
he had been misinformed as to my whereabouts and had started
out down the Chilako River in the hope of meeting me. It was not
until the Saturday that he appeared, having gone through
Blackwater. On a cold and foggy Monday, in a boat and a dugout
canoe, we took to the Fraser, on a rain-soaked run that involved
two dangerous canyons, a violent wind that brought the continued sound of trees crashing down in the woods, and heavy short
seas. We witnessed a large tree on a cliff snap off and come down
on us in the canoe, which it would have done but for a smaller tree
jumping in and saving us. Four days were spent in Quesnelle again,
mostly packing fossils and deciding which equipage to leave
behind in storage, as I would be back the following summer.
Thence a steamer to Soda Creek again and from there four long
days staging from before dawn until well after dark took us into
Victoria. On the stage with us for part of the journey was the
Premier of the Province, Mr. Walkem, a legal graduate of McGill.
A day out of Victoria there was an upset – it was only a matter of
time at that speed – and the driver got off the road and onto the
sloping side of a bank. Mr. Selwyn and I were sitting on the box
and, as it was extremely dark, I was unsure of what attitudes we
assumed in falling through the air, though to judge by the subsequent appearance of my hat I was of the opinion that I fell at
least partly on my head. As soon as the other passengers could
make an orifice they emerged hurriedly, one by one. Last came Mr.
Walkem, much crushed and for once speechless.

By the end of October I was installed again at Driard's Hotel. Mr. Driard himself had come in with the gold rush in '58, and had died only a year or so earlier, having fashioned what many considered the premier hotel north of San Francisco. Mr. Walkem's younger, medical brother, also of McGill, was boarding at the same hotel. Driard's in particular and Victoria in general were to remain home through Christmas and on to the ice break-up. Now I had stopped moving, the upcoming Centennial Exhibition in Philadelphia could move to the forefront of my mind, and looking up representative things for display became a preoccupation, starting with prime examples of the local fruit. Over the ensuing weeks the list of articles collected and purchased grew, and grew, then grew again, until one hundred boxes and barrels in need of shipping had accumulated, weighing sixty thousand pounds. Tinned fish, smoked and plain salmon, and oysters; clam and oyster shells; bear and elk skins; leather goods, tanned using hemlock; wool, cranberries, and bees; grain samples, timber samples, cedar shingles and moldings; platinum, gold, silver, copper, and anthracite; Indian food stuffs, blankets, photographic collections of Indian villages; dog fish oil, hoolican oil, all in all the hoard of an eccentric pirate perhaps, accompanied by instructions for a large map showing the provenance of all the above. Back at his desk in Montreal, Mr. Selwyn wrote to ask me to find the tallest flag staff that could reasonably be sent. I found one of considerable tallness, of all the tallness a man could want, and it flew the Dominion flag on top of the Canadian log pavilion the following summer.

While I continued in this treasure hunt, I pressganged such accomplices as Mrs. Crease, whose husband had been instrumental in bringing British Columbia into the family of Confederation, and Dr. Powell, then the Canadian Superintendent of Indian Affairs. Our searches sometimes took us into less genteel parts of the city, looking for Indian or Chinese curiosities in stores that bore little resemblance to Dickens' Old Shop, or the staff there any similitude to young Kit. The Chinese I must say are most peculiar people for importing their customs into foreign countries wholesale. Walking into their shops one saw shelves full of Joss papers, Joss-sticks, chop-sticks, Chinese shoes, and always on the stove a teapot "biling up" while on a neighbouring table half a dozen of their small cups lay in a pan of water, ready for repeated filling. I had picked up a few little items there for Mother I thought might be interesting to her and sent them with Mr. Selwyn when he returned in early November, namely two small lead caddies, each containing a sixth of a pound of tea supposed to be of very superior quality and peculiar in some way, at the rate of $3 a pound; a bundle each of two kinds of Joss papers, burned as sacrifices to the dead, the square papers representing silver money and the peculiar-shaped ones representing clothes; three very common paper fans only remarkable on account of the oddity of the figures painted on them; and two bulbs imported direct from China, supposed to be the roots of some amazingly beau-tiful flower and warranted to grow in the house in pots.

I had been in the city but a week when news of the loss of the side-wheel steamer *Pacific* off Cape Flattery came through on the telegraph. The dilapidated ship had sailed from Victoria for San Francisco while I dined at the Crease residence, and it had col-lided with another vessel in the dark. There were many Victorians on board and the sinking caused great agitation in the town. I believe of a passenger list of three hundred only one, a Canadian from Sarnia named Mr. Jelly, survived. Steamers were out all along the coast picking up bodies blown back on the coast by the warm westerlies, and one came ashore within a mile of my hotel. The shoreline was strewn with wreckage. Many of the passengers were miners on their way South to spend their summer's earnings. Among the lost also were five from Mr. Cambie's party, men I had met not two months earlier, some with intentions of going on to New Zealand. Mr. Selwyn told me that he himself had at first intended to go with the *Pacific* and fortunately decided not to do so. Hot on the heels of this news was the excitement about the murder of a Catholic priest by an Indian chief on the West coast

of Vancouver Island. It seemed to have been connected in some way
with the plague of smallpox that had caused many deaths there.

After less than a month in its trenches, I was able to vacate the
Driard Hotel and move into Mrs. Bowman's, a boarding house on
Yates Street, and I was able to fashion a bureau of sorts in my room
and tackle the swelling paperwork. I purchased a copy of Captain
George Vancouver's voyages around the world, and determined to
read them to the end. Some snow came and went, and there was
the matter of a small exhibition to organize and mount in New
Westminster (a far cry from Crystal Palace, but it was an aspect of
working for the Survey that I should have to get used to, and that
I did not *not* enjoy). Meanwhile there was background information
to be had in Victoria on my most recent travels. Along the way in
the previous months I had washed gravel from the river banks
looking for gold, and hard-panned a few times too without finding
any colour. But gold had been found on the Fraser, less than twenty
years earlier, in 1858. It happened that a much persecuted group of
Negroes living in California, hearing talk of the passage of an
impending law excluding them from the State, combined and
chartered a ship to come to Vancouver Island and there start a
settlement. Captain Jeremiah Nagle of the ship, after depositing
the Negroes and arriving at Victoria, heard of the discovery of gold
on the Fraser and purchased a specimen – a small one – and added
to it a quantity of gold dust already in his possession. On his
return to San Francisco he took measures, including posting plac-
ards on the ship and stating gold could be seen on board, to spread
reports of the discovery in every way possible, in order to produce
a rush and business for his ship. A great furor arose and all sorts of
people packed up, sold their property, and cleared out for Victoria.
Prices for landed property in San Francisco actually declined as
crowded ship after crowded ship sailed for Victoria. By mid-
summer it was estimated that ten thousand people were camped
on the edges of the city, where formerly there had been only one
or two hundred and a Hudson's Bay Post. Hundreds of skiffs were

built along the shore, as miners congregated and could not get over to the Fraser River. By August, a reaction had set in and most of them returned to San Francisco without getting any further than Victoria Harbour. Still more got up the Fraser after it was too late. Some, but only some, got good pay.

It moved into winter, but the climate there was very mild as compared with Montreal. Many of the trees still held a portion of their leaves and autumn flowers were still blooming in the gardens. However I don't think I once saw really dry plankwalks before the snow fell, and the streets were fordable only at crossings. I could excuse myself for longing for a little clear, cold, dry Canadian weather. Rain or no, my report on the Boundary Commission was now in its final stages prior to publication and there was much correspondence to and fro with Ottawa as it took shape and was assembled. I had received, along with copies of such British magazines as *Nature* and *Leisure Hour* a letter informing me that a complete account of the work of the North American Boundary Commission was to be published at a cost of $800. This had precipitated such things as a revised copy of my plant list, a printed list of errata, and my report on the prairie butterflies. I had names and corrections to insert as well from such as Mr. Hooker, the director of the Royal Botanic Gardens in London, and I had to collate the circulars I had sent out and received back concerning the congregation of locust on the prairie in the summer of 1875. (There was also talk in Ottawa of the prospect of another boundary commission, this time to settle the line between British Columbia and Alaska, if not immediately then within a few years, and I wanted very much to go up into that country and I wrote to Mr. Selwyn asking that my name be put on the waiting list.)

I made another trip to New Westminster at the end of November, and along the way took in Nelson's Mill and Burrard's Inlet which boasted three kinds of bear in the vicinity; common black, cinnamon, and black with a white spot on the breast. "The Mill" at Nelson's was the centre and raison d'être of the village and a straggling little place. There was a very mixed assemblage of persons, Europeans and Whites filling the responsible posts, Indians, Chinamen, Negroes, and Mulattoes and half breeds and Mongrels of every pedigree abounding in the lower positions. One morning I went to a scantily attended service in the reading room conducted by a Mr. Derrick, a Methodist. The reading room was a very creditable institution kept up by the men themselves, and I had some very enlightening conversations there, as well as some that made more sense to the speaker than the listener. Directly after Mr. Derrick's service I witnessed a method of killing fish by dynamite, a different style of service that was very well attended. A cartridge was fitted with a fuse and thrown off the wharf. The ensuing explosion was a dull heavy sound, but there was not much commotion of the water. This was immediately followed by the appearance of thousands of herring and other small fish jumping above the surface, not in the immediate vicinity of the discharge but in a circle around it, as if trying to escape from it. In a few minutes hundreds of dead fish began slowly to rise to the surface, which were easily secured from a boat.

Mill visiting became a habit. At Hasting's Mill, the specialty of the house was ship's spars, and they were exported all over the world. About half a mile from the mill lay the village of Granville, or "Gas Town" as it was more popularly called. Taverns and saloons were not allowed in the vicinity of the mills and so were concentrated in Gas Town for the convenience of the hands. Apparently the gaseous nature of the name referred to a man called Gassy Jack who had opened a mill there. Whilst at Moody's Mill in Squamish I bought a goat wool blanket and a specimen of "tripole earth" as it is known, which, being of a fine grain and considerably absorbent, is employed to prevent the wool from slipping while it is being rubbed and twisted between the hand and the naked knee. I was told while at the mill that the Indian women not infrequently committed suicide by hanging or choking by a cord they had made themselves. I also learnt that though the Indians on that coast did not take scalps, they were superstitious about letting anyone get a fragment, however small, of their hair. The thinking behind this apparently was that its possession gives one a supernatural power over the loser.

My intention of perusing a logging camp was thwarted several times by rain, but I did finally succeed in entering one near New Westminster. It was set among truly magnificent woods, chiefly populated with magnificent Douglas Firs with their long, clean trunks stretching up a hundred feet without a branch, as well as gigantic cedars and an undergrowth of vine maples and lichens, with moss hanging yards long from all the lower branches. The age of the larger pines was very great, often I estimated over five hundred years old. Into these woods there were lumbering roads radiating back in all direction for several miles. The roads had cross pieces embedded in them which were smeared with dog fish oil to make the logs run easier as the oxen dragged them. A tree I selected and purchased was cut up into a spar for the Philadelphia Exhibition or as it was officially known the "International Exhibition of Arts, Manufactures and Products of the Soil and Mine." December went by in a race of purchase and packing for the exhibition. I also had to calculate for the Exhibition the total quantity of gold mined in British Columbia to date, and then, almost before I was aware of it was Christmas, both in Victoria and in Montreal, and I wrote a flurry of letters, just as the replies to my first round of letters sent home in October began to arrive on the steamer. In one of these replies, besides mentioning that my friend Dan O'Hara had now qualified as a notary, Anna scolded me for not "gushing" enough with regard to her engagement. I did not, I wrote back, know how to gush on paper, but I told her if I could think of what to say or how to say it I should certainly write to her fiancé and congratulate him on his good fortune, and I wished, with a wistful heart, all at home a Merry New Year.

It especially did not feel like Christmas that year, since there was no proper winter to mark the time, only a prolonged and dismal

Autumn, with the vine still clinging to the mouldering walls and the rain and wind never growing weary; it continued moist, moister, and moistest. On Christmas Day, which was fine and frosty with a thin skim of frozen sleet on the ground, I read some Dickens in the morning as well as a paper Father had published entitled *The Dawn of Life*. (I should try at this juncture to explain the science of the affair of my father and the "dawn animal of Canada" since it was a matter of some import, and I would be remiss not to include it. Allow me therefore to attempt both clarity and condension in the matter. In 1864, Mr. Logan brought my father a fossil sample, wondering if it was mineral or animal. Father was convinced of its biologic origin, and a year later, in 1865, he formally named it *Eozoon canadense*, the "dawn animal of Canada." He believed it was the oldest fossil found to that date in Canada, and much much older than any other located anywhere in the world. Father had identified, he was sure, the missing link in the fossil record that had been eluding his peers, and in doing so he had exposed the weakness in Mr. Darwin's evolutionary theory, and reinforced the Biblical version of creation as the only answer that fit the established facts. This was a stance, despite frequent and painful opposition, that Father clove to the rest of his days, and it earned him considerable enmity. More than once I had to sympathize with him when the attacks on his professional standing became virulent or excessively public. All this transpired later. In 1875, in Victoria, I simply read his *Dawn of Life* book with much interest, and noted that it had garnered a very favourable review in the *Saturday Review of Politics, Literature, Science and Art*.) By return of post I congratulated him on his publication, and tucked in a confession that I had lost the pocket level which he had lent me and I had in turn lent to a man who dropped it on a mountain. I told Father to order another and charge it to my Survey account.

Then I unwrapped my not inconsequential sack of presents from home. I had not been able to respond and send my own gifts in any fitting way, as there was really nothing there, and even if thére had been I could not have got it safely across the Continent, although that feels like a poor excuse now, since a mirror Mother had sent to replace the one I broke in winter, and some replacement thermometers likewise sent by Father, both arrived intact. I was at least able to send Rankine, then aged twelve, some Japanese stamps and an envelope with express stamps on it of the Wells Fargo Company which I hoped was "inclusable" (if that is a word) in his collection. It was thus with some guilt that I unwrapped a portable photo album from Anna, with a photo of her at the front fully as good as any she had had taken before. I had discussed with her by letter the fact that I intended to purchase the equipment necessary for dry-plate photography and intended to use it henceforth in the field; I had first seen the apparatus used on the Boundary Commission, and its advantages over the wet-plate system were striking, gone the need for a cumbersome chest full of precious chemicals and a separate tent to provide a darkened space at hand. Words are fine instrument of record, but much more powerful and evocative when complemented by the veracity of a photograph.

Rankine supplied me with a capital diary, and Eva a somewhat peculiar cork pen-handle. Also among the gifts was a beautiful illuminated card from my Scottish cousin Ella Kemp, painted by herself with rosebuds and forget-me-nots. After the present unwrapping I walked to Esquimalt and back and then made for Dr. Helckin's to dine. The Crease household, where I might have been expected to take dinner, had all come down with measles and the second daughter had scarlet fever and they could not get servants and were having quite a rough time of it. Dr. H was of German descent, and quite one of the queerest and roughest-looking specimens of humanity I had come across. He was a most eccentric genius, going about with a great cloak of which the aperture at the front slewed round in all directions but was never exactly in front. He had a grown-up daughter, a fact my senior family members were then always keen to hear of, but she had a squint – and, thankfully was already engaged.

After New Year had passed I was at the mercy of the weather, waiting out the weeks before I could complete the second leg of my western roundabout. The geese did not all go South that winter, many remained and there were it seemed an equal number of ardent sportsmen who on Saturdays and Sundays made the whole neighbouring country resound with their shooting. If perchance they brought back one goose each they were greatly pleased. Grouse and quail had once been frequent but all the game birds had been driven away around Victoria by the concerted efforts of the aforementioned gentlemen. But the most revolting thing about Victoria was the state of the Indian element. The gentle Siwash Indians had a reserve just across the harbour and had turned various unoccupied houses in the city into warrens. They were a most degraded lot, parading in the streets in all their ugliness and dirt at any time of the day. It must have given a stranger a poor idea of the place to see an Indian dressed in a white blanket with bare legs and feet, head covered with shaggy hair never combed since he was born. Even the local geology was not up to much, with hard, hopeless-looking highly crystalline diorites (a rock fashioned in heat and laced with quartz), standing up in lumps and knobs in all directions.

The Dominion government at the time was attempting to settle the Indian question and they claimed, back then at least, to be close to doing so. They wanted to carry out a policy similar to that already attempted in Ontario, giving the Indians liberal parcels of agricultural land and bringing them together and settling them in certain given localities on small reserves, that could be increased or diminished to suit the varying numbers. However the local government in Victoria felt that appropriating large reserves to Indians so numerous as those in their territory would block up many scattered areas of the good land capable of settlement, and in some regions would take all of it. The Coastal Indians were fishermen and might not like, I suspected, to be transported away from barren coast where they get good fishing to fertile land where they could

get none. Some of the Catholic Priests showed considerable interest in the Indian reserve matter, no doubt intending eventually to
get the land for themselves.

There was only the occasional bright, or even just dim, light
in the events of the day and I was sure I could not pass another
winter there. Sometimes there was inadvertent humour, as when I
went to an amateur concert given in aid of the Reformed Episcopal
Church. The amusing part of the affair was the sudden extinction
of the gas just as a lady had opened her mouth to sing, in response
to an encore. After sitting in the dark for a while and considerable
investigation by those in charge it was found that there was no
water in the meter. I knew how that felt, for often in those months
I found it difficult to keep on writing and, having cast my net
wearily through my mental depths without so much as capturing
a prawn, I would give up and head for the rock pools that appeared
at low tide, observing the different sponges, bright yellow and
purple, delighted to be able to do so in February.

> Still I turn around and look behind
> With dimming eye on faded shore
> Loved shore where I in childhood played
> By gurgling stream or on the strand
> We strayed together hand in hand.

Another amusement was the tempest in the political teapot of
the provincial election held that February. The writ had been
dropped in the Province in large part because Prime Minister
Mackenzie's newly formed Liberal administration in Ottawa was
determined, or so it appeared, to throw away their last chance of
consolidating the Dominion by the simple expedient of constructing a railway line between Esquimalt and Nanaimo, which they had
promised to do. The line had recently a defeat in the Senate
because, there happened to be, so Ottawa claimed, an unforseen
depression in the year 1875 and the promised funds for the railway

expansion were not forthcoming. Now Mr. Walkem, my travelling companion as the reader will recall in the upset coach, was blamed for Ottawa's financial cowardice and was engaged in a political battle. I was treated to the spectacle in mid-winter of everybody electioneering and canvassing and standing in groups about the street corners button-holing each other. The two rival newspapers – like *The Gazette* and *The Independent* in Dickens' town of Eatanswill in *Pickwick Papers*, the town caught up in an election between the Buffs and the Blues – were going for each other in lively style. One day one paper would come out with the statement that the other was the "demented organ of a demoralized government" and the next day the other replied that its rival was "our low and scurrilous contemporary" and so on. Altogether the mighty system of government applied to that little place was like using the engines of Britain's Great Eastern Railway to drive a butter churn, as a certain legislator involved in the action remarked. The day after Premier Elliott was declared head of the poll after a hard contest, on February 21st according to my notebook, all the Elliotites in Eatanswill were rushing about congratulating each other while the beaten party did the reverse, whatever that may be. Both sides set to indulging in large amounts of liquid excisable articles, to the benefit of the Canadian revenue.

Undoubtedly the most watchable amusement, however, was both quicker and louder than the election. Early in April, at four in the afternoon, Beaver Rock in the middle of the harbour was blown up, where it had long formed an obstruction and hazard to shipping. Work had been going on setting the correct charge for about a year. The rock lay below the water level and by means of a coffer dam a shaft was sunk on it, and tunnels excavated into it in three directions. The whole was charged up with four hundred and fifty pounds of dynamite and about the same weight of black powder, and it was successfully exploded by electricity at the time stated. The waterside was lined with people anxious to witness the blast, which raised a considerable column of sticks, smoke, and spray to a height of sixty feet.

While I went about my solitary pursuits, completing the first draft of my Boundary Commission report and sending off Exhibition boxes of fruits and minerals and woods and such, I banked my first pay cheque from the Survey to the value of $266.66 for work up till the end of January. The family kept me informed as best they could of the passage of days back east. There was much ado about houses and homes. Plans for a summer house of our own had been drawn up, and were laid out on the desk in Father's study for suggestion and criticism and no doubt littered with barley sugar crumbs. Father had bought a property at Métis on the south shore of the St. Lawrence on which he intended to build. Meanwhile they had moved into a new house themselves in the 200 block on University Avenue that I would not see for many a month. An official visit had been made to the Harrington family, and preparations for Anna's great event were underway. I asked Mother to put me down for something useful in the wedding present line, to the amount of around $500. She wrote back suggesting a piano as a present, which I thought a sound idea.

There were about a thousand Chinamen in Victoria, about one fifth of the population, and they were useful for doing all manner of things which white men would not do. The Chinese New Year was the occasion of much Celestial excitement. They visited each other to give and receive presents, and kept open house, like any Christians, but also indulged in igniting bunches of fire crackers to keep up their Spirits, or to keep Spirits away, I wasn't sure. For two days they kept up a perpetual racket. They preserved their customs and while I was there got up a Joss-house on a small scale. An official in Customs, with whom I had frequent dealings in regard to Exhibition business, informed me that in the previous year $32,000 worth of duty had been paid on opium, which seemed to imply that it took something to console them to living there. I preferred reading in the Mechanics Institute; each to his own.

As the willow catkins emerged and the daisies covered the banks, I found that I had developed a real interest in western Indian vocabularies, beyond Chinook, and customs, and I wanted to pursue it. The notion arrived while I was giving a lecture on local geology to a crowd of one hundred or so under the auspices of the Young Men's Christians Associated (as I mistakenly called it then), an act I was rather ashamed of as I considered them somehow suspect. I made arrangements forthwith with a Dr. Tolmie in town to try and work up vocabulary sheets of some of the least known languages, and to map them according to the Smithsonian Instructions for Ethnological Observation. (It was actually twelve years before we published our results, by which time I could almost converse in several of them.) We would occasionally interview Indians at the doctor's house, in twos or threes, listing words as fast as we could and making note of tribal variances. It was in this fashion that I came to acquire quite a bag of Indian facts, both small and tall; of the local legend of a race without joints in their knees; of burial mounds made entirely of shells to a depth of ten feet deep, just lately revealed by subsidence of the land after a storm; of skeletons buried in the sitting position with the backs of the skulls flattened and distorted; and of the Squamish Indians of Burrard Inlet who believed it spoilt a musket to kill a wolf with it. One Indian who was known to have shot a wolf later sold his gun.

> But when patiently, with Science, we undo the
>   tangled scene
> And with doubting footsteps follow dim perceptions
> through the chambers of the brain
> Are we treading on an onward path, or do our
>   footsteps tend
> Through labyrinths of mind to bring us, in the end,
> To that dark verge where all we know, ends,
> In the dim unknown.

Just before finally getting away from Victoria for my summer's work proper, I made a side trip up the Leach River with Bob Ridley, a packer and a peculiar genius who had once been a sailor in Her Majesty's Navy and had interminable yarns about sanguinary battles in the old Chinese War and pirates in Borneo. He told me he had once gone gold mining at Peace River but had never struck it rich, and on the way down from the Peace got turned over in a canoe and lost his bag of dust, and two of his companions. With Ridley leading we went in through deep heavy woods and, when the track ascended a considerable way, found a number of shanties on a flat area swept through by fire, with traces of man's former presence in the shape of broken tools and crockery and more especially broken bottles, broken bottles, and piles of broken bottles. And it was there that I met a very strange man indeed, perhaps the strangest of the strange.

While I was counting broken bottles, I noticed something moving about in the stumps, or rather as it seemed to me gliding along in a certain direction, something that looked like a man but seemed preternaturally tall and to be carrying some large dark object on its shoulder. I had never before seen anything so much like a spectre. I watched it pass rapidly towards one of the cabins, then – Thump!, the sound of someone throwing down a heavy log. Then I heard "Hallo! Who's here?" and into the light of our camp fire entered the Recluse of Leach River. He was a rough-looking miner, bearded and ragged, clothes now pretty much all of a colour whatever they may originally have been, pants ending below in fringes as the result of long wear, boots decidedly demoralized and hat battered. "How de do," I said. "I have come in here to have a look at the rocks and country generally and I daresay you can give me some information about all that." "Well," he said, "I've been to Australia, California, Cape of Good Hope, England, all over New Zealand, in Natal Mexico and other places, and I've seen an awful sight of men, but touching on this river now, if that man Scott was here, he might tell ye better. He got good prospects here or perhaps on the peninsula of one of these mountains, but then he's the most deadbeat liar I ever heard. Before him I went for to prospect with a man we call Doc, though he doesn't, on the upper part of this river, and on the first day we met two bears just crossing a crick. I used this gun and I'll wager her against any in the country for throwing a ball, she has the best metal in her, yes sir. She's a condemned Russian musket and I paid jist one dollar . . ." His name turned out to be Lewis, and for a small sum I got him to show me about the country which he knew quite well. I think he had become slightly cracked from living so much alone. Sometimes, going down a long hillside, he would give a whoop, swing his "Prussian Muski" round his head and go capering over the logs with his legs flying in all directions like an armed ballet dancer.

Back in Victoria, I wrote a final flurry of letters home, the last for a few weeks, although I resolved to write at every opportunity and taking care to make long stories short, more just for reassurance to the family of my continued existence than information. While I was away visiting the Recluse, Father had sent a package containing a hammock, which would prove useful if and when I could find the proper supports for it. News came with the hammock that Agnes, Grandpapa's housekeeper, had died, which was sad news, while William would soon be home for the summer after his first year in Paris, which was good news. Also I now had a picture of Bernard Harrington, my prospective brother-in-law, to add to my portable family collection. Word came hot on the heels of all this from Selwyn, confirming, just in time, my duties for the coming season. I was to work up the coastal structure of Vancouver Island and he mentioned the sum of $2,500 as the wherewithal. I discovered I would be able to run a small schooner or a sloop for $200 a month, a pleasing prospect and a contrast to gradually wearing down a string of pack animals and began to make plans accordingly. As the weather changed for the better, carpets of buttercups appeared, the oaks started to leaf out, and the lilac buds began to colour.

Fairer than all, where all are fair
Within the flowery band
Breathing out a perfume rare
Where the tall ranked pine trees stand
In the lone distant northern land.

Increasingly, I grew anxious to leave, and watched with mixed envy a steamer, the *California*, depart one evening for the North, bound for the mines. The deck was crowded with men of all classes and in different stages of inebriation. The wharf was black with "friends" seeing them off, while the men on board were singing vociferously, shouting and waving goodbye which, given the unstable state of some of them, was a dangerous operation. The lower deck was packed tightly with mules and cattle and every inch of room long enough to lie down on was spotted for a bed, the procedure being to tack up a playing card above a sleeping place that was spoken for with the owner's name on it.

Then a telegraph from Selwyn informed me that the idea of a survey of the Island had been overruled at Ottawa, and that I was to go into the interior region again, into the Francois Lake environs and, if that was finished early enough in the season, I might take a loop line by Kamloops and the Nicola region on the way down again in the Autumn. Within the week I was anchored at sunset in Departure Bay, after a day's steaming aboard the *Douglas*, making for Bute Inlet and thereabouts as a sort of preliminary reacquaintance with the elements before the main event. The Inlet reminded me of the Saguenay but on an even larger scale, mountains eight thousand feet rising abruptly on either side. I then shuttled back to Victoria, sailing into harbour to the sound of Pacific killer whales blowing near the vessel. I listened out for the humming fish of which I had been told, a fish that makes a humming, drumming, booming noise under water and can be heard plainly in a boat, but no such piscine orchestra was to be heard. Several days of final preparation and sudden attention to forgotten details followed, and then I was once again, as in the year before, on a steamer heading for Soda Creek, which now seemed almost like an old friend.

That second official summer with the Survey passed much as the first, its slightly shorter, less robust twin shall we say. The bulk of my completed notebooks was made up as before of geological and vegetational observations, the difference this time being my more disciplined and rigorous interrogation of the native populations with a view to future publications. Rather than, as it were, going over my own tracks chronologically, let me instead attempt a summary of each facet of the journey, beginning with the hardest, the geology, and sublimating through to the ethereal realm of Indian myth and legend. My team on this adventure changed weekly, it seemed, with the arrival and departure of Indian guides and packers, who offered themselves at rates up to two dollars a day, which I was unwilling to pay, and then somehow found it in their hearts to work for a reduced, one-time-only fee. The one constant employee was Mr. Amos Bowman, a steady, quiet man ten years my senior, Canadian born, who had worked previously as a journalist and had been employed by the Californian Geological Survey, all facts in his distinct favour. I hired him gladly and had no qualms about passing over $170 in advance wages. (He later, after leaving me, both mapped the Cariboo gold fields for the Survey and purchased a large tract of land in the Upper Fraser Valley.)

Our start coincided with the beginning of the mosquito season, the battalions of the tiny nuisances reinforced by abundant shad flies. The smallest of wildlife, the relentless mosquito, became the greatest hindrance to equanimity as the miles and days rolled out. By way of distraction from the slapping and cursing, the fields of sunflowers were always a welcome sight, and I was told that the Indians took the root of the flower and ate it, as well as collecting the seeds in August and making a kind of soup with them. I recorded one farm having fields at almost three thousand feet that were capable of growing barley.

Quite soon into the journey, as the sun rose outside my tent on June 7th, my thoughts were all of Montreal, for it was on that day, to quote the handwritten certificate of the officiating minister, that "Bernard James Harrington, B.A., Ph. D., Professor of Assaying and Mining at McGill College, Bachelor, and Anna Lois Dawson, Spinster, both of the City and District of Montreal, were by license united in marriage." As I later learnt, the affair had taken place in the drawing room at home, with wreaths of lilac, Siberian honey-suckle, and cherry festooned about, while down the centre of the table Bernard's students had placed a row of specimen jars filled with lilies of the valley. Anna wore an imported dress from Scotland and the newlyweds were taken to the train station in Mrs. Redpath's grandest carriage.

(Thoughts of appropriate dress for future weddings I might actually attend reminded me that I would need some clothes when I returned to Civilization, and I made a note to ask Mother if she could order them from my regular tailor, Cathie of Edinburgh. I suggested I'd need two tweed suits with an extra pair of trousers – not lined! – for each would be about right. One suit dark and heavy for winter, the other of coarse, open textured tweed, and light coloured. The vests double-breasted and the coats with a button on the sleeve. They could await my return to Montreal.)

For my part, out in the western wilds, Anna's wedding day began with my overpayment of an Indian by fifty cents, in order to ensure that he show me the beginning of a good trail going southward. Said Indian had arrived the day before while we were drying our clothes around a large fire, announcing himself and his little boy, who was bright and intelligent looking, by firing a sort of gun salute at the heavens. He had heard the bell of my horse and thought we were rival Indians from a nearby lake, a supposition that had angered him. He was pleased to see us white men instead and was on his way down to Quesnelle with a large pack of skins to trade. Around the fire, he told us that his father had died when he was very little and also his mother and nearly all his other relatives during the smallpox epidemic about thirteen years earlier. He had buried them all one after another, but never took the disease himself, until "Konaway memaloose, nika one stop! Hiyu sick tumtum, hiyu kely" which was his way of saying "All dead, I one stop! Much grief, much lamenting." He told us that the trail we were following, since the smallpox had swept off most of the local Indians, was faint and filled with fallen timber. It was the beginning of one such trail that, for two dollars, I induced him to show us. We found the trail, after cutting laboriously through heavy windfallen trees, and I dismissed the Indian. The place we eventually reached was as dismal looking a place in wet weather as can well be imagined. We made large fires and turned in, thereby bringing to a close the day on which my dear sister got married. The next day, I found a humming bird's nest attached to a sprig of spruce and overhanging the water a few feet above it. The female sitting on the nest was very tame, and allowed me to approach within four feet. The nest was of downy material and covered on the outside in a basic colour scheme with white lichen and black moss. Inside was one very small, white egg.

The rivers were still well in flood as we battled again to Soda Creek and beyond, washing away the banks in places to reveal the underlying basalts (a dark volcanic rock) and it was sometimes as much as the steamer could do to go nowhere, sometimes standing stationary on a riffle while every ounce of steam was summoned to help her up. As we progressed after disembarking on horses and mules, in more than one instance we had to build our own bridges over water obstructions, including one across a river running down the middle of a glacier near Cherry Creek. The first mineral I investigated was silver, at Cherry Creek, an exceptionally rich ore, but despite several attempts towards developing the deposit, there was continued difficulty in following the vein. At Fort Hope, there was also a recently mined vein, richer even than at Cherry Creek, being some four to seven feet thick. This vein had been named, appropriately enough, the "Eureka."

In that country one always seemed to be going inland with an open valley to the sea at one's back, and ascending step upon step on giant terraces cut into the hillsides. These terraces had been formed, to my mind, by successive invasions of the sea, a process a geologist would call marine inundation. Several of the river valleys, the Salmon River for example, were crowned by waterfalls, the water not pausing at the foot of the fall but continuing on as a foaming rapid as far as could be seen, in fact to the sea itself. On several occasion within the terraces I found traces of black obsidian, a volcanic rock that, like flint, broke along conchoidal fractures and had been used from time immemorial to fashion knives and cutting implements. The Indians called obsidian "fire stone" or "Beci." This was a linguistic peculiarity, since beci was also the Aztec word for "knife." Could it be, I wondered, that the old Aztec word had survived so far north? For further consideration I discovered that Ta-tla, the name given to two lakes in British Columbia, in Aztec means "place of stones."

One of the enduring personalities on the trip of 1876 was Frank, who was not a Survey officer, or a member of one of the Canadian Pacific Railway parties whose path we crossed more than once, or an Indian seeking an opportunity for earnings; Frank was a mule. Frank was prone to capsizing; there was the morning he missed his footing while crossing a torrent and went off downstream some way, getting cut and bruised a little but not badly hurt. Had he gone a few feet further he would have been carried away by the main stream and then nothing could have saved him from going down over a series of rapids and waterfalls and on to the ocean. During his fall that time our sugar, rice, beans, and oatmeal got quite soaked. My plant case and camera, thanks to a good "manta" (blanket), escaped scot-free and almost dry. Later in the summer we awoke to find, as happened more than once, that the mules and horses had strayed away in search of feed. By one o'clock in the afternoon all of them were found but Frank, and it was evident we would not move that day. Then it began to hail, to a depth of about half an inch. Anxiously I sent Indian Johnny out to look for him, and he returned at six in the evening with an un-repentant Frank trotting behind. The very next day one of the horses, Dan, fell off the edge of the beaver dam by which we were crossing a swamp, into a bottomless mud hole. We thought at one time we would have to abandon him, as all our efforts could not extricate him, and he appeared to be growing weak, and he would not struggle even when beaten severely. At last, by chance, he got turned around, and after wallowing through the mud some dis-tance, he got on to the grass. I would gladly have given the men and animals a rest then, but at that point we had barely five days' food left and our bacon was almost vanished. Seven days later, with just serviceberries and salmon in our stomachs, we made Fort Fraser, very hungry indeed. The Fort consisted of several dilapi-dated log houses standing in the middle of an open flat piece of ground, old boots and moccasins and tin pans strewn all around. Groups of hungry and dejected-looking dogs wandered restlessly about in search of food. In the open poplar woods surrounding the fort a drove of perhaps forty fine cattle were feeding. We were up at a grey dawn with a long way to go, but unable to get off fairly, as Frank, stubborn to the last, had taken it into his head to go back along the trail towards a lake in search of some earlier pack animals he had met. He was once again retrieved and returned to his station, with no sign of repentance.

The man in charge at the Hudson's Bay at Fort Fraser was Mr. Alexander, a well-educated and gentlemanly man, married to a rather good-looking half-breed with a family of small children running about. I was impressed by his naturalist's eye and keen sense of natural rhythms. He believed that a really good run of salmon only comes up once every five years. Then it's very numer-ous the next year, then less, the next still less, and the next almost none before a fine run again. He was also convinced that the seasons had changed within the last eight or nine years. Formerly there had been much rain in the winter and mild weather, but the last two winters were cold and severe throughout and summer frosts, formerly unknown, were now quite common. There was mention also of a conical mound about six feet high of stony material (I suspect it was "calc-tuff" which is deposited near hot springs) with a basin-like hollow in the centre. In it were many bones of small animals and feathers, and it was said birds hovering over it hover over it a moment and then fall dead. Mr. Alexander had climbed up on the top and poked it up with a stick, and began to feel giddy. No oil was seen, but I would guess the effect was from the issue of Carbonic acid. I wish to record here also that Mr. Alexander was a man willing to do everything in his power for us, and for our circumnavigation of the lake supplied us with flour, potatoes, sugar, a little butter, coffee, and as much beef as would keep, together with fifteen pounds of bacon. We also bought some berry cake from the Indians as supplement.

Leaving Fort Fraser, the muffled descent down the Indian trail from the general country to the Iltasyuko River, where we spent some time, was very sudden, the valley under a dull sky looking shut in and very deep, filled with soaring trees and carpeted with deep soft moss. The moss seemed to absorb sound, almost drink it in, and as we moved down as though descending a ladder (with one of my eyes on Frank), and then along the valley floor, I had the impression I had been here at some other time, which was an impossibility. I thought perhaps I had read of it somewhere, and could not break loose of the notion all day until, as we paused by a large beaver pond for me to make a rather unsuccessful sketch, I realized that the valley strongly resembled one of Gustave Doré's illustrations, perhaps one I had seen in London when visiting the Turners, or perhaps in the window of the Doré gallery on Bond Street which had opened after his famous book on London had appeared while I was there.

The beavers had constructed a well-beaten trail running about one hundred yards into the woods to a grove of poplars, which they had cut down and were lying in all directions. Some of the logs had been partly cut into lengths for transport. The trail was clearly a logging one for the animals, and bushes and branches interfering with it had been tidily bitten off. The trail ended in a sort of canal, evidently improved by them to their own specifications. Any trees lying across the trail had been notched out to allow the logs to slide along through it. All in all it was an impressive feat of engineering, and I half expected to come across a pair of the rodents, plans in hand, surveying out an extension. We camped nearby on a lake's edge, and looking into the lake for evidence of life, I saw a bright bluish reflection on the lake like that cast by the moon, yet the moon could not have risen so early. Then a meteor appeared below the branches of the tree in front of me. It was equal in brightness to about twice that of Venus, and it had the general appearance of a signal rocket. It disappeared below the horizon at an angle of about fifty-five degrees.

The mosquito factor as the weeks went by, I see by the series of brief but terse one-line entries in my notebooks, proceeded as follows: bad, troublesome, very bad, horrendous, impossible. The entry relating to "horrendous" was made the day before we finally reached the Telegraph Trail, a moment of great joy for it had seemed to recede with each windfall the axe men cleared along our progress. We cut off a standing tree at four feet from the ground, squared it and at a point just at the southeast corner of Chaka Lake, about half a mile from the water's edge, marked it like this:

PIONEER TRAIL AND BLAZED LINE TO NE-CH-AKO RIVER, GATCHEO LAKE AND SALMON RIVER TO HUNTER'S CAMP. 100 MILES. G.M. DAWSON, A. BOWMAN. GEOLOGICAL SURVEY OF CANADA, AUGUST 31, 1876.

We put another smaller squared post driven in on the edge of the trail, so that the other, a few yards off, might not be missed by anyone looking for it.

When I was once more in Quesnelle in November, with ice forming along the river's edge and the mules well overloaded with samples and near exhaustion, I collected my heap of letters from the Postal Station and attempted a telegraph to let Father know of my safe return to civilization, but the line was not working, a regular occurrence, as the wires ran through goodness knew how many miles of uninhabited country and half the time were hung up on the trees instead of regular posts. When it finally did transmit I also replied to his telegram asking if I would perhaps compete for a Chemistry Professorship in Ottawa. I was still of a mind that whatever I might do eventually, it was evident both to my own credit and my sense of duty that I finish the indoor work which two heavy seasons of field work for the Survey had generated. This, I will admit now, was a delaying tactic; I had become well versed in the art of deflecting Father's good intentions for me, particularly if they meant working in confined spaces.

As I awaited a steamer out of Quesnel, thoughts of the upcoming labour of writing my inaugural Survey reports, and my own curiosity, led me to examine my notebooks with an eye trained to affix on Indian references, for it was clear that a sub-report on the subject, with an anthropological bent, was to be forthcoming. I found I had been fairly diligent, making observations from diet to religion. For example, I had learned that the black moss growing in abundance on the lower dead limbs of the trees in thick woods was used by the Indians in seasons of dearth. They saved it packed in bales during the summer and then beat it up with water, moulded it into cakes, and roasted it before the fire. In one village, the Indian women were boiling up fish heads in pots about a foot square made of wood about three-eights of an inch thick and ingeniously bent around. The boiling was accomplished by dropping heated stones into the pot. The dry fish were pressed down by hand so as to pack them in a solid mass and put into bales backed with spruce bark.

At the Salmon River we found a whole tribe of around sixty Indians on their way to Salmon House for the annual fishery. I got some of them to work for a dollar each constructing a good raft for the crossing and we got everything of ours and theirs and them and us over before dark. It was amusing to see the many dogs travelling with the Indians gradually finding themselves left alone on the riverbank. They set up the most dismal howling and after running up and down the bank finally one by one plunged in and crossed. Among this group was a very old man who remembered seeing the first white men who penetrated this part of the country, four white men, he said, each with a gun, then a novelty to the Indians, came from the east and got two Indians to go with them for a while. If it was indeed Alexander Mackenzie, he came through before the turn of the century, which made the old man very old indeed when I met him, and very young when he saw the white men.

The Indians at Salmon House were in the process of reconstructing the bridge at the falls that was necessary for their fishery which was carried on by suspending broad baskets below the brow of the falls, into which fish jumping in their efforts to ascend fall back. On the trail not far from Salmon House I noticed three small heaps of stones. The Indians had a superstition that any man passing the cairns without "potlatching" them, by which I mean making a gift to the cairn of a twig or a stone, would soon die. In consequence, of course, each cairn was covered with small sticks. The Indians believed that several "tenas" men were buried there, a race of mystical dwarfs or gnomes.

Sometimes along the trail, we would stumble on a customary Native action whose full meaning was not discernible in its entirety, but which nevertheless merited recording. At one such spot where we had stopped for lunch, an old canoe was drawn up. Near it, tied to a piece of bark-string depended from a pole, in addition to a bundle of weeds about nine inches long neatly folded together, was a piece of spruce bark, on the inner side of which was roughly drawn a figure. The Indians said that the owner had not returned and was supposed dead, and his friends had put up these signs to make it known. It being a Sunday, our Indian packers had extra devotions to perform and, in addition to the usual prayers, they had a sort of daily humming choral service both mornings and evenings, and seemed to be always repeating their prayers and kneeling whenever it was convenient.

Watching those men performing a Christian ritual over and over, or their own version of it, I understood there is in the minds and hearts of men an ancient, persistent need of explanation for the fact of existence. I am perhaps as aware as any priest of this, after twenty or more years of study of the very fabric of nature, of the vast age of the earth and its characteristics, but how this need came into being is surely beyond science to explain. As for man's place in the heavens, there must be some fundamental connecting unity of purpose and a single overarching Idea to it all, of which we have been steadily gaining insight, but we cannot, surely, integrate the whole of it. The Whole is something of which we are only partly conscious, and it is God. Whether the God, or perhaps we should call it Creator, feels and responds to our circumstantial alienation from him is unknowable, but I know I felt closer to the answer in a forest resembling a Doré than I did in St. Paul's listening to a laborious sermon.

> When alone I turn
> To where the lights of heaven burn
> My lips refuse to utter prayer.

It was among the Indians that I learnt that this attempt to fashion an explanation for the Whole manifests itself in a host, a constellation, of deities and legends. Any student who had exposure, as I did, to the persistent zeal of Professor Huxley and his championing of Mr. Darwin's ideas, would soon develop a host of question marks for the business of Creation. For example, according to the Indians, the ancient men obtained water, fire, and daylight in the following manner. There was a time they lived in the woods without any of those things, as they then all belonged to a grizzly bear. At last one man, bolder than the rest, undertook to steal the water while the bear slept, and he did secure the prize, but as he rushed away he spilt a little here and there and where the water had landed lakes and rivers remained. Then catching a silver fox, the man split up some wood and attached it to his tail, and the fox ran through the bear's fire and carried away a flame in the wood. Now only daylight remained to be had, and when the bear saw the fox stealthily approaching him again he grew angry and threw the daylight, the sun, at him, giving light to the Earth for the first time. Some of the Indian legends came in bundles, such as the great many centred around the stalwart hero *Us-tass*, and the collection known as "leprates" stories, which were Biblical in origin and had been passed on by a priest, the story of the deluge, the creation, the fall of man and so on, and then filtered through an Indian mind and finally passed on to me in Chinook jargon. One legend spoke of a "skookum (giant) ranch," meaning, I eventually realized, Eden.

Once we strayed off the trail and went far enough in the wrong direction that we walked into a village, astonishing the Natives by our unexpected appearance. There was one rather pretty little girl among them in that camp, and all the rest were decidedly plain. We found we could not communicate with them in any way, as none could speak Chinook, French, or English. (Usually at the forts an extraordinary mixture of common languages was in use by the Indians; Chinook, Canadian French, and their proper language indiscriminately mixed with fragments of English, the latter chiefly consisting of phrases that were new up there but worn out elsewhere, such as "you bet" picked up from Whites.) I wondered if we were the first whites many of those people had seen.

Our circumnavigation brought us back to Fort Fraser, where I learnt from the mail that Father was now working me up as a candidate for the Palaeontology department of the Survey, as it appears Mister Billings had died some weeks previous. (I later saw an item in one of the Victoria papers stating that Mr. Whiteaves actually attained the position, and I was not in the least disappointed. Had I been at home I should not have entered the lists at all.)

The Indians often have several names which they get awarded at feasts given from time to time. They are actually seldom called by their own names, but generally known as so-and-so's father or mother, and given the name of one of their children. If they have no children, very often their favourite dog is chosen. Nor do they mention dead people by their names, but speak of them as the father of such and such a one. This habit was not as strange as it appeared, it occurred to me, since my own name, if inverted, was Son of Daw, and my middle name was that of my mother's family. Our names also grow as we age; mine carries a necklace of letters after it; R.S.C., standing for Royal Society of Canada, for whose formation Father was responsible; F.R.C., fellow of the Royal Society, and so on. A rose by any other name does indeed smell as sweet, but to the taxonomist it is no longer a rose.

Late in September, I visited Fort St. James just for a day, and it was probably as good a sample of a Hudson's Bay post as then was extant, and the most important one in British Columbia. A Mister Hamilton was in charge, and he was helpful to me although one of his children was dangerously ill. The buildings were old, the whole having a rather dirty, neglected air, arranged in a square enclosing a quadrangle, and at a little distance the habitual Indian village. In the dining hall, half-breeds and Indians were constantly lounging about, coming in through the open door and going out at their own discretion. Opening off of the dining room was a kitchen, with a lame old French-Canadian installed inside who told me he had been there thirty-three years as a cook. The warmth of his kitchen made it the common gathering spot of the inmates of the fort. The cook, learning my profession, showed me a knoll behind the fort where a limestone outcrop was visible. I made sketches of the lovely and extensive view on several bearings from the hill, and then collected fossils and sweated back to the fort. The limestone was full of the remains of sea-urchins that helped me date the rock as

Carboniferous, and I told the cook so, which fascinated him to think his kitchen had once been at the bottom of a tropical sea.

While staying briefly at another fort, Fort George, I visited an Indian church. It was filled with narrow boards for seats, and a wooden altar covered with white calico, a few pictures and prints on the walls. In one corner there was a wooden and calico erection for a confessional, with a grating contrived out of a board rather irregularly perforated by large auger holes. On one side of the altar there was a whip hung up — a pretty formidable looking one — which was used to punish delinquents. It was then only eight years since the priests had arrived, and it was extraordinary what hold they had on the Indians, carrying them over to their side in a wonderfully short time, with whole communities repenting and being baptized in a manner resembling the early spread of Christianity in Europe.

Only two missionaries were in that district, around Stewart Lake, at that time, Pères Le Jacq and Blanchet. The former was described to me as a bigoted and meddlesome man, the latter as an ignorant and low-class priest. They depended on the Indians to furnish them with food, who received nothing but blessings for their kind offices. Though in the main amenable to the priests, some groups, such as the Rocher de Bouler Indians, laughed at other bands for their extreme devotions. They contrasted their treatment under the Catholics with those of "Mr. Duncan's Indians," Mr. Duncan being an Anglican missionary. The priests, the Indians said, had taught them prayers, and they knew them all, but they had learnt nothing else, whilst Mr. Duncan's Indians learnt to read and always had plenty of money and plenty to eat. Further, the Catholic Indians were flogged for offences by appointed officers and with the consent of the tribe. An interesting though undesired effect of the missionary's endeavours had been to inaugurate an improved form of medicine man in some places. Those hum-bugs pretended to fall into trances, as they had always done in the past, but now for effect they added supposed interviews with the God of the priests. On one occasion, I was told, one of them, on awakening from a trance, prophesied a great flood by which all would be drowned unless they followed his advice. His advice was that everyone was to go into the woods, find the largest cottonwood tree they could and make several big canoes. The medicine man then announced that if they would give him the best of the canoes he would speak for them to God on the subject of the flood and try and persuade the deity to spare them. He was as good as his word, and accordingly picked out the finest canoe – and then, after talking to God, duly arranged to have the deluge postponed!

Other medicine men did not swallow the salvation offered them whole and remained contrary. One older man, one of the Babine River Indians, a particularly troublesome lot for the priests, insisted on performing his usual cure for a very sick man, despite many of the tribe saying that the priest had warned them it was wrong to do so. But do it he would, and so after all sorts of mummeries he fell into a style of trance, putting his head into a great pan of water, into which he was supposed to exhale and expel the evil influence that had caused the sickness. He remained so long in this position the bystanders feared he had drowned, but his wife said, "Oh no, he always does this." At last, not withstanding the remonstrations of the wife, they lifted him up and found him dead. The widow would not believe it and put the body in bed and sat by it all night. Only when decay set in was she persuaded.

Three weeks later, after a hasty excursion through Kamloops country looking at quartz veins, I was aboard a steamer within a few hours sailing of Victoria, writing again to Father, though the motion of the boat, owing to a little chopping sea and the rough working engines, permitted me nothing more than a scrawl. Although I had not heard from Mr. Selwyn as to whether I was expected to remain another winter in Victoria, in the absence of his instructions I intended to follow what I understood to be the agreed plan, namely that once back in Victoria I would make preparations and leave for Montreal as soon as possible. So it was. Straightaway after docking I took a room again at the Driard, readied my luggage, bemoaned the box of broken photo plates from one of Frank's tumbles that could not be repaired, made my farewells, set my local accounts in order, and walked onto the steamer *Dakota* bound for San Francisco. From there a train heading east, and on the 4th of December, just short of eighteen months after leaving it, I arrived back in the Montreal train station and went to the new house on University Avenue, where I unpacked in a new room, with all the globes and maps and treasures of my youth installed there by Mother so that I felt in no way disturbed. I added what I could from the considerable haul from my many western months.

The house at Métis, which was to be christened Birkenshaw and had been constructed in the "St. Lawrence style," was now roofed and inhabited, gabled and porched. The primary task, Father said, had been to prune the wooded portion of the property, a chore he suspected would become an annual necessity. The pruned branches and undergrowth were dragged to the beach and piled into a bonfire, left to dry and in mid-summer Mother had announced a party, producing some Japanese lanterns and distributing them along the path that led to the shore. After the fire all the songs were sung anyone could remember, and some only partially, then the fire was doused with pails of water and the sore-throated choir adjourned to the house for remedial lemonade and cookies.

Over that winter of 1877 and into 1878, a time of national financial depression, there was a sea shift in the doings of the Survey that had considerable effect on the conduct of the field officers. The Liberals had come into power again, and the charter by which the Survey operated was under scrutiny, as happened every fifth year. The file now sat on the desk of the Minister of the Interior (an accurate description, in the case of an organization devoted to geology), and when it left the desk a new Act had renamed and redefined my place of work. Henceforth the world would know us as The Geological and Natural History Survey of Canada. The inserted ingredient of the two words "Natural

History" was the cause of the shift in emphasis in our field trips. Though Mr. Selwyn had resisted officers in the field making both hard and soft observations, as it were, observations both of the rocks and the flora and fauna, the natural wonders from forest to flight of the Dominion were now in our purview. Likewise the native distributions, customs, and vocabularies. This did not tax me unduly, or many of the others, since we had all been doing it to greater or lesser degree anyway. I was perhaps more zealous than most in my cataloguing of the Indians and their ways of life, but now I felt justified, as my interest was officially sanctioned.

Also in the wake of the new act, two things happened, one right away, one a little later. Right away, myself and three others were made Assistant Directors, and were now full-fledged government employees, with all the blessings and curses that might entail. Though it would be three years in the making, the move to Ottawa now became inevitable for the Survey headquarters. At some point in the future, I was destined to live in Ottawa as an Ottawan, and operate within stumbling distance of my masters. The Survey's link, through Father, with McGill and the Natural History Society of Montreal, both of which institutions considered him their guiding spirit, was then bound to weaken, but it had already served to bring me into the work I did indeed seem fated to perform, for which blessing I was most grateful.

———

IN THE DAYS before returning to Victoria the following Spring, I was as impatient as a racehorse. The train finally carried me out of Montreal on April 24th, 1877, and sixteen days later, having gone through Chicago, Omaha, and Provo, I was calling on Lieutenant Governor Richards in his Victoria home. Richards had sat in the House of Commons in the years I had been with the Boundary Commission, and he liked to personally welcome members of the Survey to his territory.

The journey out was as remarkable for its cast list as anything else. On leaving Omaha, people knew that they were bound to spend a few days together in a Pullman, as on a short sea voyage. In consequence, people at once became more conversational and friendly. I shared a seat with a Mr. Wise, who was connected with the railway office in Utah. Opposing us was an Americanized Dutchman appointed as Postmaster to some remote western district and travelling with his daughter, a not too ugly girl but too modest to speak. There was a Mrs. Lawrence from Washington, going out to join her husband, a doctor in Arizona. Also, another lady who soon became a chum of Mrs. Lawrence but who got off to go to Golf Hill in Nevada, where her husband was something in mines. There were also several young ladies all of whom with the exception of one were plain looking and commonplace in every respect. The one exception was returning to Oakland in California from a visit East with her mother and other members of the family; she was extremely good looking to say the least of it and clever with it.

We had a small Cabinet organ in one of the Pullmans and the musical portion of the community continued to enliven the journey with songs till we lost the music box in changing cars at Ogden. About the only tune everybody seemed to know was "Hold the Fort," so that and some of the other Moody and Sankey series, the American evangelists who wrote sacred songs, were favourites. Disgusted with the loss of our instrument, we solaced ourselves by sitting out on the platforms and steps of the train waiting for sunrises, sunsets, such as the very satisfactory one over Great Salt Lake, meridian passages, and other astronomical phenomena – and then going back indoors to shake bushels of dust and wash pebbles out of our eyes. We also observed antelope which seemed to reciprocate in most cases, and from time to time several people would dash themselves against a window to see a Jack rabbit, which never would be seen.

On we went through the apple and peach bloom of Salt Lake Valley and then into the wastes of the Humboldt Valley and creeping up to the summit of the Sierra Nevada, which we attained in the very early morning. Then the run down to San Francisco in one day, sliding along with the judicious use of the engine to keep the train from running too fast, on through the foot hills now green and beautiful with flowers and into the wide Sacramento Valley where we found ourselves in Summer, with hay-making going on, the strawberries ripe and all the trees in full foliage. Here I reluctantly left the comforts of the Pullman and in five minutes found myself alone and forlorn in a dull little country waiting room. At last four o'clock came and with it the next train, surcharged with sweating, local passengers intersprinkled with babies. We finally pulled up at the terminus at one in the morning, and some slept while I rose up at half past four to breakfast and catch the stage which started at five. The vehicle was not very reassuring as the inside was half filled with mail matter and a miscellany strapped all over the top at the back.

For fellow passengers on this stage there was a stout great-grandfather and his wife going up to Oregon to see their children; an Americo-German Jew buying skins and furs; an attorney; and a non-descript man also with a wife. Various kaleidoscopic changes in the passenger arrangements occurred, losses and gains, until the losses preponderated and I found myself alone with the driver. We drove on for three days and two nights, the longest stop being at Yreka for two hours. The road cut out for long distances like a shelf on steep grassy hillsides, complemented by impossibly steep other hills for us to ascend and descend by means of a system of the most involved doubling back and toing and froing that almost made me dizzy. I didn't know too much about all this as it was pitch dark; I only heard the brake shrieking against the wheel as we went bumping along and sometimes saw the six horses dancing on the edge of an abyss as we flew round the curves.

One begins to get very sleepy on about the third day. You are admiring the scenery – paying the greatest possible attention to it – when all at once you relapse into a state of temporary insanity with the most absurd dreams rushing through your head, till all at once you wake up on the point of jolting forward among the horses. When we stopped now and then for a break I found myself all covered with contusions and tender spots, my hands brightly polished from holding onto the iron rails and my head nearly sawn off by the edges of my collar. On reaching, at last, the Pacific, the company presented us with a last supper of clams, and I won't enter into details with the various gastronomic struggles, or the varying consequent forms of indigestion that I went through the next day. The country, however, gave the effect of a perfectly kept park, with wide fertile fields and hardly anything we would call winter. It being Sunday the day I arrived, I can characterize the region in the words of the psalmist, "Where every prospect pleases, but only man is Vile" for I never heard before so much concentrated bad language in those final ten days getting to Victoria. Yet even while waiting for the steamer from San Francisco I felt already as if I had been journeying forty years in the wilderness and was about to enter the Promised Land – via New Westminster.

While in Victoria I looked up the Creases, friends from a previous trip, and went with them on a boating party. As some people did not turn up at the last moment I found myself in for taking an oar. Despite my early training with the cousins at Musselburgh I did not then and do not now consider myself adept at rowing, being more of a canoeist. Nonetheless we got along about five miles when the excursion resolved itself into a Picknick when the second half of the party joined us overland on horseback. We rowed back during twilight and after dark. I must record here that I have always found the people in Victoria to be very kind, both to each other in general and to me in particular.

In mid-May the *Enterprise* bore me to New Westminster, then the redoubtable steamer *Royal City* carried me to Kamloops, my centre of operations for the summer. On the Fraser we raced the *Royal*'s rival ship *Glenora* all forenoon, races along competitive routes not being uncommon then. After docking I went by stage and buggy with driver Steve Tingley, well-known in the area, and at last came by steamer into Kamloops by moonlight, across a perfectly calm lake.

Learning that the self-same steamer was to battle the unruly North Thompson the next day, I remained aboard for a brief side trip. In the late afternoon the timbers below the frustrated boiler furnace caught fire, and we halted at some rapids to put out the blaze. On our return I saw an old Indian sitting and cooking something in a pot, three dried fish beside him on a pole. He sat with his back to the river, stirring away, and though we passed within a stone's throw of him he never indicated that he noticed us. Further on, I conversed with some Indians from the deck, near a coal deposit beside a Reserve an old miner had mentioned in Victoria. The Indians, however, seemed determined to keep the location a secret. Back in Kamloops, anxious to start, I went directly to the camp I had telegraphed ahead to set up, to look over our pack animals. Seven of the mules were crippled and useless, so I went to the Indian Reserve to discuss the idea of buying horses with Chief Louis, their leader. He was in a sweat lodge with a friend, and we held a conversation through the blankets, during which he promised to bring over some horses that evening. (The chief eventually came to Ottawa, where we met again, and went on to England in defense of his people.)

The intention was to occupy the next few months with three expeditions in the Nicola Valley, the name I eventually affixed myself to the series of lakes between mountains we were to survey. The Survey actually had seven parties at work in the region, of which mine was but one, scattered along the proposed Canadian Pacific Railway routes by the Fraser and Thompson Rivers, with the intent of having a complete map of the area surveyed by autumn and then selecting one railway route as best.

Three men formed my party this season; a Mexican packer called Jacinto whom I had travelled with before, a Lytton Indian with the habitual name Johnny who did the cooking, and a white man called Douglas who carried the rocks and hammers, attended to my horse, and put up the tent. Douglas was a very quiet man of a mild disposition and he saved me much trouble.

And so, a few days before the beginning of June, the rigging was fitted to the horses and the packs made up and we put our best feet and hooves forward. The season was a remarkably early one, probably two weeks in advance of the norm. The chokecherry was already nearly past its prime, the Canadian violas were in looming thickets by the water, and the amelanchier was on show in its favourite moist places with its fruit fully formed. I was glad at heart that the daily round of collecting, pressing, and photographing had begun again after a winter of suspended animation.

The first notable feature we encountered was rather a puzzle – Stump Lake, a large sheet of water with many of its eponymous stumps now submerged, some of them charred, extending far out into the lake. The Indians reported that some of them still living could remember when there was no lake there, and within the memory of the settlers around it water had ceased to flow from it. My own feasible explanation was that of an original subterranean outlet through which the water entered and then later passed away, and which had subsequently become blocked.

Though it was one of my favourite aspects of travel, photography proved difficult in the early stages of this trip with massive clouds hanging around most afternoons, birthing passing showers and squalls. I was cheered a few days later when, at supper, an Indian messenger appeared with the mail from Kamloops. My fellow surveyor, Ross, had sent the messenger with a note that I should give the man five dollars and some supper before he left, both of which instructions I performed.

The pursuit of coal exposures and iron ores within the mountains sometimes produced interesting auxiliary results. For example, on the mountain east of Coldwater, about six miles down the trail to the town of Hope, an encouraging target, there lay an Indian Camp, and after a little trouble I secured a youngster to guide me to the summit, just over five thousand feet, up where the aspens were just opening their leaves. My guide could not locate the main seam of iron, however I did put my finger on some interesting glacial traces.

A word or two here, of a geological nature, concerning glacial theory and the migration of ice. Geology is the science of clues, of solving mysteries, much as the Edinburgh physician Dr. Conan Doyle does in his Sherlock Holmes stories, which I read in serial form in the *Strand* magazine when they were published perhaps a decade ago, although Mr. Holmes is now of course "dead." The harder parts of Canada, the land beneath our feet, contain indications as to the form of her distant past, and it is this I and the Survey attempt to discern, both for the sake of pure knowledge and in service to such industries as the railways. I also recall a sentence from my notebooks at the School of Mines, which read along the lines that "Sooner or later, everything moves," an admonishment to not forget that the earth is in a perennial state of rearrangement, and that the wrinkles and scars that she gained then are partly visible now; one must follow the arrows back and arrive at a possible solution.

In the case of ice, Canada has much in storage in its attic, and both Father and I spent many hours wondering where and when and how far this ice, these glaciers, had moved in the past. When my guide on Iron Mountain (a name I provided for the previously untitled formation) inadvertently led me to marks of passing ice down near the United States border, I was naturally anxious to find a few more confirmations – or denials – of our theory.

By the side of the trail on Iron Mountain there were projecting masses which had been sculpted into ridges, like those on a forehead, by the passage of ice. Finding the hieroglyphics of obviously large ice formations flowing southward and elbowing past the projecting rocks, at a point almost a mile above sea level, helped me to further visualize the depth and extent of the great sea that

Father and I both believed had filled the land this far south as the northern ice had melted and vast detached icebergs had roamed here, leaving their mark.

When the guide and I returned to the Indian camp, the women were busily engaged in gathering the wild onion, just before it burst into flower. They wandered about in the woods with baskets on their backs and a crutch-like stick in hand with which the plants were uprooted and then tossed over the shoulder. The onions were then raised up in the trees around their rather large wigwams to keep them out of reach of dogs and other larger wildlife, the stalks put in bundles very neat and clean looking that appeared cured. They were black and more like seaweed than anything else, having been steamed in holes in the ground with hot stones and dried for future use. The process was said to render them quite sweet.

On the trail, I have always found the distance between un-common sights to be short. The uncommon becomes the expected, and that is in no small part of the joy of the journey. An example. While in camp one evening at the fifty-seven mile post from Hope, a small band of cattle passed through. Two very young calves, birthed along the way, were tied up with gunny sacks and slung on a horse, with their heads and one foreleg each projecting out and hung on either side of a Mexican saddle. The drover explained, when we asked, that further back he had had to kill two calves that were unable to travel, causing his cows to always want to go back down the path where they supposed the dead calves were. And so he had found it less trouble to carry the live calves on in this fashion. The horse carrying them seemed in no wise embarrassed by his strange load, and when the drover stopped, he strayed about feeding as though barebacked. Not so the anxious mothers who followed the horse lowing loudly and looking earnestly at their calves as though they did not know exactly what to make of it.

We travelled on down the continuing wide valley and gentle slopes of the Coldwater River, the Douglas firs increasing, with pine grass for the horses tangled here and there with pea vine. One evening while asleep a large band of cattle came up behind and nearly ran over our camp, which was when we discovered where we had put it – directly on a cattle trail. The cursed rain was either already there or on its way no matter where we went, and evenings were invariably clothed in gently, persistently shed drizzle, just for a change. The horses, tied by their halters to a long rope stretched between two trees, stood disconsolately in the wet, with their thoughts no doubt, poor things, on dry bunch grass or the flesh pots of Egypt in some form.

The canyon of the Coquihalla River was magnificent, with its wooded or nearly bare cliffs rising abruptly from the river to a great height, and beautiful cascades pouring down over them in many places. The river itself worked towards the sea in the bottom of the narrow tortuous valley with a steady roar. In several places, years ago, great snow slides had descended the sides, sweeping a broad, clearly defined veldt completely clear of timber, the trees smashed off so close to the ground that scarcely any prominent stumps remained. At the foot of the slope the trees were piled in a tangled splintered mass of the most confused character, giving out the idea of an almost irresistible force.

The next day we made Hope, moving down a hilly trail lined with salmonberry trees with a strong wind blowing up the Fraser River that we were told was the usual thing from pretty early in the morning to sundown. Hope was a picturesque place, bound on every side by abrupt mountains. There were altogether maybe twenty-five white people there, with a larger but variable number of Indians. It was a place of some importance in the mining days but had dwindled down to become one of the quietest places on earth. The steamer, which called twice a week each way, constituted the only relief to the monotony of life.

By contrast a nearby Indian village was very neat, with pretty little whitewashed houses and small garden patches, fields, and orchards. A man called Yates who was with the Hudson's Bay Company told me that while a few years earlier there were about two hundred and fifty Indians in the area belonging to the Church of England, that number had dwindled to less than sixty, the rest having gone over to the Catholics on account of the shabby treatment meted out by the Church of England missionaries. Mr. Yates had lived in Hope for some thirty years without ever returning to Victoria. He was, naturally, well posted on the history of the place and could supply all the dates of events with as much importance as though he spoke of the history of a lost empire. Hope seemed to occupy two hundred and seventy degrees of his horizon. He was an Orkney man, a class of Amiable Hudson Bay Fossil, specimens of which were scattered all over the northwest.

From Hope we moved upward towards the summit of the Cascade Range, passing over a stony bench on which rhododendrons were abundant with magnificent heads of pink flowers. Tier upon tier of snow-clad mountains lay to the north and south, none of them going up much beyond the timber limit and, looking down the valley we beheld the Skagit River, a mass of foam winding along below us with white flowering raspberry still abundant on the sides. After three days of ascent, we reached the summit on June 16th, having left camp at half past five that morning. On the second day of the climb we passed a man called Wardle who was the Kootenay Mail Carrier and then another man, "Captain" William Bristol as he called himself, who farmed an eponymous island west of Hope, but who in his heart was also a mail man, having formerly run an express canoe mail service and a stage coach.

At the summit, I got the camera down and took three photos of the panorama, though it was cold so, business completed, I was glad to descend to Powder Camp. The camp's name came from an incident involving prospectors who were packing out a campsite when it caught fire. There was a rush to throw the blasting powder into the nearby creek, which was thankfully successful just prior to explosion. The place was much quieter when we were there, and I was able to write up my observations and survey notes. This was a constant chore predicated by the lack of a good map, which it thus fell on me to prepare, which in turn made it necessary to keep a careful running survey during the entire summer, since I'd been unable to secure the services of a suitable scientific assistant, the whole of the work therefore devolving onto my shoulders.

Our next port of call was at the ranch of Mr. J. Hayes, an American who had come into the Okanagan territory in the 1860s. On the map his ranch is marked now as the town of Princeton. He was a quaint enough character, who had mellowed with his years, isolation and location leading him into oddity. His first question to us was whether we would not take something to drink, and he urged us to take a glass of milk, whereupon a small tumbler was produced from a cupboard with dried traces of former quenchings; a quick wash in the bucket and then the tumbler was filled to the brim with milk that hours earlier was still in the udder, and which was certainly very good.

Hayes was tall and lanky with a stoop and the general appearance of a typical Yankee. He was concerned to discuss his garden, which appeared to have run out, although latterly he had grown cabbage, cauliflower, cucumbers, squashes, beans, and more. The potatoes in the last season it seemed "grew all to tops and not to bottoms." Manuring did no good, and though there were still some gooseberries and asparagus in there they were "all the time petering and petering and going back instead of ahead." He sold me a sample of gold containing some platinum, and then showed us his large magnet, which he admired. "She draws powerful, I tell ya," he said, "but she won't touch that platinum" as if this proved the platinum to wilfully possess some extraordinary property of resistance to ordinary forces.

Soon after leaving Mr. Hayes with one last drink of milk we were in rattlesnake country, or so my Indian guide told me, and then Jacinto killed one while looking after the animals, to confirm the statement. The rocks were very provoking thereabouts as we moved towards Osoyoos, being as they were all slides at the bases of the mountains with nothing to be seen of bedding up above, and it shook my faith in all the previous fixed formations I'd seen to find all these beds so much jumbled together. Another mystery with an elusive solution, and of course that was what I had come for.

> Oh! for a fossil, some poor shell
> That died upon an olden shore
> But yet in whispered voice can tell
> — last hollow throbbing of a bell —
> Of the ancient ocean's roar.

The soil too had become more alkali, as indicated by the proliferating rye grass. It was generally very thickly populated country; one could hardly put one's foot down without treading on a large black beetle or an ant, and the grasshoppers nimbly kept out of the way of one's feet, while occasionally dashing themselves violently into one's face, coming in stern first under all sail in a good breeze.

Then we came into the wide, flat-bottomed Osoyoos Valley, expecting to see settlement of some sort, but we could see none and did not know which way to take. We could see two narrow land bridges – glacial eskers is the correct term – crossing the Osoyoos Lake which was about nine miles in length, one in the middle and one at the southern end, like a vast mathematical "equals" sign drawn on the lake. The valley looked to me then like another example of a great channel that had drained a current of melting ice, populated with icebergs like model boats on a park boating lake. I was just on the point of camping at a little stream when out of the corner of my eye I discerned a house, and steering towards it soon saw another one. These were the families resident there, exactly two in number, Judge Hays as he called himself and a German called Kruger. Both had run up considerable holdings. I accepted Mr. Hay's invitation to dine with him, and I had, for a change, a capital dinner off a real table with a clean table-cloth. While we were dining a packer called Newman arrived with news of an Indian rising to the south in Oregon. Refusing to go on a reservation, the Nez Percé tribe were making a fight of it as they retreated.

Moving up the Okanagan Valley towards Penticton, again the name the rancher there had called his spread that had broadened out to include a settlement, Indian Johnny remarked on a particular bird singing away merrily in a tree. That bird, he said, "*wa-was all same Siwash la langue*" a curious phrase being a mixture of at least three languages roughly meaning, "that bird sings in each place where it is in the dialect spoken there by the Indians." I believe that he believed himself, as well. The bird apparently was saying "Halo Capswallow!" which was in fact Chinook for "Don't steal!" The bird, or one of its relatives, caused some amusement the next day when, in order to cook lunch, Johnny took a wooden bar off a fence and broke it up for the fire. Shortly afterwards the moral bird, perched on a tree near us, kept reiterating his sung advice not to steal.

Okanagan Lake was a truly beautiful sheet of water, and I searched out a place to bathe. I thought I had spotted one when I suddenly came on an Indian woman sitting in a state of nature, going about her ablutions. She seemed a little put out at being caught thus, but wisely sat still. On looking up a little further I saw paterfamilias and a whole brood of children occupied in the same way. Retiring a little I called to the gentleman, who obligingly put on his unmentionables and came over to answer questions about a swimming spot. I went to the suggested location and had a good bath in the lake, under the patronage of a water snake about a yard long who swam up and looked at me. He was a brown fellow with dark spots, very graceful and pretty. Then the rain began again and the trail twisted on and ascended in heavy rain. Our motto among us became "If this is a *dry* climate, let me try a wet one."

The Vernon Brothers, Charles and Forbes, had been in charge of the Coldstream, the most prosperous ranch in the Okanagan Valley, for six years when with their permission we camped alongside the estate's little flour mill. The house itself was in what I might call the "Cacouma" style, and only Mr. Charles Vernon was presently there, an English gentleman and ex-officer who did some farming and mining, besides attending to various public duties such as Justice of the Peace, land commissioner, gold commissioner and such. His brother had accepted the position of Minister of Public Works in Victoria, and so Mr. Charles was living there. We dined with him one evening, an event for which he himself made an excellent cake and he told us the story of settlement roundabout, that the valley was a sort of Arcadian retreat. The first settler, called Cyprian Laurence, came there around 1860, and many others had been there nearly as long, mostly half-breeds, speaking French, but there were some French people from Old France at the Okanagan Mission. They all seemed comfortable enough in their way, seventeen families in all, and there was a school with about twenty scholars, again all half-breeds; on our way to look at the Vernon mines, we had met some of them with lunches and books, neatly dressed. A little log church with a tinkling bell gave out a few notes every evening. There was still plenty of land thereabouts to be had by simple preemption or by purchase from the government for a dollar an acre.

A side excursion to Cherry Creek to examine some interesting rocks was called for, and I informed Mr. Vernon that we would thus reunite in about eight days. On the first morning I stood on a hillside, making a sketch of the country when I heard suddenly, where all before had been perfectly still, a *crack* followed by a *krr* then a *wish smash*. A great rotten old tree had fallen without any provocative cause whatsoever; one of the wood ants must at that moment have gnawed through the last fibre that made the difference between standing and falling. We arrived at the Cherry Creek formation soon after, and it did indeed have a silver load and some diggings, and I got a fine specimen of the ore, but got no colour when trying for gold. I made a survey and found a broken sluice ditch, and some small amount of gold in black sand. The company working this mine had had the name "Christian."

Returning to Vernon's we moved about his property for several days, which is what it took, given the extent of it. The layover included a Sunday spent reading a selection of Mr. Vernon's weekly budget of papers and periodicals from all parts of the world. I noticed then and have noticed in all my travels before and since that Sunday layovers have a demoralizing effect, and one makes a later start on Monday than any other morning of the week. Mr. Vernon, on being asked while we sat up late talking, said that if he desired to sell he would expect $2,500, presumably the maximum price.

While Mr. Vernon embraced the traditional use of horses as transport and labourer, when we camped at the next ranch along the trail, Ingram's Grand Prairie, we found quite a different quadruped in use. During the recent gold excitement in the Cariboo region, Ingram was enterprising enough to buy some eighty camels which were shipped from the Amoor River in Siberia. One of the vessels transporting them became ice-bound and the animals starved, while the other ship managed to land twenty-four of the dromedaries at San Francisco. When they arrived in the Okanagan, they were voted a nuisance and prohibited on account of the fear which horses and mules entertained of them, rendering it impossible for those skittish animals to pass the camels. Three of the camels were still there when we were at Grand Prairie, the others having been killed or lost. Unfortunately the three remaining ones were all females, and all born in British Columbia. They worked well as draught animals and withstood the winter admirably. Their hair was said by Ingram to be worth a dollar a pound in New York, so there was a profitable culture in that at least.

Many miles had now passed in the saddle and I was grateful that our next survey would be of Little and Great Shuswap lakes and we would therefore switch to canoes. First there was the need for a canoe, and I found one at the ranch of Mr. Whitfield Chase, the first white man to make a home on the lakeside. Mr. Chase said we were welcome to it, but it was ten miles away and so two Indians were sent to retrieve it, one of whom I also hired to accompany us on our circumnavigation. He was a smart fellow with the appropriately nautical name of Noah. On getting the canoe out of the water I realized there was much work necessary, so I went over to the nearby Indian village to see if they had any. I had seen them out fishing on the lake, generally two or three canoes at a time, and a snatch of their peculiar grunting sort of song would proceed across the water. They caught a small species of whitefish in abundance on a hook and line and ate it with potatoes, spreading the fish on a piece of cedar bark and eating it without condiment of any kind, and using two hands when it came to the extraction of the numerous little bones. The Chief, whose name was Andre, was anxious that I walk around his garden first, especially to see his "ians," his onions, and with many well-meaning words as to the *Klooshness* of his *tumtum* (the happiness of his belly) he pulled up a handful of the largest of his little onions and with a majestic wave of his arm presented them to me. I took the opportunity of reciprocating by presenting him with some tobacco, but still it seemed there were no canoes to be had.

So, we set to work in earnest on the big old canoe, which I dubbed the *Pseudomorph*, an apt name since it denoted the replacing of one mineral within a rock by another, while retaining the same overall shape. We collected gum, used it, then nailed strips of blanket and tin over the gummed and caulked cracks, scraped and shaped her bottom, made oars and paddles, strengthened her with thwarts. (I had almost by accident become a boatbuilder, which was just as well later on when, in the Yukon, we were hundreds of miles from anyone and faced with yet another boat crushed by rocks.) When we first put her in the water she leaked badly and had to be taken out again, dried by fire and gummed inside and out, and by dark she was seaworthy. In the morning we made for the island in the middle, Copper Island, and feeling sure that the usual monsters would be credited with inhabiting the lake and the island I proceeded to inquire of Noah and found that it was even so. A creature

THE AGE OF THE WEST.

"all same as bear" lived under the water and ate Indians, while in the winter many little animals somewhat like horses came out and ran about on the ice, leaving dung. After a day on the water without leaks, I pitched my tent within a few feet of the water's edge and looked out on the lake as I wrote my notes, the water lapping rather sullenly on the gravelly shore.

The lake became more fiord-like the next day, and a poor dog, nearly starved, was on the shore, evidently abandoned there. He seemed half afraid to approach us, but considered himself left in charge of things, and his weak barking was a rather poor defiance as we landed. At his rear was a wonderful profusion of berries; black berried haw, ripe; service berries, rather over-ripe; berries of the large white flowering raspberry in great profusion; wild cherries; red huckleberries; black raspberries; pigeon berries; and sarsaparilla berries.

It was raining when I awoke on my birthday, my twenty-eighth, which gave me an excuse for a longer lie than usual, then after noon we travelled on to the former site of the town of Seymour, where there was only the ruined walls of one house standing. It was a romantic and pretty spot for a town, but the end of the Big Bend gold excitement had laid it to rest. In 1864 Governor Seymour had sent a party out to blaze a waggon trail to the Kootenays, and they had found gold along the way. In the ensuing rush, Seymour on Shuswap Lake was the steamer dock where goods and men trans-ferred for the overland trek to the gold fields. The fields ran dry in just two years and the twenty or so buildings of Seymour began to decay one by one.

By mid-August we had come full circle, the shore line being not much short of two hundred miles, and were back in Kamloops with all of it surveyed; the "Cruise of the Pseudomorph" had ended. I collected a fair bag of letters, but only had time to sketch out the barest of replies as the next trip was soon underway. There was a debate back in Montreal as to whether to send Eva to France for the winter, and my opinion was sought. I thought that perhaps the trouble and expense of sending her might not be warranted by the probable result, and she could make a sight-seeing trip some other time with myself or William. A sight worth her seeing right then would have been the salmon running. We'd seen them from the canoe going up over the bars faster than we could count them, thousands in an hour, after they had run the gauntlet of the canneries below where they were being canned at the rate of 70,000 pounds a day. They were still hundreds of miles from the sea and we saw them again periodically in various stages of spawning, sometimes spent and turning red and dying with their heads pointed upstream to the last.

I made two more trips, one on horse, one in canoe, that summer before we turned back for home, one about forty-five miles up the north Thompson River and the other a fairly swift one around Kamloops Lake. Johnny had sprained his wrist which led to my having to replace him, which led to an amusing incident when the replacement innocently put on the dining table, among the condiments, my bottle of insects in sawdust and alcohol. On both trips I had become more aware of the need to collect samples, especially of coal. Mr. Selwyn had written asking for such as these for yet another Paris Exposition was due to take place the following year.

I heard the story of one particularly unpleasant superstition from one of the ranch owners who had employed some Indians in ditch digging. He noticed that when they came into camp at the end of the day they would jump several times over the fire and tie up the legs of their trousers before going to bed. This arose from the notion that a small, very abundant lizard, if it caught sight of a man, would follow him steadily by his tracks until, catching up with him when he is asleep, it would enter by a certain orifice and kill him, hence the various rituals. When they saw the lizards during the day they would take forked twigs, and impale them and tie the ends together with grass, and stick it upright in the ground, the lizards drying to mummies shortly thereafter. On the canoe trip I had three Indians, the addition being one called Bill who was minus his nose but had lately been paid off for some gold and in the matter of clothes cut me out altogether.

I had stepped up my geological examinations, and perhaps allowed my concentration on those alone to blind me to other natural distractions, and it was almost the death of me. On ascending a slope in one place to examine a terrace of older rock that I believed would reinforce my glacial theories, I heard a movement just as I opened my compass. Looking down I saw a large snake fully four feet long, moving slowly. As his head, though threatening, was turned away from me, I finished reading the compass, took a look at him and left. He precisely resembled a rattlesnake, but had no rattle. Johnny explained that while the true rattle's bite is almost always fatal unless immediate measures are taken, the snake I saw had a bite that was frequently not fatal. The beast I saw looked so much like a rattlesnake that I thought it must be a variety of the same. Later I found out that Johnny was mistaken. It was indeed a rattlesnake!

The next few days I devoted a fair amount of time in the evenings to pulling together the geological evidence I now had to hand, and the days were spent in surveying and hunting, taking readings from Polaris and on one occasion the object of the chase was — a badger. He looked around in an inquiring way before I shot him.

Being now close to the Hayes outfit again, I wondered about getting there post haste as the weather was deteriorating, but then some fresh water shell fossils turned up in some loose stones in a river bar and I thought it important to trace them. I set off overland with a local Indian guide to find the source of the origin of the fossils upstream, which indeed I did. Wishing to cross the river and see the rocks on the other side, the Indian volunteered to carry me over, and stripping off his boots and britches he seized a stick and presented his back to me to mount. We crossed successfully though owing to the depth of water I got my feet wet. Going up on shore a short distance I found an exposure with some plant and insect fossils, and encouraged I fagged away at the rocks, with the rain now coming down in good style. Standing out in the rain in a wet linen coat with a straw hat and puggery down one's back is not pleasant, especially while Mr. Indian crouched under a log, endeavouring to preserve from the elements those parts of his person left uncovered by the absence of nether garments, was gently hinting that *wake Si-a copete Sun* ("sun nearly finished"). I did not want to give up and was rewarded with some fish scales, the first vertebrae remains yet found in the Tertiary beds in the area. Finally, wrapping up my treasures in a handkerchief, I crossed the river as before and reached camp just before dark.

It was startling to me, extrapolating from those fish scales, to discover that the face of Nature then was so much as it is today. In the interim, nearly all the large species have perished, and whole continents have changed, and yet an observer, conveyed backward to a scene of those days, would have to examine closely many of the plants and animals and their inter-relations and complexities to make out the difference from those with which he was familiar. For instance, I found some little water skipper fossils that day that looked as though they might have skipped just yesterday instead of countless years ago.

I had intended to make Lytton by the middle of September, and came close to doing so. The journey there seemed littered somehow with bones. At the mouth of the Coldwater, about a week beforehand, many Indians had collected from different parts of the country. I could not quite understand at the time the nature of the "play" they were making but it was some ceremonial reburying of the dead. I met one man on horse who had his brother's bones done up in white cloth behind his saddle. I later learnt that this business of reburial was a long-standing Thompson Indian practice; the grave of a relative was re-opened two or so years after death and the bones wiped clean and put into a new suit, a skin robe, or a blanket. There were two main camps of Indians there for the feasting, separated by a few miles, with the *klootchmen* (women) dressing up in their best and dancing while the men sang, then the men danced to the drumming, imitating different animals.

Then an Indian guide we had hired on a temporary basis showed us the bones of his unfinished house, on the Coldwater River, which he had built but abandoned fearing some white man would come along and pre-empt the claim. He had formerly had a house and a little farm back near the mouth of the Coldwater but a white man called Chapman came and pre-empted the land, against which there was of course no redress. It seemed in my mind that there had already been too much of this sort of thing in the Nicola Valley.

In Lytton itself, since we arrived cold and wet, I gave myself the luxury of staying at the Globe Hotel, and after a good supper and sleep went across town to a point between the Fraser and Thompson Rivers (which meet at that town) to see a reported Indian burial place so ancient that the living Indians knew nothing about it, and did not even count the dead there as their friends. The mound was roughly oval and pointed to the junction of the two rivers, being about one hundred and fifty yards long and a third that width. It was composed of sand, with tufts of bushes and yet one large tree on the lower end. The prevailing strong winds had ripped the mound up in many places, and this natural action had bared the remains. The internments along the summit and slopes were several hundred in number. The bodies were generally in the sitting position and the skulls showed no signs of compression, although many of them crumbled to pieces on handling and only some of the older ones were worth removal. The most important people, judging by the quality of the implements lying nearby, seemed to have been buried near the crest of the ridge. Yellow and red ochre paint lay near the bodies and in one case the head had been thickly covered in red ochre. No iron implements were found, only copper and lead, and it seemed that it must have been abandoned as a burial place about the time of the advent of whites to the Coast, or even before. Altogether it was a wonderful display of bones and implements, and we gathered quite a number of the latter and returned to Lytton. After dropping those packs off, Douglas and I quietly went back to the mound and appropriated seven skulls, the best examples we could find without resorting to excavation. We carried them back in a gunny sack and packed the whole collection in a couple of boxes for Victoria.

It now remained only to make the slow run for home. I was up, with first dawn to make the long drive into Kamloops, and was delayed just a little by the straying of the horses, who seemed to find that part of the country too big for them. That night there was heavy rain that turned to snow, and when dawn broke the ground was completely whitened and the trees loaded. The next day I was surprised and disgusted to find the ground again covered with snow and a snow storm raging, but there was nothing to do but get off, as we were low in feed. In the evening I had a rare bad headache, caused by handling dynamite which we had used in endeavouring to split up a great log for firewood. On then to Lillooet, a busy place, full of packers and pack trains and business and bustle and Chinamen working in the fields thereabouts. The scenery around the town was very fine and quite the style for a tourist resort if only it had been less out of the world. Our trek was accompanied by the harsh *crock*, or half *caw* or even sometimes *creak*, of the Clark's nut-cracker, and every now and then one could be seen jumping to the ground, seizing one of the cones of the great ponderosa pines and flying to a limb, where it held the cone steady in its claws and proceeded to extract the seeds by repeated blows with its pick-axe bill. Meanwhile, on a nearby limb, the great blue jay set up a tremendous, ugly screaming, although by its plumage it is a perfect dandy among birds. In this theatre of bird-scream we made camp on the Bonaparte River and, hungry as a wolf, I ate well from the coyote we had bagged, and tried to sleep, but I was pleasantly distracted by the aurora, which was the best I'd seen in a long time.

We were up on a plateau now, and in viewing the country across the Thompson River I could suddenly see how the land had buckled and folded up in the post Miocene era, and how the waters had drained from it as that happened, leading to this arid country where wood for a simple camp fire was so hard to find. I made as many

notes pertaining to my vision as I could before it began to fill with
questions and doubts. I wanted to get a photograph of it too, and
I sent Douglas back a ways to act as a figure to give dimensions.
When I gave him the signal that all was over he began to run back,
but suddenly jumped sideways; he had almost stepped on a large
rattlesnake, which had been near him when he stood still but only
began to rattle when he moved. At camp that night Douglas, unfortunate as usual, pitched the tent in the dark in his hurry on a bed
of cactus and gave us twenty minutes work clearing the hateful
prickly pears with a shovel while they stuck to everything like burrs.

The valley of the lake below the camp next morning was filled
with great rolling masses of drifting mist, from which the mountains
rose like those pictures one sometimes sees of the world floating in
a mass of clouds. In descending we soon became involved in the mist,
but steered northeastward by the dim image of the sun, until we hit
the waggon road south of Clinton that ran into Kamloops, surveying as we went, past lakes and pools full of shy ducks, and got there
just at sunset, the poplars fringing the river brightly golden and
purple shadows filling the valley. After a buggy ride the following
day in search of copper which I never found, just some nacreous
schists (nacreous implies having a mother-of-pearl lustre) we moved
on to dinner at the Spence's Bridge inn, where the local general store
owner sold me some fossils from Jackass Mountain.

The familiar steamer *Royal City* subsequently carried me down
from Yale to New Westminster, where I attempted to get a room
at the Colonial Hotel. A great ball was in progress there given by
the fisheries, and the waiters and many others had partaken freely,
so securing a room took a while. I stuck my head in the drill hall
where the ball was going on and enjoyed the decorations, prettily
done out with flags and nets. Another steamer the next day, the
Enterprise, bore me into Victoria and the Driard Hotel, where my
status had been elevated to "regular." A carpenter and I spent a long
day packing and overhauling my specimens into as few a number of
boxes as possible, which we got down to twenty-one.

By the next mid-morning I had drawn a draft from the bank, paid all my bills, telegraphed Mr. Selwyn that I was on my way, and driven down to Esquimalt with Dr. Tolmie, and made promises to come back the following season to pursue our mutual interest in western ethnography. Down at the wharf the harbour was gay with war vessels, the *Shah*, the *Opal*, the *Albatross*, and the *Rocket*. I got away on the *Dakota* and at around ten in the evening we rounded the light on Cape Flattery, and I was heading home.

—

THE FOLLOWING SUMMER, as a matter of course now, found me again in the West, with plans this time to go further still to the Queen Charlotte Islands. The trip had a significant difference in personnel from previous outings. Father and Mother had assailed me into letting Rankine come along. My brother was, they thought, in need of benefit, as he was already showing signs of his taciturn and sometimes contrarian nature. He was then fifteen, almost a man, but still fourteen years my junior, and ripe for adventure and an extended trip away from home. I could recall my own eagerness, at that age and perhaps earlier, to go West, so I did not wish to deny him the same pleasure. It is a long train journey across the continent, however, and Rankine proved to be a singu-larly reticent travelling companion. When anything particularly pleased him he only chuckled internally or whistled. I hope to improve him in the skills of being a fellow voyageur, as once one had the skills and could practise them the best information and offers of assistance came that way.

When in San Francisco we went to the Chinese theatre, where I had not been before. It was well worth seeing, though the music, composed of peculiarly reedy and squeaky notes, mingled with tones of horns and gongs was anything but enjoyable. The first part of the performance was a comedy, which to those who did not understand what was being said seemed long-drawn and stupid and not funny at all, especially as much of the conversation was carried on in a sort of sing-song. After this came to a happy end, an exhibition of tumbling began which was quite wonderful. The dresses throughout were wonderfully gay with silver, gold, and silk. The audience was almost altogether of Chinamen who seemed to enjoy the display heartily. The atmosphere was rather dense with tobacco smoke before we left, which was about eleven o'clock, and how much longer the fun lasted I do not know.

By the time we reached Victoria Rankine was already beginning to look sunburnt and well, though still thin enough. I brought him with me to meet Captain Lewis of the Hudson's Bay and he assured Rankine that the natives of the Queen Charlottes were not to be feared and that we should go up there at once as the weather in the Spring and early Summer was best. Around the town, I investigated the "Quartz excitement," an attempt to develop quartz mining for gold, which had absorbed all the capital in the Cariboo region in various more or less precarious speculations. I suspected that were the Survey to make assays in the region there would prove to be less to it than met the eye, and that someone would soon have the ungrateful task of endeavouring to bring down the expectations of the people to the level of common sense. (The excitement collapsed shortly when the assay results were made known, and thereafter that style of "vein mining," or should that have been "vain" mining, received a severe check.)

The schooner I was expecting to hire to take us to the islands was blown ashore in a squall and so much damaged that I made arrangements for a replacement, the *Wanderer*, a ship of about twenty tons, belonging to a man called Sabiston who said that a new suit of sails for her was all that was needed. She had plenty of beam and was built originally as a pilot boat. Sabiston was a young man, a Nanaimo pilot's son, efficient enough though perhaps a little opinionated. A man called Williams, who knew the Queen Charlottes well, came with the boat, and lastly came the cook, a sailor who went by the name Dutch Charley. Rankine was impressed with Dutch,

The Wanderer *in the Queen Charlotte Islands, 1878.*

Haida village, Queen Charlotte Islands, 1878.

commenting that he was going to be quite a success, as he cooked very well and kept things beautifully clean, besides wasting very little, which led me to wonder how well Rankine had observed our cooks in Montreal. While I was discussing estimates for getting away with the Captain, Rankine was making comments on the fewness of good-looking girls in that part of the world, especially in contrast with their abundance in San Francisco. The best looking and there-fore most highly esteemed he had yet encountered was a Miss Macdonald, daughter of the senator of the same name who had travelled over on the railway with us.

The next week was a frustration relieved by small flecks of gold. Rankine acquitted himself well, as did Miss Macdonald, at croquet at the Governor's home one afternoon, but the Queen's Birthday celebrations, on May 24th, interfered with fitting of the sails to the *Wanderer*. On the day of the celebrations we walked up Clover Hill in the morning to see a Base Ball match and rifle firing, and in the afternoon wandered up the Arm to watch the races and regatta. The Indian canoe races were especially interesting, stem-ming from the excitement and vim with which the competitors went to work.

The sails were ready at last by May 27th, the mainsail and the jib bent on in the morning and the foresail received its last stitch and was bent on in the afternoon. We said goodbye for the second or third time to acquaintances in the street and I almost surprised myself to find that we were really off, beating out of Victoria on the 27th of May, 1878, as the light faded from the hills, touching in their turn with a rosy tint the distant Olympian mountains. We steered northwestward through the villages of giant kelp for the Queen Charlotte Islands, cutting first around to Nanaimo, after a brief sojourn spent on the reefs close to Portland Island waiting for the kindly tide to make and lift us off uninjured. We sailed all day through beautiful islands, with here and there a settler's house on some good spot of land, and many a humble shanty and potato patch of the Indians, whose canoes might be seen with a little bag-like sail shooting before the wind from one island to another. The row of coal-hauling vessels lying at the wharves in Nanaimo harbour, with the occasional rattle of a truck of black rock descending into their holds as they were loaded, emphasized that we were in a coal country, where one of Nature's old store houses was being ransacked for the benefit of the present generation. (When we were on the Queen Charlottes, it was my main object, for the Survey, to define the area of the coal measures there.) Also in Nanaimo there was a delay while Mr. Sabiston spent some time run aground, or, as Rankine put in a letter home, "our bold Captain lives here, and has very recently married, so I am afraid that we shall be here all morning."

Judging our craft not sufficiently sea-worthy for the rough outer coast of Vancouver Island, which is exposed to the full sweep of the great North Pacific, we were obliged to voyage by the inner channels and series of connecting fiords which characterize the coast. Well adapted for steam navigation, and wonderfully picturesque and grand to the eye, the channels, such as the Goletas which we beat along all night, were tedious for sailing vessels. The wind blew either directly up or down the channel, shut in by its mountain walls, and what with calms and the rapid and constantly changing tidal current, we spent many a weary hour at anchor, or even retrogressing as we did in Plumper Bay, where we were forced to go ashore for water to a spring, the sound of which could be heard from the schooner as it trickled out from the roots of the cedar tree. The sea was beautifully phosphorescent when touched by oars, when we made the crossing, and Rankine called the drops "water stars." Although the ever-stretching length of time it took to reach the Islands was an annoyance, the journey was not without highlights, and the hidden depths of the sea, as well as its superficial areas, provided entertainments.

With the distant Prince of Wales Mountains on our starboard, with much snow there upon, and floating on past Alert Bay, we overhauled a canoe containing, besides a number of Indians, a white man, who was there for protection as they passed the pirates who made their living off Cape Mudge. The pirates would not attack a fellow white man. One man was rowing the canoe with a short pair of oars, while the others paddled in the old style, their faces daubed with ochre and other pigments which gave them a peculiarly repulsive appearance. One woman had a broad mark in red ochre on her upper lip, in the place where a mustache ought to be, and she looked very comical and defiant at the same time. The occupants of another canoe later boarded us, and among them was one called Chip (or so I thought; he was actually pointing out he was a "Cheap" or Chief) who had saved the lives of several white men in a little vessel anchored in a sound. Indians were about to massacre the crew when he warned them. He had no other object in visiting us than to tell his story, talk a little, and beg some tobacco.

The inhabitants of the deeper waters regularly made their presence known, porpoises and sea lions sporting about in the calm water, disappearing and appearing among the long rollers, as whales breached repeatedly in the evenings. While Rankine had the line out at sixty fathoms for halibut, he spotted a fur seal, which compensated somewhat for the halibut he never caught. When hauling a line up on another occasion, from about six fathoms down, I could see a huge many-rayed starfish coming up which dropped off at the surface, revealing that it had been feeding on a silver dog fish, a parrot-beaked thing of remarkable features. Only the head and shoulders of the dog fish remained, so I surmised it had taken the hook and then been snapped off behind by some larger fish, probably a shark, and the starfish had then appropriated what was left.

A little further on we caught, on a rock, a young seal with the placenta lying near it, weighing already about thirty pounds, quite active and seemingly well able to take care of itself. It sprawled about the deck when we got him there, uttering from time to time its peculiar cry of "mwha," a sort of watery burgling "ma" in a plaintive tone. At times it became quite vociferous and then relapsed into silence. At first it shrank from being handled, but it got used to it and even seemed to enjoy being caressed. Williams tied a halibut line to it one morning and threw it over for a swim. It did not like the operation, and when it was about to be repeated in the afternoon it immediately seemed to realize the position when the rope was brought out, and set up a great noise. Thrown in nonetheless, it swam well enough but tried always to regain the deck by attempting to climb the side until hauled in again, when it was quite content. For an animal but one day old it certainly showed great intelligence, sprawling up to one's legs and pressing its nose on one's boots and smelling them carefully. It even appeared to follow one when one went away. Dutch Charley tried feeding it on oatmeal and water, then rice and water.

A southeasterly breeze laden with rain carried us down Millbank Sound and into Bella Bella, at noon on June 8th, the town being on a particularly broken part of the coast and due east of the southern tip of the Queen Charlotte Islands. The Hudson's Bay post at Bella Bella was prettily situated on a gentle hillside, with a small stream falling into the bay near it, and a sloping patch of garden for which most of the soil, I was told, had been carried in from some distance. A remarkable target-like white erection on one side of the harbour had a painted board below which stated that it was in memory of BOSTON, A BELLA BELLA CHIEF. Mr. Boston was a head man from the Thirties who was considered sharper and shrewder than the others. Also in the town, which had quite a rep-utation on the coast for canoe building, was a very large specimen, just lately finished sixty feet long and much better finished than the one which had been bought for the United States Centennial Exposition and displayed in Philadelphia. The one I saw was valued at $200 and the Indian who made it expected to be able to sell it to the Fort Rupert Indians for that sum, although to my eye it was of real little use but for imposing on State occasions.

Anchored just off the harbour, we were visited by a canoe full of Haida Indians, and these were the first I had met, though there would be many more. They were three days from Skidegate on the

Queen Charlotte Islands, and had dried fish oil and gulls eggs for trade with the *tillicums* (the people) when they got to Victoria many days hence. To my surprise they also had some fossils for sale which were intended for Mr. Richardson at Victoria, if he happened to be there. They were quite happy to sell them to me.

Sixteen days had thus already been occupied in just bringing us to Bella Bella and, abandoning therefore the idea of visiting first the north end of the Islands, I decided that we should lay across immediately for their southern extremity. The extreme length of the Queen Charlotte Islands is one hundred and eighty miles, with a greatest breadth of sixty miles. To allow the reader to picture the islands in their entirety, it is useful to imagine the embryo of some giant beast, laid in the Pacific Ocean near the coast of British Columbia, with its large eyeless head facing that coast and its limbless tail hanging below. The traverse across the sea to the southern tip was eighty miles, and while making it we were first becalmed, rolling miserably in the swell without wind for some time, and then, not without some discomfort and danger, we weathered half a gale from the northwestward which blew hard all night and took us thirty miles to the north. On the twelfth of June, I woke early to find that I could see Cape St. James; we had completed our voyage of nearly five hundred miles from Victoria and after beating slowly all morning in a light breeze, we cast anchor in a snug bight between the silent wooded shores of a cove in Stewart Channel, the space of. water which separates Prescott Island, the most southerly, from Moresby Island. The largest island of the chain is the most northerly, Graham. From the south we would wend our way to the northernmost point, through Darwin Sound, to Skidegate, into Masset Sound and up to Cape Knox.

In 1882, some four years later, I published in *Harpers* magazine an account of the tour Rankine and I made in the *Wanderer* around the coast of the Queen Charlotte Islands (the Queen in question was the wife of George III). It was a privilege to appear on their pages, and if the reader will indulge me I intend to reproduce the greater portion here, with certain infiltrations of my own necessitated on rereading. The principal subject of my article was the Haida themselves, the most western of tribes, and the concerted study of them I made as I moved deeper into the ethnography of the peoples who lived here in the time before surveyors and science.

I would enshrine a thought in verse
That it may live though I shall die
To speak down all the after years
To stand above the mist of tears
Like some white mountain seen afar
Beyond the scope of heaving sea
Like the wreckage on the shore
To show this sea was sailed before
That ye may pass by light of day
Where I perchance am cast away
In tempest and in night.

Along the coast of British Columbia, as I already knew, the Indians were almost exclusively fishermen, engaging in the chase to a very limited extent, and seldom venturing far into the dense forests, of which they appeared to entertain a superstitious dread, peopling them in their imaginations with monsters and fearful inhabitants. While some of these tribes were little improved, or had even deteriorated from their original condition, others were moderately industrious, and apply themselves to work in various ways. Of the tribes inhabiting the coast, the Haidas, a compact group, were in many respects the most interesting. The Queen Charlotte Islands, which they possess, are separated by wide water stretches from the mainland of British Columbia, and the southern extremity of Alaska to the northwest. Their comparative isolation and homogeneity meant that the Haidas, while distinct from most other tribes of the coast, are in language and customs so nearly the same in all parts of their own territory.

During Captain Cook's last voyage in the Pacific he considered that a lucrative trade in furs might be opened between the north-western coast of America and China. Consequently, though the existence of a part of the Queen Charlotte Islands had been known to the Spaniards since the voyage of Juan Perez in 1774, it was actu-ally the traders who followed in the track of Cook that made most of the early discoveries on that part of the coast, and it is they who first came in contact with the Haidas. The earliest notice of the Haidas I was able to find lay in one Captain George Dixon's illus-trated and mapped narrative, *Voyage Around the World*, bearing the date July, 1787. Dixon first made land on the islands near their northern extremity, in the vicinity of North Island, and gives in his subsequent narrative a detailed account of his meeting and intercourse with the natives, and his trade with them for furs. It was Dixon who named the islands, Queen Charlotte being the name of his ship, which in turn was named for the Queen.

When first visited by whites, the population of the islands probably exceeded seven thousand. Toward the beginning and during the earlier years of the present century the Queen Charlotte Islands were not infrequently visited by trading vessels. The sea-otter, however, the skins of which were the most valuable articles of trade possessed by the islanders, had become very scarce through continuous hunting, so few vessels but mere coasters had called at any of the ports for many years back. When we visited, the popu-lation had dwindled to around two thousand and included in that number were many who, while now living elsewhere on the coast, still called the islands home.

The climate of the Queen Charlotte Islands is excessively humid, and they are almost everywhere covered with magnificent coniferous trees. Mountains 4,000 to 5,000 feet high rise in their central portion, and they are penetrated on all sides by dark deep fiords with rocky walls. To the northeast, it is true, a wide stretch of low and nearly level country occurred, which may some day support a farming population, but at that time its sombre woods, filled with dense undergrowth, and barricaded with prostrate trunks in every stage of decay, offered little to induce either Indian or white to penetrate them. The Haidas, therefore, though culti-vating small potato patches here and there along the shores, were essentially fishermen. Few paths or trails traverse the interior of the islands, and of these some formerly used when the population was greater were clearly abandoned.

The halibut was found in great abundance in the islands, and it was particularly on this fish that the Haidas depended. Their vil-lages were invariably situated along the shore, often on bleak, wave-lashed parts of the coast, but always in proximity to produc-tive halibut banks. Journeys were made along the coast in canoes skillfully hollowed from the great cedar trees of the region, which, after being worked down to a certain small thickness, were steamed and spread by the insertion of crosspieces till they were made to assume a most graceful form, and showed lines which would satisfy the most fastidious shipbuilder. In their larger canoes the Haidas did not hesitate to make long voyages on the open sea; and in former days, by their frequent descents on the coast of the main-land, and the facility with which they retreated again to their own islands, they rendered themselves more dreaded than any tribe from Vancouver to Sitka.

In their mode of life, and the ingenuity and skill they displayed in their manufacture of canoes and other articles, the Haidas did not differ essentially from the other tribes inhabiting the northern part of the coast of British Columbia and Southern Alaska. In the Queen Charlotte Islands, however, the peculiar style of architecture and art elsewhere among the Indians of the west coast appeared to attain its greatest development. Perhaps with the greater isolation of these people, and consequent increased measure of security, the particular ideas of the Indian mind were able to body themselves forth more fully. The situation of the islands, and the comparative infrequency with which they had been visited for many years, had at least tended to preserve intact many features which had already vanished from the customs and manufactures of most other tribes.

The permanent villages of the Haidas consisted generally of a single long row of houses, with but a narrow grassy border between them and the beach, on which the canoes of the tribe were drawn up. In front of each house stood a symbolical carved post, while other carved posts, situated irregularly, and differing somewhat in form from those proper to the houses, were generally memorials to the dead. Such a village, seen from a little distance off, the houses and posts grey with the weather, resembles a strip of half-burned forest with dead "rampikes."

The general construction of houses with the Indians of the northwest coast is everywhere nearly the same, but among the Haidas they were more substantially framed, and much more attention was given to the fitting together and ornamentation of the edifice than elsewhere. The houses were rectangular, and some-times over forty feet in length of side. The walls were formed of planks split by means of wedges from cedar logs, and often of great size. The roof was composed of similar split planks or bark, and sloped down at each side, the gable end of the house facing the sea, toward which the door, an oval hole cut in the base of the grotesquely covered post, opened. The poles, which we call the totem post, but to the Haidas are known as *kcchert*, were forty or fifty feet high. Stooping to enter, one found that the soil had been exca-vated in the interior of the house to make the floor six or eight feet lower than the surface outside. One descended to it by a few rough steps, and on looking about observed that one or two large steps ran round all four sides of the house, faced with cedar planks also of great size, which had been hewn out, and served not only as shelves on which to store all the household goods, but as beds and seats if need be. In the centre of a square area of bare earth the fire burnt constantly. The smoke mounting upward passed away by what we may call a skylight – an opening in the roof, with a shutter to set against the wind, and which served also as a means of lighting the interior. There were generally four of these laid horizontally, with stout supporting uprights at the ends. They were neatly hewn, and of a symmetrical cylindrical form, and were generally fitted into the hollowed ends of the uprights. The uprights were often about fifteen feet high, with a diameter of about three feet; and it is only when we became acquainted with the fact that a regular bee is held at the erection of the house that we could account for the movement without machinery of such large logs, a puzzle which Rankine remarked on right away. The building bee was accompanied by a distribution of property on the part of the man for whom the house was being built, a custom well known on the West coast by the Chinook name "potlatch." A house accommodated several families, each occupying a certain corner or portion of the interior.

It was the carved posts, however, which constituted the most distinctive feature of a Haida village. To make one of these, a large and sound cedar tree – probably three or four feet in diameter – was chosen somewhere not far from the water's edge, felled, trimmed, and then moved down to the sea. Being launched, it was towed to the village site, and by united labour dragged up on the beach above high-water mark. It was then shaped and carved, some of the Indians being famous for their skill in this business, and earning considerable sums by practising it. The log was hollowed behind, like a trough, to make it light, while the front was generally covered with a mass of grotesque figures, in which the animal representing the totem, or clan, of the person for whom it was made takes a prominent place. It constitutes, in fact, his coat of arms, and may in some instances be gaily painted. When all was finished the post was taken to its place, and firmly planted in the ground, to remain a thing of beauty till, under the influence of the climate, it becomes grey with age and hoary with moss and lichen.

The peculiar type of art most fully displayed on the carved posts was found more or less in all the manufactures of the Haidas. The neat and even elegant wooden dishes which formerly served all household purposes embodied always some peculiar animal form or grouping of forms more or less complicated or contorted.

Though the artist might well be able to copy nature faithfully enough when he tried, as witnessed in some of the masks used in dancing, he in most cases preferred to follow certain conventional ideas which appeared by long usage to have become incorporated with the native mind.

Not the least curious of the customs of the Haidas, and probably with some religious significance, were those connected with dancing ceremonies. These appear to be divided into six classes, which were designated by as many barbarous names, not necessary here to mention. Of these I was fortunate enough to see one, the *Kwai-o-guns-o-lung*, a description of which, given nearly as written down at the time, will serve to illustrate a class of performances once common among the native peoples, but now almost everywhere passed away.

Landing after dark from our boat at the southern end of the fine sandy beach on which Skidegate village fronts, we found that part of the town quite deserted, but could discern a dim glow of light at a distance, and distinguish the monotonous sound of the drum. Scrambling in the dark by a path zigzagging along the front of the row of houses, and narrowly escaping falls over various obstacles, we reached the house in which the dance was going on. Pushing open the door, a glare of light flashed out, previously seen only as it filtered through the various crevices of the house. Entering, we found ourselves behind and among the dancers, who stood within the house with their backs to the front wall. Edging through them, we crossed the open space in which the fire, well supplied with resinous logs, was burning, and seated ourselves on the floor amidst a crowd of onlookers at the further end. The house was of the usual oblong shape, the floor covered with cedar planks, with the exception of the space in the centre for the fire, and the goods and chattels of the family were piled here and there in heaps along the walls, leaving the greater part of the interior clear.

The audience filled almost every available space, squatting in various attitudes on the floor, men, women, and children of all ages.

The smoke of the fire escaped by wide openings in the roof, without causing any inconvenience and its glow brightly illuminated the faces and forms of all present. The performers, about twenty in number, were dressed according to no uniform plan, but attired in their best clothes, or at least their most showy ones, with the addition of certain ornaments and badges appropriate to the occasion. All, or nearly all, wore headdresses, variously constructed of twisted cedar bark, and ornamented with feathers or, in one case, with a bristling circle of the whiskers of the sea lion. Shoulder girdles of cedar bark, coloured or ornamented with tassels, were very common. One man wore leggings with fringes of puffin beaks strung together, which rattled as he moved. Many, if not all, held sprigs of fresh spruce and were covered about the head with downy feathers, which floated in abundance in the warm air of the house. Some had rattles, and added to the din by shaking these furiously at the accentuated parts of the song. Five women took part in the dance, standing in front in a row, and were dressed with some uniformity, several having the peculiarly valuable cedar bark or goat's wool shawls made by the Tshimsiens. The headdresses of the women were all alike, consisting of a small mask or semblance of a face carved neatly in wood, and inlaid with pearly haliotis shell. These, attached to a cedar bark frame, and trimmed with gay feathers and tassels, stood before the forehead, while at the back in some cases depended a train with ermine skins. The faces of both men and women engaged in the dance were gaily painted, vermilion being the favourite colour.

The performer on the drum – a flat tambourine-like article formed of hide stretched on a hoop – sat opposite the dancers and near the fire, so they could see each other's movements. The drum was beaten very regularly with double knocks thus, turn turn, turn turn, turn turn – and the dancers kept time in a sort of chant or song, to which words were set and swelled into a full chorus or died away, according to the notions of a leader who stood among the dancers and who, besides marking time, now and then gave a few words of direction or exhortation. At every beat a spasmodic twitch passed through the crowd of dancers, who scarcely raised their feet from the floor, but moved by double jerks, shuffling the feet a little. After ten minutes or so the master of the ceremonies gave a sign, and all suddenly stopped, with a loud *hugh*! The dance was resumed by the perspiring crowd at the signal of the drum which struck up after a few moments' rest had been allowed. The crowd of gaily painted, gaily dressed savages, by the kind light of the fire, presented, on the whole, a rather brave and imposing appearance, and when excited in the dance the Haida may yet almost imagine the grand old days to remain when hundreds crowded the villages now occupied by tens, and nothing had eclipsed the grandeur of their ceremonies and doings.

The fundamental narrative of the origin of man and the beginning of the present state of affairs is the most important of their myths. Very long ago, they say, there was a great flood, by which all men and animals were destroyed, with the exception of a single raven. This creature was not, however, exactly an ordinary bird, but – as with all animals in the old Indian stories – possessed the attributes of a human being to a great extent. His coat of feathers, for instance, could be put on or taken off at will like a garment. The name of this being was Ne-kil-stlas.

When the flood had gone down, Ne-kil-stlas looked about, but could find neither companions nor a mate, and he became very lonely. At last he took a cockleshell from the beach, and married it. By-and-by in the shell he heard a faint cry like that of a newly born child, which gradually became louder till at last a female child was seen which, growing by degrees larger and larger, was finally married by the raven. From this union all the Indians were produced, and the country peopled.

The people as yet had neither fire, light, fresh water, or the oolachen fish. These things were all in the possession of a great chief, Setlin-ki-jash, who lived where the Nasse River now is. The chief had a daughter, and to her Ne-kil-stlas covertly made love and visited her many times unknown to her father. The girl began to love

Ne-kil-stlas, and trust in him. At length, when he thought the time ripe, he asked for a drink of water. The girl brought the water in a closely woven basket, and he drank only a little, setting the basket down beside him, waiting till the girl fell asleep. Then quickly donning his coat of feathers, and lifting the basket in his beak, he flew out of the opening made for the smoke in the top of the lodge. He was in great haste, fearing to be followed, and a little water fell out here and there, causing the numerous rivers which were now found. But in Haida country a few drops only fell, like rain, and so there are no large streams there today.

Ne-kil-stlas next wished to obtain fire, also in the possession of the same powerful chief. He did not dare appear again in the chief's house, nor did the chief's daughter any longer show him favour. Assuming the form of a single needlelike leaf of the spruce tree, he floated on the water near the house and, when the girl — his former lover — came down to draw water, he was lifted by her in the vessel she used. The girl, drinking the water, swallowed the leaf, and shortly afterward bore a child, no other than the cunning Ne-kil-stlas, who had thus again obtained entry into the lodge. Watching his opportunity, he one day picked up a burning brand, and flying out as before by the smoke hole at the top of the lodge, carried it away, and spread fire everywhere.

Ne-kil-stlas of the Haidas is represented in an almost endless series of grotesque and often disgusting adventures. The collection and study of details concerning the habits, customs, and thoughts of a people semi-barbarous, and disappearing before our eyes in the universal menstruum of civilization, may seem to be of little importance but they lead into a wide and interesting region of speculation, one that embraces the question of the origin and interrelation of the American aborigines, their wanderings, and all the unwritten pages of their history, which we can hope to know only in dim outlines even by the most careful inquiry.

In regard to the Haidas, what has been the origin of the highly conventionalized art which their works exhibit, and the social customs which, with a power almost as strong as that of fashion among ourselves, causes them to devote so much of their time to ceremonies apparently meaningless, but which serve to form the bonds and rough working machinery of society among them? Have they developed slowly in a community separated from the human stock at a very early period? Had they never been brought face to face with a superior power, would they have grown in the course of ages into an independent civilization like that of Mexico or Peru? We can never hope to answer such questions fully; but we know there were on record several instances of Japanese junks, driven by the prevailing winds and currents, being carried across the whole breadth of the North Pacific. Also, the passage across the Bering Strait to the north is short, and even at the present day made on the winter ice by the Esquimaux. It is therefore more than proba-ble that people with their rude arts may from time to time have been borne to the western coast of America, and that it is to Eastern Asia that we must look for the origin of its inhabitants.

By the end of August, two and a half months after making our way northward by degrees, we stood in a little bay named Bruit, the water casks full, and all prepared for the crossing due east, which took a day, a night, and a long day under sail, whereafter we were in Port Simpson on the mainland, and Rankine was able, despite the darkness, to go ashore and hunt up our mail. When he was back on ship with a considerable sack, we had the pleasure of sitting in my cabin below decks reading news from home dating from three months back, while the everlasting rain beat against the deck. We had become quite accustomed to precipitation and the dampness everything had about it, so much so that if I put away a pair of boots for a few days, on looking them up again they generally had a coat of mould outside and in.

Standing on the dock at Port Simpson, my gaze towards the Islands, one could say I had undoubtedly left my mark there, for in the course of my survey I had cause to give names to several of the features, and in one case in particular was able to achieve the pleasant juxtaposition of naming Lyell Island, in honour of my old professor Sir Charles, which formed the eastward flank of Darwin Sound. My days at the London School of Mines were also commemorated with the naming of De La Beche Inlet, after the school's founder. Others of my betters within the fields of exploration and the natural sciences who remained on the topography were the naturalist William Carpenter, who received the "order of the Bay," Juan Perez the Spaniard in whose century-old trade wind we were sailing, who got a Sound, and geologist James Dana, also an Inlet. In the ship's hold was a goodly stock of natural specimens, animal and mineral; otter skins, seal, coal.

We got under way for the trip back to Victoria on the first day of September, sailed all day and were blown all the way back to where we had started through the night. Rankine had an appointment with school back in Montreal in a few days, and so after an evening spent with two of the local missionaries, Duncan and Tomlinson, he decided to stay and catch the first steamer for which Mr. Tomlinson was also waiting. I called in the next day to find Rankine at breakfast. I bid him farewell till met again, and provided him with money to carry him back to Montreal. I requested him once on the train not to get off and spring on again, a habit of his, more frequently than was absolutely necessary to preserve his mental and bodily health. I noticed that he received all these hints with considerable reserve, and saw that he had made his mind up to do just what he liked. After buying a barrel of "oolachens" or candlefish, a much valued spawning fish that was so oily that I had seen it dried and used as a candle, we set sail. With Rankine gone, I needed a replacement in crew, and I hired an Indian boy at the rate of $20 a month plus the $10 return fare from Victoria.

I had no trouble keeping the Indian boy busy, as with Rankine on his way home (the steamer the *Grappler* passed us on the way down with him aboard, on September 8th,; extrapolating from there, I reckoned him home by October 1st) I had full attention to give to the natural world we were sailing through, and I kept up with my photographs of record, for which a corner portion of my eye was on constant alert. On a small island in the Klemtoo Passage I tried to get what would have been a quite artistic photo, looking north at a curious effect of kelps and the reflection of trees in the water, but it was rather an act of faith to expose an "Extra Sensitive" plate for ten or fifteen seconds and get away with a picture.

The photographing of natives was sometimes also an act of persistent faith. We had called in at Quatsino, a village in an inlet on the northwest coast of Vancouver Island, and I was out in the boat collecting some not very attractive fossils when I wandered into a village where all the people of it had gathered in front of one of the houses. As I came up they all joined in a repeated chorus of *Cla-hoya tyee?* and *Klooshe!* – "How do you do, chief" and "good" in Chinook, which was all the Chinook they had, and their own language I could not understand. Evidently they seldom saw strangers and appeared in their manner quite apprehensive that I had all sorts of power and might want to use it. The women all had their heads deformed in the manner peculiar to that tribe, having been bandaged up in infancy so as to assume a conical aspect. They appeared all very poor, wretched, and dirty, about the most miserable and degraded Indians I had seen. Most of the men appeared to be away. I continued in search of the drift coal in a brook I had heard of, and found some, and on my return stopped to take a photograph, but had endless difficulty in getting them to understand what was wanted, then to get them to go to the right place and finally to get them to sit still. I got some reason into them at last by offering them a biscuit all round if they would sit. Two men came down to the schooner afterwards for the biscuits, and one agreed to be my guide the next day. He was perhaps twenty years old with a cross eye and a long queue or pig-tail which he wore round his head, having ceased from cutting his hair in the hope of becoming a medicine man.

It had been a summer of conversations with Indians, long and short, including a long exchange I had with one especially troublesome woman who was part of a benign boarding party that swarmed the schooner one day and insisted on knowing the name of everything. The longest and perhaps most philosophical exchange occurred on that trip back to Victoria, in a village in Seaforth Channel called Ka-pa, which lay behind Grief Island. The chief of the village, Ham-Chit, came out to us on our arrival with a neat wreath of red-stained cedar bark about his head. He was very intelligent and had a long conversation with me after supper. He said that the Indians were always talking among themselves about their decrease in numbers. Long ago, he said, they were like trees, in great numbers everywhere. Yes, they fought among themselves, as he said the white men fought among themselves. Some were killed, but always more were born and the whole country teemed with them. Now the white men had come and the Indians *chaco Motherloose*, which is Chinook jargon for "have died." He pointed out to me the former extent of his village and contrasted with its present shrunken size. Yet there was plenty fish, plenty food and they had various things from the white men which they did not know before. The Indians did not now fight with themselves or the white men, only for a few years when whiskey was introduced among them, not long enough to do much harm. And yet they die. The Indians did not know how to explain it, but, he said, *Klunas saghalie tyee Mamook* — "I don't know what God is doing." The next night, when I again spoke with Ham-Chit, he asked me for some old copies of the *Illustrated News*, and a cup of flour to make paste to stick them up in his house. (I am sure if I had stayed another day he would have asked me for a brush.)

Two days on, anchored in a snug cove at the very tip of Vancouver Island, I had drawn the ship's boat onto the beach to try and find out where she was leaking. She had begun to be rather frail and strained throughout, by much contact with rocks and hard usage. As I was doing this, the most doleful crying and wailing was kept up by some women in one of the nearby Native village houses.

I asked what was happening and learned that it was the ceremonial mourning for a little child who died a few days earlier. The women were relatives and went on with their work more or less steadily while uttering those heart-rending cries, a sort of wailing mingled with interjections and sentences probably referring to the deceased.

Interspersed with the quest for coal and the vocabulary of the Haida, as we wove our way through the islands and made ports of call, moments of natural, poetic beauty would arrive without warning in that magnificent landscape. Held captive by a wind that lay dead ahead and a running ebb tide, I went on land with the boat in a spot called Bull Harbour, on an island off the Vancouver Island northern shore and crossed a narrow neck of land towards the distant roar of surf. On gaining the coast I was well rewarded for my trouble in finding a magnificent sea falling in against the steeply shelving portion of a shingle beach. The simultaneous advance, rise and tumultuous break of the great blue seas, as they arched up, fringed with little rainbows as their edges became fretted and misty, was truly grand. The impressive sound of the stones and pebbles along the whole beach roaring as the broken wave retired brought vividly before one the process of the destruction of continents and the immense sum of work which must be performed by an eternally busy agent like that. The scene almost realized that of a dream I remembered once having of great waves breaking on a beach. No explanation can be framed of the sentiment called up by the display of such never-ceasing force, and I could only fall back on Tennyson,

> Break break break on thy cold grey stones, oh sea
> And I would that my heart could utter
> the thoughts which arise in me.

The month of October was occupied with tracing the coast-line of Vancouver Island as we scudded along it towards Victoria, first partially on the western coast and then down the eastern in its entirety. The Indian nation contained within the island borders

were the Kwakiutl, and they spoke a collection of closely allied languages I was able to chart, much as one might survey adjoining
regions. I took some "shore leave" in Fort Rupert, where some two
hundred Indians were living, and the resident whites were Hunt
and Hall, the former the Hudson's Bay man, the latter God's man,
who had only just arrived, and was not well acquainted yet with
the local Indians. I had a sheaf of mail awaiting, my second of the
season, which brought my knowledge of Montreal up to the end of
August, and in addition a letter from Rankine mailed from Victoria
to say he was safely arrived there and intended immediate departure for Montreal. The Montreal news included hurrahs for
William, who had suffered brilliant achievements at the Paris école,
and was now, despite the disadvantage of youth, applying for a post
at the University of Toronto (in which he was non-successful). On
the other hand, there was no news from Mr. Selwyn – who had not
favoured me with a line since I left the Survey offices – as to the
state of my report on the travels of 1875–76 which had been printed
but not proofed.

Fort Rupert could claim a fine harbour and I put in a day of
fossil collection, then we proceeded in search of the Su-quash coal
fields and Alert Bay where I was invited into one of the long houses
and there beheld what at first sight I took to be a giant's eating
utensils. The colossal bowl was two feet high and twice that in
length, cut from a solid block of cedar with two Indian figures clasp-
ing it with their hands linked. The spoon was about four feet long,
with the handle bent around at the end forming a bird's head, which
was grasping a frog. Both bowl and ladle were in fact feasting
vessels. The Indians were in the midst of a potlatch, and singing as
the distribution of blankets and bread took place. The songs of
those people carried almost exactly the same tunes and intonations
as the Haida peoples.

The *Wanderer* bore us down the coast to Nanaimo in a series
of fits and starts, the fits taking the form of visits to mines or
coal deposits, the starts getting Mr. Sabiston sufficiently *compos*

mentis to up anchor and away. In Nanaimo, I descended into the Chase River mine at Nanaimo with Mr. Bryden of that company to see the inner workings; the bullish force pumps removing the water, of which there was little, and the dragon-like ventilation furnace removing the gas, again of which very little, and no safety lamps were used, except by firemen making their tours of inspection. The coal seams being mined ranged from the minor to the major, from two feet up to a thickness of twenty, and small trucks were winding their way up full and back down empty in a tireless chain of give and take. All this I had studied not too many years previous, on Jermyn Street and in the Coal Exchange, drawing out on paper in miniature what now loomed and clanked before me at life-size, and the experience made me very glad that I had chosen to work above ground, and not have to inquire, as the miners did when they came to the surface at the end of their shift, how the weather had been that day. Not only did I know all too well how the day had gone, but more likely than not I had taken its temperature, barometric pressure, and retained the figures in a notebook.

Leaving the smoke of Nanaimo well behind, the captain made a straight run for home port, reaching the Dodd narrows just in time to get through with the last of the ebb tide. The rest of the day we made fair progress and by nine p.m. were abreast of Narrow Island. I worked long into the night, packing specimens as we carried on sailing right through to sunrise and on past Saanich Inlet while the wind held in the forenoon, but in the afternoon it fell off leaving us practically – and appropriately – becalmed at Trial Island about dark. Drifting on with the ebb tide, however, we finally got a little air to push us in, and we made fast in Victoria Harbour at eleven p.m., and I took my sponge, brush, and comb and went up to Driard House, where all were still awake, and I secured a good room. I was not sorry to conclude that chapter of my marine experiences, and I stood for a while just looking with admiration on a bed with clean sheets!

I awoke in those clean sheets refreshed and with a list of things to accomplish before either quickly leaving for Portland or holding on and taking the regular steamer to San Francisco at the end of the month. I compared my long list with the urge to get back to Montreal, and the list won out. I got all the stores and specimens taken out of the schooner and arranged them in one of the Hudson's Bay storages on the wharf, settled accounts with Williams, Charley, and Indian Johnny, and that evening had a very civilized dinner at Judge Grey's. Grey had represented New Brunswick at the Confederation Conference, served a session in Parliament, then went west to the British Columbia Supreme Court. We discussed possible routes the railway might take through the mountains, and the Judge favoured Kicking Horse Pass. Feeling it unwise, and unable to speak as anything other than a member of the Survey, I kept my counsel.

A spare carpenter was easy to find on the next day, being a Saturday, and I had him remove the flooring in the schooner that had provided the extra storage, and set him to work closing boxes while I addressed them. There were a deal more of the finely crafted blankets the Haida used as currency than I had supposed, and I first had to clear them all at the Custom House Building. Later I took a turn in the Chinese quarter to look for china, and then settled with Sabiston and was glad to get rid of him. Unfortunately I had to return to the schooner the next day to get him to sign a new receipt, the original one being defective. After that things improved with the arrival of Dr. Tolmie, whereupon we set to and conversed the rest of the day on Indian vocabularies. The good doctor arranged for a man called Haida Mills to join us in the few days to come as "linguistic assistant" and Mr. Mills did appear, though more than once I went down to the Indian quarter to look for him. Aware that we would be in need of good maps for our eventual reports, I went across to the Land and Works Office the morning after and rooted out several of their best ones, which were still pretty sketchy, which could serve as a basis for my own additions and began to make tracings, a task I could see would need more than a day to complete.

I dined that evening with a Judge and a Governor, then went back to the hotel and wrote a long letter to Professor Huxley, of a philosophical nature. While on the *Wanderer* I had grappled with a book by a German professor of botany in Strasbourg, one Oscar Schmidt, whose book-length essay *The Doctrine Of Descent And Darwinism* commented on Darwin's own application of his evolutionary theories to man himself. As Schmidt wrote and I copied into my notebook, "Nay, Darwin himself has now gone further, and, to the terror of all who can scarce imagine man except as created shaven and armed with a book on etiquette, he has sketched a certainly not flattering, and perhaps in many points not correct, portrait of our presumptive ancestors in the phase of dawning humanity." Schmidt's book held much information, but I found the tone and some conclusions first annoying and then repugnant. I wrote to Huxley in the hope that he, who had befriended and studied Darwin more than any man, might shed some light for me.

As I moved about the town in the forenoon, theories of descent still alive in my mind, several people came up to me, commenting that they had seen the article I wrote in the *Evening Standard*, the Victoria newspaper, describing Victoria and all its glories. Several of the commentators politely wondered why, since I had been there four years, I had only just discovered and written about the city's salient features. I hastened to buy a paper, and solved the mystery with a turn of the page; brother Rankine had published a description based on his experience of Victoria the previous summer, and it was being attributed to me!

In the final day or so before the *Dakota* again bore me away, a parade of faces appeared before me and receded, some at the dinner table, some in offices; a former British officer who was now quarrying for marble; an Archdeacon with questions on Indian matters; a banker; a minister of mines; a bookseller to see if I was interested in his line of Report journals; and finally the welcome face of Mr. Bowman, who operated the local livery stable and in whose buggy I made the trip to Esquimalt to catch my steamship. I left on the

Dakota promptly at noon, on a ship for once with a slim passenger list and plenty of room everywhere. It was a clear sunny day, and I was treated to a magnificent view of Mount Baker and the serried peaks of the coast range. We made San Francisco in three days, and I departed on the Central Pacific Railway the next, making the change at Council Bluffs for Chicago, thence Detroit, Stratford, and Toronto and into Montreal on the 10th November. There I learnt that Mr. Selwyn had fair excuse for his non-communication; he was in Paris almost all that year attending the third Paris Exhibition, the biggest to date, and at which he served as President of the jury of Maps and associated apparatus, and at which Mr. Bell, a fellow Nova Scotian, displayed his device for sending speech direct over a long distance, a machine he was calling the "telephone." Mr. Selwyn and I did not meet up again until the January of 1879.

—

I HAVE NO great recollection of the winter and early spring of 1879. In those exploratory years that took me through from the age of twenty-four to thirty, the details of domestic life has become buried over the intervening years under an accumulation of vistas and landscapes that had in my younger self resided only as unformed dreams.

In April I went West for the Survey. The immediate object of that season's exploration was to obtain all possible information as to the physical features and economic importance of the region from the Pacific coast through seventeen degrees of longitude to Edmonton, on the upper part of the Saskatchewan River. For a great part of this distance, however, the exploration was necessarily limited to a single line of traverse. I was charged to determine to what extent the said traverse offered advantages, and disadvantages, for the passage of the unreeling line of the Canadian Pacific Railway. Several surveying gentlemen connected with the railway were associated with me in the field.

The expedition occupied in all a period of seven months, extending from the 8th of May to the 9th of December. Our starting point was the familiar Port Essington at the mouth of the Skeena River on the coast of northern British Columbia, reached by steamer on the 6th of June. From then to the end of December, when we arrived at Winnipeg, Manitoba, my time was continuously occupied in exploration in a spectacular region without any recognized means of conveyance.

Our water voyage up the initial tidal portion of the Skeena, a somewhat-travelled stretch, took us without much trouble to the horticultural line of division at Quatsalix between the coastal and the interior fauna. The damp-loving devil's club and the skunk cabbage became scarce at that point, and the wild crab apple disappeared, while the pines and aspens took over and became abundant on the river flats, and the soap berry inhabited the slopes.

The Indian village of Kit-wan-ga soon appeared on the right bank, the houses of a style usually found on the coast, but not nearly so large and well-finished as those of the Haidas. Ten carved poles, giant tent pegs, anchored the village, none very striking in design. The river then forced us through its strongest rapids, and then it forked dramatically at Hazelton in several directions, where the Indians had erected a new village of half-a-dozen barn-like buildings a quarter of a mile downstream from the old one, a little further away from the traders. They spoke of putting up some new poles soon, something I would have enjoyed observing, but this was not a ethnological mission, and we pressed on. The river was from here scarcely deemed navigable, even for light canoes, and the large canoes that the Indians of the coast hollowed from cedar were generally employed. They had remarkably elegant lines and were not, as might be supposed, heavy or cumbrous.

Above the forks, the ascent of the river required the utmost skill, dexterity, and strength from our crew. Paddling was of little use; tough hemlock poles, pointed and hardened in the fire, served better and so we impelled foot by foot against the rushing water, till some place too strong or deep was, whereupon we made a dash for the opposite bank, or the shore of some island, and poling recommenced. Occasionally it became necessary to drag the canoe up along the banks by the branches of trees and half-submerged shrubbery.

The eastern trail from the Skeena to Babine Lake follows closely an old Indian route, and had recently been cut and improved by the Provincial Government. The Indians made a regular trade of carrying goods and provisions across to the lake at the rate of four dollars a hundred pounds, which was the load usually carried by a man or a woman. In many cases they could take much more than that. Having a considerable quantity of baggage we were obliged to hire a motley crew of these indefatigable Indians, twenty-three in all, including two women. Several dogs were also pressed into service to carry the articles belonging to the Indians themselves.

One part of the trail crossed the Watsonkwa river by means of a bridge the Indians had built themselves. The river flowed below us through a steep-sided trough with the impetuosity of a torrent, and I admired the handiwork of the bridge which was of a style known as "suspension." The footway was hung from the superstructure by a series of vertical poles with hooked ends, the lashings, I discovered, made with telegraph wire left by the Western Union Company when they abandoned their overland line. Our crossing was carefully observed by a mountain goat, whose friends seemed to be everywhere as we progressed.

At the summit of the trail we could see Babine Lake stretching far to the East like a silver ribbon and we made the descent through country bristling with windfallen trees. The lake, I learnt from our carriers, is called Na-taw-bun-kut, which simply describes it as long, but the French servants of the Hudson's Bay Company called it Babine in allusion to the fact that the Tinneh Indians living on it had the custom of wearing a wooden labret or lip-piece in the lower lip. We went the length of Babine, which connected to the Stuart which we traversed, and we arrived in

Fort St. James in time for July 1st, on which day we ran a Union Jack up the flagpole and entered the horse races in the afternoon.

At the Fort we met up with the pack trains of horses which had been sent by the Canadian Pacific Railway from Kamloops, and they were for the prosecution of our survey to and in the Peace River Country. We left the Fort on July 8th, a combined party aggregating seventy-four pack and twenty-two riding animals, making for Fort McLeod. Mr. Selwyn had gone over this same route in 1875, while I was in Southern British Columbia, and I carried his report in my saddlebag. We reached the Fort in six days, whereas he, subjecting the ground to more careful scrutiny, had taken ten. The region had formerly yielded large numbers of skins, of marten and mink, but since the extensive spread of fires, the biggest around ten years earlier, the animals were scarce, except for the bears.

The next river to cross was the Parsnip, which we accomplished on July 19th, the animals swimming across without incident, all else ferried across in a boat we had brought with us from Fort McLeod. The gentlemen connected with the railway then began their descent of the Parsnip in the boat, while I set out the next morning by land for our intended rendezvous in mid-August at Dunvegan, going via the valley of the Pine River, which ran through the Rocky Mountain Range. I calculated the total distance which a railway line would have to follow through the Pine Pass to be 108 miles, 93 of which were classed as easy work and 13 as heavy work. Along the way several of us were constantly employed in advance on horseback looking for fords or cutting trail. At the summit of the pass we found a small cottonwood canoe cached at the side of the river, and so I named the mountain we were on Canoe.

I had hoped to meet Mr. MacLeod with the railway party coming westward to meet us, but though we reached a likely crossover spot at the Lower Forks of the Pine on August 7th, he was not there, nor had he left a note. We fired a number of shots in the calm of the evening to bring in any Indians who might be in the vicinity but without success, so we continued on. On the twelfth, we emerged into a valley, the first prairie country we had seen where the grass in some places was as high as the horses' bellies and already ripe and turning brown at the tops. The hillsides were gay with summer flowers such as Castilleia, Aster, and Solidago.

After travelling a few miles through this park-like country we caught sight of a couple of Indians who immediately plunged into a thicket and were next seen on the top of a hill about half a mile off running away as fast as they could. Our party was doubtless enough to disturb the equanimity of two timid Beaver Indians who had perhaps never seen mules before.

Two of our men pursued the runaways to their camp and returned shortly to our camp, followed by a number of men, women, and children who were curious and hungry. These were the first people besides our own party we had seen since leaving the Parsnip River twenty-four days previously. They were slight in build, and coarse featured with a pleasant expression. Lithe and active but comparatively weak, showing a considerable resemblance to the woodland Cree.

On the 15th we unexpectedly met Mr. McLeod with a few horses and men on his way westward. We camped together, made arrangements for the remaining explorations, and then went our separate ways, which brought us into Dunvegan the next day. We were then in the heart of the Peace River country, which I later calculated to be a tract of about 31,550 square miles. That summer had been one of excessively heavy rainfall, with cold raw weather in the early summer months, but notwithstanding that, on our arrival at Dunvegan small patches of wheat and barley in the garden presented a remarkably fine appearance and were beginning to turn yellow. The potatoes in the vegetable garden were quite ripe, and dwarf beans, cucumbers, and squashes were flourishing.

I did not linger at Dunvegan and, my eyes on the dwindling season, hastily organized two small parties, one going northward with Mr. McConnell, while I set out to the southward on Monday morning, having with me a packer, three British Columbian

Looking down on the Athabasca River, an etching from my photograph, 1879.

At Fort McLeod with the Survey party, 1879.

Indians, and a half-breed as guide. We crossed the Smoky River, then the Ghost River, and then the Rivière Brulé and came into the Grand Prairie at the Wapiti River. It was clearly an exceedingly fertile region, of a deep rich loam which it is impossible to surpass in excellence. Buffalo trails still scored the sod in all directions and scattered bones were numerous, though the animal was no more to be seen. The Indians stated that the extinction of the buffalo was not entirely due to the introduction of fire-arms, but that all the remaining ones were killed many years ago by an excessively severe winter when the snow was over the buffaloes' backs.

I wanted to make a geological run of a few days down the Wapiti of about fifty miles to where it met the Peace River, then down the Peace for another one hundred and twenty, and thence to the mouth of the Smoky. There was a possibility of the railway running either through the Pine River pass, or that of the Peace River, and I wanted the Canadian Pacific to have sufficient data to make a choice. The rest of the party then returned to Dunvegan and we duly made our excursion, mapping the Cretaceous beds as we went. When we were about six miles above the Smoky I realized we were at the point where Sir Alexander Mackenzie built a post in the autumn of 1792 and wintered in a house built for him, preparatory to his exploration of the then unknown country to the westward, in his search for a trade route to the Pacific. In the Spring, his Indian wife bore him a son there.

> The mist is upon the river
> And the moon, the waning moon
> Looks down on the dimmed mirror
> Where all the ice will gather soon.

Horses awaited us at the mouth of the Smoky, where we cached the canoe again, perhaps for some future explorer to use, and rode back to Dunvegan, arriving on August 30th and met up with the Canadian Pacific contingent. The beans, cucumbers, and squashes in the garden had been cut down by frost, but not completely killed, and the potato tops were also slightly nipped. The wheat and the barley were being harvested.

On the 5th of September our party, including Mr. McConnell who had returned, and the revenant Mr. McLeod's, struck out for the Athabasca River, in the company of a guide who promised to take us to Sturgeon Lake. We were obliged to use a long detour around a mass of burnt woods and windfall that was difficult even in winter on snow-shoes and quite impracticable for animals in any other season. At the lake we were greeted by Cree Indians living in rough log-houses, who cultivated small garden patches. All the men were away on a hunt and we despaired for a guide, until I procured a lad who agreed to take us to where one of the hunting parties was operating, and we could hope to find a man acquainted with the country, which we did. He brought us, after several days spent penetrating a very difficult stretch of terrain, to the banks of the Athabasca at a stopover point known as Drift-Pile Camp.

A party from Edmonton was supposed at this juncture to be on its way from there, with provisions to enable us to complete the season, but there was no trace of them. I turned my attention to planning my descent of the river. We set fire to a great pile of drift-logs on one of the bars in the river, and sent out one Indian up and down the river to seek for information, but all with no result. It was further unexpectedly found that no cottonwood trees suitable for making a canoe existed in the valley, and as the river was quite unsuited to a raft, by reason of it swiftness and the number of shoal bars, it was difficult to know in what way the programme could be carried out. It was finally decided to use the canvas cargo covers and blanket wrappings in the construction of a canoe. To this all hands devoted themselves for three days, when we had the satisfaction of seeing a large vessel, properly framed and strengthened, which when painted over with a mixture of bacon fat and spruce gum was nearly water-tight. I had great difficulty in persuading our last Indian guide, Antoine, to accompany me down the river. Having at last induced him by offers of good remuneration, and waited a day till he provided himself with a sufficient supply of moccasins for the return journey, commenced the descent on September 30th. Besides myself, the occupants of the canoe were a Mr. McNeil of Victoria, Antoine, a Cree Indian with whom we could not converse, and his little son, about twelve years old. We had about twenty days supply of provisions, which we hoped would carry us to Edmonton.

In descending the river we kept a sharp lookout for traces of the provisional party from Edmonton, and at length we noticed a newly blazed tree, and on landing found a note attached to it, written by a Mr. Brown. They had reached this point over a week earlier, having travelled three days on foot from where they had left their horses in a region impassable from dense masses of fallen timber. Their supplies had also become exhausted and they had turned back at once for Edmonton. It was therefore fortunate that we had not depended on them for supplies or assistance.

> A grove of tall and silent pines
> Where moss receives the tread
> Where the shadow darker lies
> The leaves are piled of seasons dead.

We soon found that our guide had forgotten nearly all that he had ever known about the river but, having no choice, we pressed on regardless. The stretch to Old Fort Assiniboine, a distance of thirty-three miles in a straight line, was characterized by the presence of numerous and large islands, and the current, previously rapid, became tranquil as we neared the old fort. It had been abandoned for many years, and it seemed that not too long ago even the ruins of the building had been destroyed by fire. Six miles beyond the site of the fort the river turned suddenly to a northeastward course, and continued with little deviation to the mouth of the Lesser Slave River.

On arriving at the mouth of the Lesser Slave River, on October

6th, I discovered that none of the other railway parties abroad in the region that season had made a running survey of the Lesser Slave and that it fell to me to fill the gap in the exploration that would otherwise remain unfilled. We therefore applied ourselves to the task of ascending the river as far as the shore of Lesser Slave Lake, which Mr. McConnell had already studied, and after four days of arduous labour, in cold stormy weather our task was accomplished. I had hoped to obtain photographs and sketches of the lake, but after waiting in a very uncomfortable camp during the afternoon of October 10th and the morning of the 11th, with no abatement in the storm of wind with flurries of snow which had begun on our arrival, I decided to set out on our return. On the 12th we ran all the rapids safely, in a blinding snow storm, and camped early in the afternoon on the Athabasca River, as the air was too full of snow to allow me to take bearings from point to point on the river. The next morning the air was clearer and the air was populous with wild fowl on their way southward – ducks of several species, geese, cranes, and swans.

In its aspect as a possible railway route the country between that dreary camp and Athabasca Landing, our next point of call, I made note as we progressed that a route that first crossed the Athabasca River by means of a bridge 760 feet long and about forty feet high was feasible, and that from there it would be best to follow the right side of the Athabasca valley, notwithstanding its somewhat sinuous course, where the bank was suitable and no heavy slides occurred.

The weather was now cold and wintry, with several inches of soft snow on the ground to greet us at Athabasca Landing, on October 14th. The time appointed for my rendezvous at Edmonton with Mr. McLeod was at hand, but exploration into the practicability of the Rivière La Biche for railway purposes remained to be determined, and no time was to be lost as it was mid-October and the river might at any time become partly choked with ice and impassable. We were so fortunate as to find at the Landing a free-trader about to set out on his last trip to Lesser Slave Lake with goods, and we were able to purchase from him a small bark canoe. I dispatched Mr. McConnell, with a half-breed named Adam Caillon to descend the Athabasca, ascend the Rivière La Biche, and make the best of his way to Victoria or Edmonton after reaching the Lac La Biche settlement. He was successful, and my acknowledgement of his report and efficient assistance should not be omitted from these pages.

From Athabasca Landing to Edmonton the Hudson's Bay Company had constructed a rough cart road for transporting goods inland, and this brought us with relative ease to Edmonton, the Fort that constituted the terminal point of our surveys for the season. After a few days spent in making the necessary arrangements and selecting the strongest of the animals, we set out – fifteen men, thirty-four horses and mules, eight Red River carts, and two buck-boards – on October 25th, to make our journey of nine hundred miles to Winnipeg. At Duck Lake, on November 12th, the carts were exchanged for flat-sleds, a heavy snowfall having taken place, and on the 2nd of December after a wintry journey of thirty-eight days across the plains, we were glad to find ourselves at Winnipeg and again within hearing of a railway whistle.

It was a journey of limited adventure down a long and winding road that, measured by the calendar, was the most time-consuming I had taken, and the longest I suspect I shall ever take. Having completed the exercise, it was clear to me that the region encompassing the Peace and Saskatchewan Rivers and Edmonton, where settlement was advancing, was one of very great fertility where crops were providing wonderfully favourable returns, and it possessed all the elements necessary to enable it to become, at some not very distant date, a populous province of the Dominion.

> Oh God, upon this close of day
> Thy sun descending in the West
> I know not what words to pray
> But ask that all mankind be blest.

THE BRIEF SPAN OF THE HEART

—

THE WEST AND I had become well acquainted in the four years I spent out there. In fact, by my calculation, of the fifty-six months prior to my return in December of 1879, I had spent only nine in Montreal. In the Survey's warehouse lay the stacks of packing cases I had dispatched back from the field, and the shelf of completed notebooks in my office at Gabriel Street was much longer than my not particularly long arms. I set to unpacking my specimens, my samples and mementoes, as well as the accumulation of facts, figures, and thoughts in my mind, and the days lined up like soldiers, each with their own *petites idiosyncrasies* but appearing much the same in their uniforms of snow white and then leaf-green.

The first publishable piece of work to come off my desk was a report on the harvestable trees in British Columbia, and then I plunged myself into considerations of the whole problem of glaciation. As I reviewed the evidence, it became clearer and clearer, as though one theory, that of drifting ice, was melting away even as another was hardening, namely that the last glaciation had extended further down the continent than either I or Father had previously thought. It had been fenced in by the Rocky Mountains, but passing like a shaving blade over the lowland prairie. Father and I had many a discussion of this, and we, in the end, had to agree to differ.

Next I began, though I suspected it would be many months before it was finished, the study of the Haida and other western Indian tribes, with especial attention to the investigations of Dr. Tolmie and myself into tribal vocabulary. It was at that time that Father made his remark about my writing talents being wasted on reports, when I should be better occupied writing a popular tome, a journal of my travels perhaps.

So one year yielded to the next and in 1880, for the second summer in a row, I remained in Montreal, a non-posting that felt close to imprisonment. I did not find being trapped in the inclement heat and crowded streets of the city at all equal to being abroad in free movement in the woods. The solitude, being less "natural," was oppressive. The people one met day to day were no more to me than so many nine-pins. Father and Mother in particular would stir people up to ask me out, and I repeated several times that I wished they would not do so, as I hated going out. I came to loathe going to dinner especially, my skill for small talk eroded by the silence of great forests. So, I wrote on in my simple reports, noting, for instance, that the Indians called the Milky Way *Ya-ka-tsool-k* meaning *the snow shoe track*. Christmas came again, and I took my joyful responsibilities seriously as the eldest son to show a good example to the children, encouraging the writing of thank-you notes and leading the singing and carpet games. I enjoyed doing so, but in the New Year I let Mr. Selwyn know that a third Spring without a western journey in the works would be most taxing.

I did manage some relief from Montreal at the end of the summer of 1880 when, as promised years before, I took my now sixteen-year-old sister Eva on a sight-seeing tour to Scotland, London, and Paris. In Scotland, where we took a boat down the Caledonian Canal from Inverness, a most beautiful run that Eva caught in a nice little sketch, I caught up with my cousins and Eva met many of hers for the first time. Cousin Ella joined us later in London which city I had not seen for seven years. This time, things went at a pace I was not at all used to, and I realized that I was having trouble keeping up with the enthusiasm of my young sister to "do it all." I did not seem to have time to do other than make arrangements and rush about places that were generally uninteresting when got to, such as the hours we spent in South Kensington Museum, a sort of nightmare vision of endless passages, statues, pictures, and stairs. The night after, I must admit, we went to Madame Tussaud's on Baker Street which we both enjoyed. Ella came on with us to Paris after London, where we all went up the Eiffel Tower, and down again, and I can confess to being quite worn out on our return in September to Montreal, where we were able to see Anna's new baby for the first time.

Back in time for the changing of the leaves, I learnt that Mr. Selwyn had larger problems than my itchy feet and intellect with which to deal. When the Act redefining the mandate of the Survey had gone through in 1877, our removal to Ottawa became probable, with its attendant opportunities for Members of Parliament to interfere directly in our operations rather than at arm's length in Montreal. There was much displeasure at this eventuality, it being almost viewed as an insult to the city, and the campaign to prevent the move raised the calibre and robustness of its arguments. Some said that the renowned natural history museum Mr. Logan had bequeathed the nation would be starved of oxygen, and that likewise the great University of McGill would be weakened by the loss of so prestigious an ally as the Geological Survey. Besides, Montreal was the greatest centre for mining capital in the country, not Ottawa, and disconnecting it from the organization dedicated to locating the raw resources for those mines was foolhardy. Selwyn summed up the case against the whole shenanigans when he wrote to the minister stating that "the Survey's removal to Ottawa could not fail to operate in every respect most prejudicially."

Despite our relentless resistance, the Government went ahead the next year and found and purchased premises in Ottawa for the Survey, in a luxury hotel that had fallen on hard times on Sussex Drive. The Parliament Buildings were visible from the upper windows and the Minister's office a mere five-minute walk away. I recognized the building when Selwyn described it to me, because it was there that the Marquess of Lorne had staged the inaugural exhibition of the Canadian Society of Art which I had attended. The purchase of this building, a concrete act from which the government would have difficulty retreating, nevertheless had the effect of propelling the opposition into greater effort. Father wrote a strong personal letter to the Prime Minister (Sir John A. was still the nation's leader then) but it was to no avail.

So it was that in May of 1881, all around me in the Survey offices on Gabriel Street, men were packing up and carefully labelling boxes, some marked as FRAGILE! and others, those holding the ore samples destined for the new museum in the new building, marked HEAVY! I too packed and inscribed my boxes, but I would not be there to open them. Mr. Selwyn had heeded my pleas and I was off to the west, travelling to Toronto, then Chicago and finally arriving in Bismark, where I lingered long enough to write to William to arrange for the *Witness*, Mr. Dougall's temperance newspaper that has been a family reading staple since the days when it was a mere weekly, to go to my address at Fort Macleod. William was to be trusted in this duty, being of all of us most like Father and steady in his affairs. It was in Bismark that I discovered that the baggage workers had nearly dismembered my camera, but I was able to reconstruct it later in Fort Benton, after many days winding westward on the Missouri River.

I had not up to that point experienced anything so long on water as that trip up the Missouri River. We seemed to spend almost as much time ashore in a bar, the crew gleefully indulging in a sort of stampede of profanity. The steamer's engines were running through thirty cords per diem, so we were wooding two or three times a day. There were several small herds of buffalo lower down the river and innumerable Indians, including most of Sitting Bull's people.

He drew the pathways for the bison on the prairie
And in the sky marked the way of birds,
    and winds, and rainstorms.

At one point we spotted thirty buffalo on the far side of a long spit round which the steamer had to go. A party landed (not I; I chose to sit quietly on board and record the operation) and trotted about a mile in the heat and clouds of mosquitoes, only to witness the animals swimming the river on the other side. The steamer, however, had by now rounded the spit and scared the animals back towards the hunters, who at once set up a fusillade at close range and succeeded in killing one near the bank, while badly wounding another. Some men went after the wounded creature. The boat tied up to deal with the kill, and the party returned long after dark, unsuccessful, and somewhat unsettled by the rattlesnakes they had heard making themselves audible among the stones.

Although it seemed at that point that, like Ulysses, we would be forever travelling in a boat or in a stage through a series of either damp or dusty adventures, never reaching our destination, we did reach the dock at Fort Macleod constructed on an island in the Oldman River. The Fort at that time consisted of a barracks square surrounded by some low rambling buildings and thirty or forty low-roofed long buildings, and some storehouses. Originally built eight years earlier with a complement of around one hundred and fifty Mounties, it had not grown much, although it had managed to cork, as it were, much of the local whiskey trade, which trade the Mounties had been charged with eradicating. There was one shop, run by the Bakers, a hardy couple prepared to weather the adventure. The populace was sparse, no more than two people in each house on the average and most of them half-breeds. Nearby was a large camp of Blackfeet on their way north to their agency for the treaty payment, all very poor, ill clad, and dirty. Later in June than I had hoped I was again a man and a notebook unravelling the nature of the western Dominion. Expeditions such as this one in the Missouri watershed were now taking on a familiar rhythm. At the beginning of each trip my face would undergo a ritual first peeling, then reach a state of equilibrium that would maintain itself until I was indoors and pale faced again.

The mosquitoes were exceedingly bad that year. After years of travel in their company, one got accustomed to them and came to regard them as just another necessary element of the atmosphere. But between horse flies by day and mosquitoes at night the horses got barely any rest, and we let them set the pace. At sunset they would come running back into camp from their pasture in search of a smudge. A month later, we were back in Macleod and there was a budget of letters awaiting me, little packages of comfort, some containing amusing epistles from those members of the Montreal literary group with whom I then corresponded.

With the research to the east of the Fort done, a northern circular tour down the Bow River was the next item of business. At the mouth of the Bow I shot an antelope while an Indian who was travelling with us shot two, giving us an abundance of meat all the way. I asked the Indian for the reason behind our fortunate hunt, and he explained that his fellow tribesmen were for the most part gone from that country, concentrated now in the mountains, and the antelope had become plentiful as a result of their drawback.

By the time autumn was setting in I was again back in Fort McLeod, arriving for once without a gnawing hunger in need of immediate service. We got into McLeod the day after the Governor General left, which I counted as lucky as all the attendant fuss was well over. A number of Blackfoot had come to meet with the Governor, and the day before they and most of the inhabitants had staged some horse racing. Against the odds, an Indian horse won one of the races and the natives gathered in nearly $1,000 in bets, owing to the unexpected result.

From McLeod I went up into the Rocky Mountains, worked northward one hundred miles or so, then billeted in Fort Calgary, which seemed to get no closer the more we travelled towards it, until we were right in the gate. The situation of Calgary was remarkably beautiful. The plateaus there retired to some distance from the river, which was bordered by wide flats thickly covered with bunch grass and well-adapted to agriculture. The river was fringed with trees, and from the higher points in the neighbour-hood the Rocky Mountains were still visible.

> The yellow grass in billowy lines
> Is warm in the sun and still
> Where mountains afar with crag on crag
> Show purple and blue on the far sky line
> Through the still hot air comes thin and clear
> The distant sound.

I returned to Montreal in October, boxes filled with coal samples still in transit behind me, and took a few days to catch up with my parents and sibling and to undergo the usual professional debriefing with Father. Mr. Selwyn wrote to say that, should I come then to take up my position at the new offices of the Survey in Ottawa, I might be a little ahead of their preparations for me, and find matters a trifle untidy. But I was determined to leave Montreal for personal reasons which were at that stage of concern only to myself, and so in late November a short train journey took me to Ottawa, the city already sporting a healthy blanket of snow.

On arrival, I went at once to the Grand Union Hotel and got a comfortable enough room. I realized, standing inside those hotel walls, walking about in the hotel corridors watching others come out and in, that I had become a nomad, happier on a forest floor than the fourth floor, and more used to the sound of a tent flapping hard against damp ground than a flag rope beating on a ceremonial pole. I wrote to Anna in this mood, declaring that I wished I had a rapa-cious appetite for money or something that would keep me going somewhere else than in Ottawa. It has always struck me as particu-larly pleasant to be connected to the production of something useful, say potatoes or horse shoes, and to know that if you stopped exerting yourself one day, you'd have nothing to eat the next.

I was thus inclined to take my time searching for permanent quarters, and occupied a corner of Mr. Selwyn's office on Sussex Drive while carpet was laid in my prospective bureau, or some such delay. As I recall, it was the chimney in Mr. Perry's office, soon to be mine, that had caused the trouble. Some sort of back draft was established which filled the space with gas and Perry was forced to evacuate and the room shut up. However, the poor man went back into it for a moment to get some books, and was thoroughly poisoned by carbonic oxide and rendered very ill for some time afterwards. Steam heating apparatus was fitted into the building shortly thereafter and the threat from rebellious chimneys reduced.

I soon came to the conclusion, as the Christmas season of 1881 approached, that Ottawa was even duller on a Sunday than Montreal, and not so large that it was easy to get far away from any central point; one always felt oneself to be right in it. Civilization, it seemed, had already lost its charms for me, so recently returned from the wilderness, and my Survey work that I could classify as really necessary was scarce. I was in search of a motive for action. Consequently, though I had scarcely sat down, I mentioned to Mr. Selwyn while we were both at our desks, that I would very much like to explore the Liard River, which had been an abiding wish since I returned from British Columbia in 1879. He replied that in the new year he would consider it, which I took to mean I should pause awhile before asking again.

That Christmas in Montreal – I only got away from Ottawa on the night before Christmas Eve – was an unhappy affair for me, more depressing yet than any I spent as a boy in my room in McGill. Brother Rankine had returned from London a few days before I arrived, not a cause for the dumps in itself, but my mood no doubt made it seem as though he were the cause of it. In fact, mine was a depression of another sort, of the painful variety that follows the sting of unrequited Love. A heart I sought, one I had known for some time and had wrongly assumed contained an equal affection, had been won by another, a man not of scientific background but a lawyer and a writer of considerable note.

My mood remained forlorn, my sense of self-pity exaggerated, when I took the train back to Ottawa in mid-January of 1882, and disembarked at the bustling Broad Street station and hailed a carriage. We trotted past the stacks of timber by the sawmills and the lines of single working men like me marching towards them. I had found rooms at Victoria Chambers on Wellington Street and went straight there, and in the evening made the short walk, no more than a block, to the Rideau Club, where I had taken a membership and could always expect to find one or several fellows with whom I could converse and take the pleasure of relaxed company.

At the office, an official request from Sir Alexander Galt for information, resulting from my western explorations of the previous summer, lay unanswered on my desk. Sir Alexander was a friend of the family, and Eva a strong friend of one of his several daughters, and another daughter, Amy, was a member of my mother's reading club which met regularly over the cold Montreal winters. Sir Alexander had written to me while I was on the Missouri, enclosing a map and wondering if I might mark it up with the likely coal deposits I had gone there to chart. I had drafted a hasty reply from the field, sitting on a packing case, wondering if he might wait until I had returned East. Now, by dint of many hours solitary work in the Autumn I had reached the preliminary stage of my report on the Western coal reserves, and had drafted them out in two sections. With one hand on my own shoulder, as it were, pressing down, I fashioned a reply to Sir Alexander. The wording did not come easy, as I was in some ways attempting to play two roles simultaneously, that of loyal employee of the Survey as well as that of a public servant beholden to another of elevated status and power. In the former letter, Sir Alexander had mentioned that he would expect to make a professional charge for the report, so I began forthwith by stating I would prefer receiving no remuneration for it, on account of my connection with the Survey. I stated only that I was glad if I had been of use to him and I hoped it would aid in the great progress of the northwest, to which my efforts had been directed since '73.

The snow, like some slow frozen wave moving in reverse, ebbed, slushing around for a while, and then the first crocuses appeared early on Parliament Hill, and Society came out of hibernation. I was able to store my beaver coat for another nine-month, tail and all. Still melancholic in private but obliged, Janus-like, to show another face in public, I spent a musical evening in late February at the Selwyns', where Mrs. Harrison played the piano. I was always glad to see Mrs. Harrison, she too possessing a sort of agnostic soul. She was very astute as well as musical (in contrast to Mr. Harrison, who looked like an owl and had roughly the same amount of musical wit about him) and after her recital we were able to find a corner – always my favourite part of a room – and talk. Our conversation could not be keep off the rocks on which my heart had so recently run aground, and I fear I talked on a little too much. She listened bravely and then gave me, dear lady, some return towards peace of mind.

Back in my rooms later that night, I took up the pen and wrote to Mother and apologized for being so cross and unpleasant while I had been home at Christmas. I confessed to her that it was difficult to be otherwise when one finds that he has arrived at the end of all in life that is worth calling such and hoped for, but I did not lay out the full nature of what I had suffered. I also knew that my failure to go to the club with Rankine, on that ghastly Monday when I had learnt of my forced retreat from my hopes of love, would be taken as a slight against him, and I had no wish for him to think that. The real reason for my behaviour she had swiftly divined, to be sure, and so I asked her firmly not to reply to the letter, but to ensure that Rankine knew the cause of my ill manners lay elsewhere than with him. I also asked Mother in that letter to mail on the two mother of pearl studs I received as a gift from the former object of my heart, which I had now decided to keep. I have them still. I knew, however, that I would not soon be happy again in Montreal. Several times over the next few weeks, Father came to Ottawa to assist in the preparations for a major meeting of the American Association for the Advancement of Science, of which he was President and which he had invited to Montreal that year. Both he and Mother had spent months on it, Father commuting back and forth between home and Ottawa to arrange funds and maintain support from the Governor General. My behaviour at Christmas was not discussed.

I gradually decided to take a piece of Mrs. Harrison's advice and go east rather than west. I would tour Europe. I duly applied for and arranged a leave of absence from the Survey in April, ostensibly for the purpose of going to Germany and France to visit some mining districts.

The decision made, I was restless to leave, but my days quickly filled with the details of hosting the Association meeting. I decided to give the delegates their lunches in marquees on the Parliamentary Square, behind the buildings, and have the meeting rooms decorated and the furniture not all covered with dust cloths as was usual in the summer. The meeting went off without incident and then, towards the end of February 1882, all the boxes of specimens arrived from the last western trip. I was able to offer some skins to Father for the Redpath Museum; a black-tailed deer pelt, a mountain sheep, and a buffalo skull. The museum, then in the process of construction, took its name from its benefactor and a family friend, Mr. Peter Redpath. Its opening later in the year would happily coincide with the twenty-fifth anniversary of Father's appointment at McGill, and would at last provide a suitable showcase for his treasured collections. When we had arrived in 1855, Father had in tow several boxes containing his collections. He had inquired whether the University had a museum, and was shown a desk drawer in which was a handful of poorly labelled items! He vowed then that the University would one day have a worthy building.

It was not until mid-March that I was able to begin serious planning for the grand tour, and report to Father that I had taken passage on the *Sarmatian*, leaving Portland May 4th. On the same day I secured my passage, I gave a lecture to the Little Literary and Scientific Society, co-opting one of my old papers from the Ladies' Course in Quebec for the purpose. I must admit I barely paid attention to myself; they, fortunately, were not so rude.

By late April I locked the desk with very little work left atop it, and spent a day or so in Montreal wearing a brave face, where Father and I were able to discuss the death of Charles Darwin, who had passed away at Down House in Kent on the 19th. He had been buried a few days after in Westminster Abbey — Father pointed out the irony of a church burial for the man who had in his eyes refuted much of the Bible — not far from Sir Isaac Newton. My former teacher Mr. Huxley had been one of the pall bearers, and I knew he must be feeling the loss of his old friend and I determined to drop him a note when I was in London. I caught the train down to Portland at the end of April to catch the steamer, which came into Halifax harbour just before dinner on the Friday. William, who had seen our funnel from his boarding house, met me at the wharf. Over dinner we were able to discuss our respective future plans. William was working in Halifax under contract to a Mr. Plunkett and his Syndicate for the location and supply of coal reserves for the Pictou branch of the Windsor and Annapolis Line, designing some boring tools. Although he had doubts about its management, he felt himself reluctantly obliged to see it through. I noted that the railway line, once built, would pass within earshot of our birthplace in Pictou, and William said he had often seen it in the course of his work.

When the conversation turned towards me, to my going Continental for the better part of a year, I put a fine shine on things, which I had decided to cast as a mixture of work and pleasure, and of general education. I referred to the different mining districts I intended to visit, including those in France of which I knew William had some knowledge. As to my specific travelling plans, the when and where of them, I explained, as I had to the others, that I felt making any decisions as to the order in which they were to be visited would deprive the trip of all the pleasure therein. William had discovered a new system for learning languages and had gone ahead and ordered the German system for me. We browsed the requisite books that had arrived at his home just the week before, and which I intended to absorb along the way. The German I already knew wouldn't fill a waistcoat pocket, so I was pleased at his forethought. On the next day, we collected Mrs. Selwyn, who was already down in Nova Scotia for the summer, and took the carriage round the city, arriving at the pier in time for my two o'clock sailing on the *S.S. Sarmatian*, which was loaded up with the mails and the Inter Colonial train passengers. Halifax glowed in the young summer sun as the ship pulled out; ahead lay the continent, and several months spent in my own company without fixed date of return.

On the fourth evening out of Halifax, I felt the machinery below me stop, and went on deck to see what was going on. I discovered we were not far from another large steamer, the *Catalonia*, a Cunarder, which had signalled us to come to a halt. It turned out she had a broken shaft and was quite helpless. By daylight, it became clear that the passengers, excepting those too sea-sick to move, would have to be added to our list. In making the climb down one rope ladder on the *Catalonia* and up the one on the *Sarmatian*, complicated by the lifting of the smaller boat by the swell, several ladies seized the opportunity for fainting. Ninety cabiners were thus crowded in with ours, some gentlemen having to make do with intermediate class rooms or even the hospital. Among them, as it happened, was a Mrs. O'Reilly with her two children, whom I had known in British Columbia. We took the *Catalonia* in tow for a day and night, by which time she was patched up enough that they could at least keep her head to the wind. Rough weather came on and almost everyone was prostrated with sea-sickness, and I had the deck to myself as we came into Liverpool and a still bed in the Adelphi Hotel, followed by a night out with the Rudolfs. When I saw cousin

Ella Kemp in London, where she was staying for a while, I suggested again to her the idea of passing part of a winter in Canada, as a way of relieving her delicate disposition from the persistent trouble she had with the damp and cold of a Scotch winter.

The channel crossing was one of the smoothest I could recall, and after a pleasant re-acquaintance with the gastronomic pleasures of Paris, I moved south, travelling quite off the general English tourist beat, where I scarcely saw any English-speaking people. Most of the tourists were away in Switzerland, or under the impression that it was or should be hotter elsewhere, although the heat had not arrived yet to any great extent. The throng, conspicuous by its absence elsewhere, reappeared when I alighted from the train at Le Puy, south of Lyon. There I stood, like the rest of the town, in the shadow of the cathedral poised on the summit of Mount Corneille, an edifice said to be as old as Europe itself, much visited during medieval times by pilgrims making their way to Santiago de Compostela.

The town interested me for its outstanding combination of spirituality and geology. It seems that, prior to the arrival of Christianity, an enormous "dolmen," a standing stone, stood atop the sacred hill Mount Corneille, erected by persons unknown. Sometime between the 3rd and 4th centuries A.D., so the story went, a local woman suffering from an incurable disease received visionary instructions from the Mother of Heaven to climb the mount where she would be cured by sitting on the great stone. She was. Appearing to the woman a second time, Mary gave instructions that the local bishop should be contacted and told to build a church on the hill. When the bishop climbed the hill, he found the ground covered in deep snow even though it was the middle of July. A lone deer walked through the snow, tracing the ground plan of the cathedral that was to be built. Convinced by these miracles of the authenticity of Mary's wishes, the bishop completed construction of the church by A.D. 430 and the great dolmen was left standing in the centre of the Christian sanctuary and was consecrated as the

Throne of Mary. In the eighth century, however, the pagan stone, known as the "stone of visions," was taken down and broken up, the pieces incorporated into the floor of the church in the Chambre Angelique, the "angels chamber."

The habits of a working life, once engrained, are hard to ignore, and the notebook I had brought thinking only to enter superficial observations, now also became the repository of poems and remarks from a deeper place. It lies open here before me, retrieved, without much trouble, from storage, but rather harder to return to in mind, particularly the poems.

> Pitiful pitiful sad hearted one
> Going thy little round sun after sun
> Dark grim and pitiful, millions untold
> Toiling and weeping till hope hath grown old
> Toiling sad hearted till evening is come
> And the lips that could murmur of sorrow are dumb.

"Pitiful, pitiful, sad hearted one," is no way to begin a first page, and yet I did so and the black edges of the mood I was in through those months is reawakened by writing out those lines again. Poems are spells, surely, capable of transporting the one who penned them back in time, be they willing to go or not.

After leaving Le Puy I found myself in Montréal; not my home town but its original French namesake, which lay in the valley of the river Aude. Like my home city, it too had felt capture and war, and at approximately the same point in history. Not long after Cartier had stood on Mount Royal, Montréal "senior" was attacked by Huguenots, and held for a year and a half until it was purchased back by its own inhabitants. Ten years later the Huguenots overwhelmed it again; this time the Duke of Montmorency rode out from Carcassonne and after killing fifty of its defenders retook it, whereupon the townspeople swore allegiance again to the King.

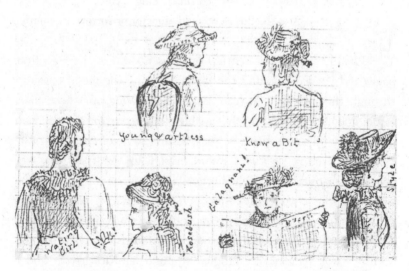

Two sketches from my notepad, made during my Europe journey in 1882.

At Toulouse I took a ticket on the Chemin de Fer du Midi — the circular excursion comprising Luchon, Bayonne, Bordeau, Montauban, and back to Toulouse. The principal source of amusement on a train is looking through the window onto a world that, until that moment, one has never seen before and will never see again. For example, through the window at Cette, I saw men and women loading barges with coal from railway trucks, the coal being carried in baskets on their heads. One of the women chose that moment to turn her head towards the train, though the basket did not move, and we exchanged glances, for the first and last time.

At Bagneres de Luchon, at the foot of the Pyrenees, I knew there lay one of the greatest health resorts or "établissements thermaux" in France, with ten thousand visitors every summer drawn like dried fish to a town of four thousand, with its forty-eight Roman hot mineral springs impregnated with sulphate of sodium. Here I halted up for a few days.

The valley was small and closed in with pretty high mountains, the baths surrounded by well-kept gardens free to everyone. After bathing, one could cleanse one's purse at the magnificent Casino, where you either became a subscriber or paid a franc a day entrance as I did, and hence were entitled to all the attractions of a good club such as the Rideau in Ottawa, including reading and writing rooms, post and telegraph office, even a small museum of Pyrenean objects and models of mountains. In the mornings there was music in the gardens, and it came in the window of the splendid writing room where I composed several pieces of poetry.

Grey hairs grow thick, some honours fall
But that one day when you and I
Were on, is still the best of all.
So, now come death, or chance what may
In downward slope of passing years
I hold the memory of a day.

While there at the healing baths I took an excursion on a train to a nearby small volcanic lake. The people there were dreadful beggars; we must have had at least twenty at different times begging in the carriage window for coppers. The last miles had to be gotten over on horseback, and you had to bargain for your horse. At the little rim of the lake the man in charge of the horses, who called himself a guide, though no one else could, required something to drink at our expense after his arduous exertions. The privilege of looking at the lake cost a mere thirty centimes. On the return, the horses needed oats, as did the stable boy, the coachman, and the guide again, since he was now freshly exhausted.

> I feel a great regret of love
> For those who gave me birth and strive
> To do their duty, dimly seen
> Amid the stress of life.

From Toulouse, it was on to Lyon, where I was able to collect quite a body of letters, some only two weeks old, including a substantial one from Father. I knew that he found my journey to Europe "deficient in any definite aim," and he could not resist asking me, this time in a letter while I was still out of the country, if on return I could undertake either some or all of his workload. As he had admitted to me recently, he found himself manifestly older and less able for work, and Mother was also not as strong as she was. He had worn himself out, arranging and hosting that annual meeting of the American Association for the Advancement of Science.

While I could not help but detect the anxiousness in his plea, Father stressed that my taking a post at McGill need not interfere with my field work in the West, as the following summer the railway would be open across Canada quite to the Rocky Mountains, and it would be logistically easier for me to work there in the warmer months. Indeed, he would even like, before going, to have a run out there himself. But his concern remained that his life's work, the

Redpath Museum, would fall in the hands of strangers. Close to completion and due to open later that year, Father knew that with his museum he had created a truly noble teaching plant, perhaps the finest natural history collection in the country; his dilemma was that while he railed against employing inferior men, the means were not there to employ superior ones. I wrote to say I would give the matter some thought, which was true but evasive.

Also in among the letters at Lyon was a rare one, from Eva, telling of William's engagement. By this time, to his relief and mine, he had cleared Halifax and those men of uncertain trust he had contracted with, and was back in Montreal working for the Dominion Bridge Company, where his work was appreciated and his prospects good. An ideal time, then, for love to strike him. Eva, who had just turned eighteen, put it this way, "William the prudent and wise is, it seems, destined to be the first to sacrifice himself and settle down." It appeared that while William was in Halifax, an Englishman and his family, a major in the army who at one time guarded there for five years in charge of the commissariat and were revisiting, stayed for almost a month at the same boarding house as my brother. Their eldest daughter, Florence Elliott, nineteen years old to my brother's twenty-four, proved as Eva put it, "fatal to William's peace of mind." He posed the question and eventually, though not too long an eventually, received his answer. I believe now that William held back from telling me the news himself, as he was then more acquainted with my own affairs of the heart than was Eva.

As I suspected there would be, there was an earnest, well-meaning letter from Anna inquiring as to the state of my heart. When the matter of romance had, at least as far as they were concerned, blown over, Mother and Anna had set out to find me a replacement as the best method of healing me. The general impression was that I should quickly settle and marry, and a Miss B.G. had emerged as the candidate most likely to prove interesting to me. Their kind assistance, as I informed Anna by return of post, in a letter I found painful to compose, came quite too late. I would not marry ever, I said. One does not love twice, and ashes could not be burnt back again into coal by any process I knew of. Had I been ten or fifteen years younger, I told her, I might have begun life again, but I was to become thirty-four in a month's time, and I was old enough to know my own mind. I had never thought life was worth much, and it had taken me nearly three years of false hope to find that mine was worth nothing to me.

Looked at from the best point of view, the end of the affair certainly relieved me of some embarrassment, having nothing to hope for, very little to fear, and no belief in anything besides the automatic and mechanical part of me that remained scarred but intact. I knew that when I got back to work, some day, I could go on with a certain painful exactness in the groove I had made. Obviously, one must do something to gain one's daily bread so long as one is unfortunate as to need it, and as one grows older one becomes more and more contented to be a machine as one becomes less capable of feeling either pleasure or pain to extreme. I once read, somewhere, that there are three stages in a career. The first is when people say, "He will do great things." Secondly, "He might do . . ." Third, "He might have . . ." In my own case, I can say that I was faced with an uphill fight, and fought it out inch by inch till I found myself . . . at the bottom. Until failure came, I never found anything worth doing that could be done without putting your whole life into it. But when failure did come, and under those conditions, it was final. I knew that I would very much rather be happy than otherwise, but there is a text that says "What does it matter to a man if he gains the whole world and loses his own soul." Well, then.

I wrote words to this effect to Anna, and asked her to understand and not go to the trouble of endeavouring to gather up spilt milk. And, as time proved, the matter was not spoken of again to me, although I am sure others spoke of it within the family.

I felt that despite the many miles I had put between me and my affairs in Montreal and Ottawa, I had learnt nothing and forgotten nothing of the irrational emotion we call love. I began to think I might as well be grinding away at maps and reports in Ottawa as squandering money which others might use better. One day, perhaps, I could make for the extreme northwest, where I hoped several years of my life would be passed before the relentless tide of civilization and the national quest for the raw materials overwhelmed me like a returning glacier. Already, on my last trip to the Rocky Mountains, the railway making and settlement building going on there made me feel something akin to what the Indian must have felt when the white man took possession of his pastures and drove away his game. In a few years, I felt certain, there would be no part of the northwest untrodden enough to be interesting. So, I went home for Christmas, the ghost of Christmas past not entirely exorcised, but its bell rang so faintly I could hardly hear it.

> The streams and springs of life in every land
> Draw down by one great river to the sea
> And all the bonds that time and chance on change
>   have wrought
> Are broken down and melt in one true thought.

THE AGE OF THE NORTH

—

IN THE YEARS following my return from Europe, I made good on
the vow I had outlined in my letter to Anna; I directed my energies to my work and my family, and let affairs of the heart sink, like
fallen trees, to the bottom of my thoughts, there to gradually
harden and most unlikely to ever resurface. My duties and
thoughts were focused at the Geological Survey with my appointment as chief assistant director in 1883.

Shortly after, Father, not to be outdone, received a richly
deserved Knighthood for his services to just about everything, but
to education, religion, and science in particular. For a while I
addressed all my letters to him "Lord Fossil of McGill," which jest
he took well. Several times when I was out with Mother, until my
ears grew used to it, I would scan the crowd when someone addressed
her as "Lady Dawson" wondering quite whom they might mean.

Over the next three years I was engaged in periodic forays into
personally assigned "pieces" of the Dominion that had been drawn
up and numbered according to a large map on the Survey's library
wall, the pieces of the Canadian jigsaw that remained, even then,
largely unexplored and mapped to our satisfaction. As the Survey's
men fanned out and turned stones, there was still one area I had
been anxious for a generation to penetrate, and I felt, by 1887, that
I had earned the right to go there; in fact I felt I was overdue. It
was the Yukon District. There, at last, I could guarantee that most

of humanity would be elsewhere, and that the solace I sought in nature, which knew nothing of my demons, would be bountiful.

So, in the Spring of 1887, I embarked on what I must ruefully now regard as the trip of my lifetime, my finest year of travel. (I say ruefully for I may wish for another like it, but judging by the example of my predecessors in the position of Director of the Survey, Logan and Selwyn, who lasted twenty-six and twenty-seven years respectively, I am unlikely to escape my desk quite that far and for that long again.) Knowing I was going into uncharted territory I sought the wisdom of others and wrote to Mr. W.H. Dall, a correspondent I had first made contact with in 1875 when talk of mapping the Alaska and Yukon border had briefly flamed, then died. He was at that time my counterpart in rank in the Geological Survey of the United States, a body founded in the same year as Canada "confederated" if that is the correct verb. Dall is known to the general public, if at all, for the sheep that bears his name (there is also a porpoise that carries that honour) and I esteemed him and his knowledge of the Yukon.

The Yukon district, in strict geographical terms, is bounded to the south by the northern line of the Province of British Columbia, latitude 60; to the west by the eastern line of the United States territory of Alaska; to the east by the Rocky Mountain Ranges, and to the north by the Beaufort Sea. Thus defined, it has a superficial extent nearly equal to that of France and ten times that of Nova Scotia. Our expedition was to be the first major contribution to our knowledge of this wide country.

Mr. Dall's stock of knowledge was certainly ahead of mine, for on the death of a colleague by sudden heart attack in 1866, he had taken over an expedition to map out a telegraph route on the Yukon River between Russia and North America, via the Bering Sea. Dall wintered over and survived (a prospect I might be forced to take up, though I did not wish for it) and in the next year the Alaskan territory was purchased by his country for the sum of around seven million dollars. Quite how this figure was reached I know not, but because of it Dall was then able to continue his explorations and sail the coast of what was now his homeland in a schooner he respectfully called the *Yukon*. He informed me by reply that he had in fact taken his honeymoon in the Yukon a mere eight years before I was to "get up there." (He agreed with me in a post-script that fixing the boundary between Alaska and northwest Canada apparently, after two decades, remained impossible to accomplish, though he did not agree, as I had indicated, that it required only a willingness on the part of the Washington Government to bring it about.) As part of our mission, I was tasked to determine the point at which either the Yukon or its sister river the Pelly crossed the 141st meridian, which constituted the boundary between the Canadian North-West Territory and the American Alaska, and I had employed a Mr. Ogilvie, a Dominion Land Surveyor, to perform this overdue feat. As I told Dall, the real reason for a Canadian expedition into that place at this time was that the headwaters of the Yukon River were attracting more and more attention as a gold-mining district, and that the Dominion of Canada should know something of its geography and geology before it was invaded by fortune hunters.

One or two days after I had written to Dall, I received a heart-felt letter from Father on behalf of the family wishing me the highest prospects for my journey and the best of results for my explorations. He was also, without saying so directly, communicating the anxiety my parents felt at the undoubted dangers I was about to face. He wished with all his heart, he said, that he could come up to Ottawa to shake hands with me once more before I left, a sign of his mixed feelings of trepidation and pride. Just before I left to take the train west, Father wrote again to pass on the news of Rankine's arrival in Australia, though I had no idea he had gone there. He was working, it seemed, as a ship's doctor and appeared from his letter to be in good spirits, a piece of good news to take with me, as was the recovery of several of Anna's children from an invasion of measles. Less than a month before Father wrote, Anna had given birth to her sixth child, christened Bernard after his father, and there had been the threat of contagion, but all was well. Ever the gardener and observer, Father also informed me that the snowdrops and crocuses had sounded the Spring fanfare in the centre bed at McGill, the only one thus far with some soil exposed; winter was hanging on in Montreal like a lodger not anxious to retreat. Mother also wrote a day or so before I was due to take the rail out, enclosing an air pillow and some socks.

I left Ottawa for the Yukon on the 22nd of April 1887, travelling for the first time all the way to Port Moody by the Canadian Pacific Railway, and thence to Victoria. The irregularity of the Alaska mail steamer at that time of year meant that we were unable to reach Wrangell, a small town on the frayed coast of Alaska, until the 18th of May. Wrangell is the Indian gateway to the Stikine River, on which we would go inland.

Once there, our party split into three, like the prongs of a fork, with my colleague from the Survey, Mr. McConnell, given the task of gathering the finer points and precise shape of the Stikine River while I, as expedition head, would cross into the Yukon Basin by way of the upper reaches of the Liard River, so named for the species of poplar tree that grows in wild profusion along its banks. Mr. Ogilvie's border-locating assignment I have already mentioned.

On May 19th, my party obtained passage on the first steamer that year out of Wrangell going up the Stikine River, and there was quite a crowd of around forty Chinamen on board going to the mines; the Chinese, we were to discover, often outnumbered the whites when we came across miners working for gold.

The entranceway to the Stikine River, the portal into *terra incognita*, was quite undistinguished, a saltwater inlet with wide tidal flats sitting between bold islands, the sharp, rough boundary ranges of the snow-dabbed mountains surmounting them. (Always, it seems, in my life, mountains in the background.)

> Through this dim portal, cold in stone,
> I turn and must walk alone
> My choice was made
> There are two ways to worship God
> I chose this high austere retreat
> And left the path where busy feet
> Of men and women come and go.

The Stikine was big and swift, a confident river difficult to climb, full of little rapids. Our little stern-wheeler had scarcely sufficient power to make headway, but we made progress chain by chain, and there was the pale green blush of Spring among the cottonwood trees. Slowly, on the right bank, the blinding absence of feature that is a glacier came towards us. As we sailed closer, it became apparent as three divided glaciers united at the mouth. The middle one, aptly known as the Great, filled the bottom of its valley, which was itself half a mile wide, spilling out in a fan with its face rough and crevassed with broken ice rucked up into spires. The miners on the steamer said that at one time the glacier extended right across the river, which flowed under an arch of ice, while steam from a hot spring on the other side drifted across.

> Blushing on some mossy bank,
> Where days are long and woods are dank
> Or crowded thick 'twixt lichened stones
> Where some old glacier laid his bones
> Where the tall ranked pine trees stand
> Their nodding bells are swung
> In the lone distant northern land.

Somewhere along the way our ship's rudders were damaged, and needed repair. There was no cabin accommodation and we therefore, at about eight o'clock in the evening of the first day, crept into an old Hudson's Bay post, abandoned since 1873. We

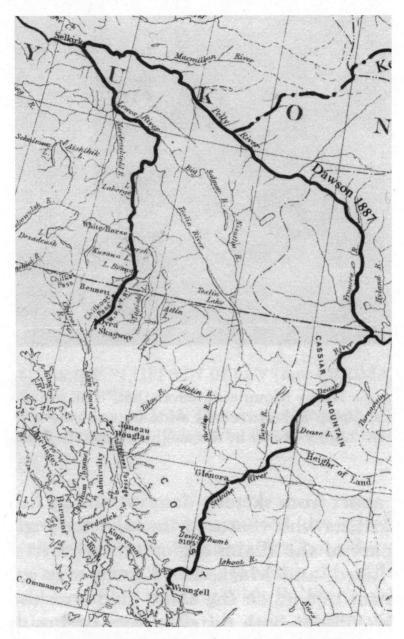

The route of the Yukon Survey of 1,300 miles I made in 1887.

On the hill behind Telegraph Creek, Yukon, 1887.

A hopeful gold prospector, Yukon, 1887.

trooped off the boat and bedded down on the shore, though a sort of twilight lingered nearly all through the night. We woke, or were awoken, between three and four in the morning, stretched out our cramps, and reboarded like so many bipedal cattle.

The next day took us through a series of canyons: first the Little, which, by comparison with what came after, it was; then its neighbour the Klootchman, which was of no special impediment; finally Devil's Club, which was in a calm mood that day. When, like a cork out of canteen, we came out of the gorges, there were burnt stumps of cottonwood, some six feet in diameter, on the riverside flats. The valley opened up then and the mountains seemed to bow and retire, the salmon-laden stream of the Clearwater coming in by several mouths. From here, we were told, the Indians had long canoed, portaged, and canoed again all the way to the sea.

Thirteen miles short of the wharf at Glenora, the scenery became peculiar, volcanic. The first bar in the river I had seen being worked for gold came up, and I learnt that some men had taken thirteen ounces a day out of there. More steadfast and steadier work was in progress on one or two little farms nearby, capable of growing all sorts of vegetables except the tender ones, their surplus supplying the true gold of nourishment to the panners. The trees in early bloom were scarcely behind Montreal or Ottawa in their advance into the season. We tied up at Glenora but no sooner had we done so, or so it felt, than we cast off again, as though the Captain was anxious to make headway before the current became angry.

As the steamer slowly fought its way towards Telegraph Creek, the head of navigation on the Stikine, I read through the notes I had brought reviewing the history of gold mining in the region. The traditional Indian inland waterways, one of which we were now travelling on, had always been jealously guarded by the Chilkat and Chilkoot coastal Indians, who carried on a lucrative trade with the interior "Stick" Indians, and who held those people in a species of subjection. Though the existence of these routes to the interior were known by reputation to white prospectors, the pervasive hostility of the coastal Indians to the passage of whites had long prevented their exploration.

Then, in 1869, a Mr. Whymper posted notice that minute specks of gold had been found by Hudson's Bay men in the Yukon, but not in quantities to warrant a "rush." The first white man who crossed from the coast to the headwaters of the Lewes River, upon which I intended to be travelling in a matter of weeks, was George Holt, in 1878. Holt was a prospector and a romancer of considerable inventive powers. Accompanied by Indians, he followed the river down (downriver in the Yukon District implies travelling north, as the rivers run that way in search of the Arctic Sea) and then tracked over an Indian trail, returning by the same route. On his return, he reported the discovery of coarse gold, by which he meant nuggets of gold larger than a wheat grain, but none of the later miners moving in the same general area was able to confirm Holt's statement in this particular. He was afterwards killed by Indians at Cook's Inlet, in 1885.

Two years later, in 1880, a prospecting party, under the leadership of one Edward Bean, taking advantage of kind relations established with the Indians by a United States Naval officer, built a flotilla of boats and on the Fourth of July set out downstream on the Stikine. One of the prospectors, a man named Steel, later claimed he found bars yielding two and a half dollars a day in a small stream well inland. Then, in 1881, four miners got as far as the Big Salmon River and ascended it for two hundred miles, finding a little gold all the way along its course. (This I consider the first discovery of paying placers in the district. The term placer, I should explain, refers to gold which is imbedded in softer material that is or was once related to a river, such as clay or gravel. If the river is alive and running shallow on the surface, so too may be the gold, but it can also be found in old river beds or even below the bed where a river once ran.)

In the following years the miners began to spread throughout the country, hitting pay dirt in varying quantities on the Pelly

River, on the Stewart, and on Forty Mile Creek, and the word spread rapidly through the south. Indeed, while foolishly attempting to hasten out the news of a big coarse gold find on Forty Mile Creek, and cash in his considerable stash, a miner named Williams froze to death on the Chilkoot Pass in January with the gold still in his pack. Soon thereafter came reports that it was possible, though rare, for a miner to collect gold to the value of one hundred dollars in a single day. In a little over five years, from the time the four miners went up the Big Salmon until our arrival, the extent of country over which gold had been found was very great, and I expected we would find it had extended even further as the draw of gold fortune pulled men deeper and deeper. It only took news of finds such as the one of a nugget of fourteen ounces, obtained in Defot Creek, to tug the prospectors ever northward. The glow of gold in their eyes was lighting up the northern sky like an aurora.

> Where long neglected mountains stand
> Just crumbling into shreds
> And laying bare on every hand
> The treasures of their beds

Though it was eleven miles northward from Glenora to our next stage, the cold seemed less extreme when we reached Telegraph Creek on May 25th, and the outlying rock concurred, muting from blackish quartzites to sandstone. Here, after several nights sleeping rough on the shore under a net of stars, we were able to catch some rest in roofed accommodation. Not too far north of us, as a bird might go, lay Dease Lake, the centre of the Cassiar mining district, and it was there I intended to construct our boats for the trip onward. Then I learnt from miners coming downstream that the agent up ahead I had contracted to have our cut wood ready was still short of completing his task; indeed, he had not started. I sent Mr. Johnstone from our party off ahead on foot to the lake to cut timber, while Mr. Lewis went back to Glenora in search of barley for the mules we would require on later treks. In the meanwhile, I climbed several of the nearby basaltic hills and columns and took time with some sketches. Perhaps it was the first time those hills had yielded to the pencil.

> The clouds brood low
> Among the shattered peaks
> Each rugged crest floats its white banner to the sky
> The hills are seamed and old and grey
> Writ with deep rough-mannered runes
> Graved with lines from their Graver's art

Five days in all passed, and then the mules were shod. The first day of making our own way on foot and hoof we made a drive of six hours, camping under aspens and willows on thin clays and rough grass. The red-dogwood and strawberry were in bloom, their colour like flame. The next day's push of fourteen miles took us onto a high plateau with a gently undulating surface, several small streams hurrying across it southward. On June 3rd, the day began at a height, according to the barometer, of 1,800 feet, and ended with us five hundred higher and not much further on; our Indian guide spoke of an ancient bridge his ancestors had built to our left, strung over a bad canyon, but, assessing the risks and the weight of our packs, I decided against, and we did not take it. The river valley on our right as we walked was a mile from rim to rim, the Stikine River below swift, muddy, and defiant like a piece of rope.

Finally, on June 5th we reached the head of Dease Lake, and found the greater part of it still covered with ice. The lake was named all the way back in 1834 after Peter Warren Dease, the Arctic explorer who had hiked with Franklin and whose death on his farm near Montreal I could recall reading about in the *Witness*. We had to sail the long stretch of the lake to its mouth, and then travel downstream on the river of the same name, but would have to wait while the season warmed up. We made a camp out a ways from the trading post, at the foot of a twisted fold of volcanic rock topped with limestone, and there I found a piece of impregnated serpentine which, if I look up from my desk, I can see in a display case, reflecting the lamplight. A man with the contrary name of Merrifield came into our camp from Telegraph Creek with three miners and two Indians packing their blankets, and gave us the unsettling news that there was a persistent rumour of Indian trouble in the Yukon.

The persisting lake ice contrived to defeat a foray I wished to make up the lake in an Osgood canvas boat (a style of craft which folded up in a concertina fashion into a small compass, made by the Von Saal company in London) and so our camp held us another night, which proved fortuitous. Mr. Johnstone, returning from his timber-scouting expedition, walked in, having abandoned his small boat on the opposing side of the same ice that had us dammed, which was shrinking rapidly. He reported also that there was the means of boat-building ahead.

> The mist is on the river
> The moon, the waning moon
> Looks down on the dimmed mirror
> Where the ice will gather soon.

It was not until the 9th of June that we were able to reach our resting spot, Whipsaw Camp on the west shore of Dease Lake. Whipsaw was a lumber point on the shore six miles short of Laketon, a small settlement where two men Johnstone had retained were busy sawing lumber for our boats. Seven days were here busily employed in constructing three boats for the purposes of the expedition. Our carpentry was hasty yet efficient and by noon of the 16th our fleet was ready. With no delay, we launched, celebrated the absence of leaks, and by the evening of the same day, a strong wind having broken up the remaining barrier of ice, we reached Laketon on the left bank of Dease Lake.

Having worked his way up river behind us, at the pace suited to a careful surveyor, Mr. McConnell now joined us, with a crew of five Coast Indians with regional knowledge, hired to work for the Survey in my boats and get us to the Liard River. While I de-briefed McConnell, a thorough man, the steamer bearing supplies came in from the head of Dease Lake and I made purchases according to budget and packed them. Two days later we set out from Laketon in quite a little flotilla. The party was now at full complement and included, beside myself, Messrs McEvoy, Lewis, and Johnstone, plus two Tshimiam and three Stikine Indians, all good boatmen. Unfortunately, two local Indians hired as expert guides and to help in portaging, deserted a day or two after we set out.

One, two, three, four little lakes in a line, strung pearls of calm held apart by stretches of tortuous, swift current, took us along the Dease River to Sylvester's Landing. Here I took the opportunity to ask Mr. Sylvester in person about the facilities we might hope to find lower down. We made almost forty miles down the Dease the next day, our best day so far. As we poled along, the snow got less and less, and the grass and the cottonwoods seemed to grab the chance to grow, with small sage and sassifrage and lupins at their feet in full flower. Mr. Sylvester mentioned that he wintered over his horses there without cutting hay for them, and they came out fat in the Spring.

The valley continued to open out as we boated through a series of dark mornings while the mountains took several steps back, finally becoming invisible from the river. The first stands of larch trees appeared as the air became more humid. Then, after only a few pulls on the oars, we quite unexpectedly found ourselves at the mouth of the Dease River, with the Liard, the next rung in our ladder, just ahead, and beyond that, the Pelly and Lewes Rivers.

For the explorer, the pertinent journals of those who have gone before in a region are fine companions. At the threshold of those two great rivers, I took from my pack a small pamphlet entitled *Discovery and Exploration of the Youcon (Pelly) River* authored by an officer of the Hudson's Bay Company, Robert Campbell. Mr. Campbell had made his arduous journeys in the 1840s, and his account of them had only just been printed, in pamphlet form, two years before, in 1885. An admirable man who, still alive at that time, had answered my questions addressed to him with comprehension, Campbell was often at my side in word and deed in the weeks ahead. He had arrived at the self-same point on the Liard River to which we had come in late May of 1840, "with a canoe and seven men, among them my trusty Indians, Lapie and Kitza, and the interpreter, Hoole."

The relative ease with which we had come down the Dease to its mouth and its confluence with the Upper Liard became a pleasant memory as we struggled along the Liard through a series of canyons. One such canyon, a mere three miles in length, a narrow cleft in the earth with walls rising straight to the sky for five hundred feet, took us a whole day to get through, including four portages at the higher stages of the water, all of us lifting the boats over points of rock that would have gutted any of our vessels. The Indians told me that gold had been found on a terrace above us, the schistene rocks there having yielded $4 a day and I marvelled at the tenacity of the miners who would venture there to make their claim.

Our daily travel for the following few days on the Liard, a river with a current averaging five miles an hour, was never more than ten miles; the river would bend first this way, then that, as though changing its mind on a whim. Each day presented us with a new diorama of rock formation, sandy beach changing to great quantities of lignite in the banks, some of it laminated with amber, then an abundance of limestone that provided some obscure fossils, and after four portages of our heavy wet loads and boats, cliffs of shattered white marble.

This difficult forward progress was exacerbated on the 3rd of July, when our two remaining Stick Indians decided to go no further. Persuasion had no effect on them, and with some sense of disappointment I made them give up part of a sack of flour which had formed a portion of my advance to them, and let them go. Despite this setback, perhaps fuelled by determined annoyance at their desertion, we had several days of satisfactory progress and thus came, after a dozen days and forty-five river miles, to the meeting place of the Liard and the Frances Rivers.

Once past the Upper Canyon of the Frances River, the waters divided into numerous channels running around flat islands resembling giant pebbles. According to Campbell, Frances Lake lay not far ahead, and we paddled, poled, poled and paddled, the waters being relatively pacific. After earning twenty miles in two days in this exhausting fashion we camped amid thickets of wild roses, wondering how far it might still be to the lake, sensing or hoping it to be near at hand.

The next day, the 8th of July, almost immediately after leaving camp, we found ourselves in the lake with ice hemming the edges an eighth of an inch thick, and a beach which uniformly ran round it adorned with piles of artistic driftwood. The whole mass of water was clearly held in by morainic accumulations. Few lakes which I have seen, and I can modestly claim to have seen a great many, surpass Frances Lake in natural beauty. Campbell felt the same, writing "we entered a beautiful lake, which I named Frances Lake, in honor of Lady Simpson." Lady Frances was the deceased wife of Sir George Simpson, Chief of the Hudson's Bay Company, and was herself in her time an adventuring canoeist.

Three miles from its lower end the lake bifurcated, forming two nearly parallel, extended arms about eight miles apart, rather like the wishbone of a turkey. The arms were separated by low, rounded mountains, the culminating point of which was Simpson's Tower, again named in honour of Lady Frances. To the west of the lake lay another set of rounded mountains, which I was pleased to name the Campbells.

As was becoming the habit, our first order of business after erecting the tents and eating was a search for the site of an old Hudson's Bay Post, as described by Mr. Campbell in his pamphlet.

Abandoned since 1851, this one turned up just above the narrow entrance to the east arm, completely overgrown, though the outline of the old stockade was still visible, with bastions at the corners, and I made a note of its dilapidated state for the company. The scenery of this arm of the lake, even in that beauteous place, was singularly striking, bordered as it was on its east by the towering, almost overbearing Too-tsho range. One peak within that range was found by rough measurement to attain an elevation of over 9,000 feet. I had the pleasurable honour to name it Mount Logan after the Survey's founder Sir William, himself a towering geological figure.

It was into the westerly arm of the lake, however, that we ventured with intent. I asked for slow progress so that I could sketch the scene, including the mountains of which a great number were now visible. As I sketched, I examined the shores for signs of Campbell's trail, the old Indian one by which he had made it across land to the Pelly River, but to my embarrassment, partially as a consequence of not having the Indian guides, we reached the swampy flats that denoted the termination of the upper lake, without finding it. Retracing our route, I located the remains of a large boat which had evidently been burnt on the beach, near an old log cache of the Company. Here was our trail. I gave the men the next day for washing, and we dined on the lake-trout, white-fish, pike, and suckers fished from the lake in abundance.

The following day, everything not absolutely essential was separated out and the greater part of our camp equipage stowed in a cache constructed for the purpose. The boats were hauled out, and over the next two days we carried our remaining stuff to a point some miles up a stream above the cascades, and sent off two of our Coast Indians in the Osgood canoe to track the winding stream, while the rest of the party found their way along the valley with heavy packs of one hundred pounds weight in very hot weather with innumerable mosquitoes as companions. The portage was about sixty miles, and eventually we reached Findlayson Lake, and we constructed a raft there on which we floated to the lake head. On the 29th July, we had the satisfaction of reaching the bank of the Pelly River. On his arrival at that position nearly a half century earlier, Mr. Campbell had given the river its name, in honour of Sir H. Pelly, a Governor of the Company.

At one time, I will now gladly admit from the comfort of the future, I had scarcely dared to hope we would reach there, so numerous were the difficulties we encountered. But they were behind us at last, and after a brief spell of relief I took inventory and was pleased to note we still had nearly a month's provisions for four persons, our instruments, a small camping outfit, a canvas cover from which a canoe might be constructed, and the tools and nails for building a wooden boat, should that prove to be necessary. All photographs and related equipment were intact. The weather was very fine and warm, nothing Arctic about it. There was spirit enough to go on.

Our coastal Indians, who had for a long time been very uneasy because of their distance from their village and the unknown character of the country into which they had been taken, were here paid off, and to their great delight allowed to turn back, taking one boat with them.

As a dangerous rapid was reported to exist on the upper part of the Pelly, I took the decision that before proceeding we should construct a canvas canoe, in preference to building another heavy boat, which might prove impossible to portage past the rapid. Having completed the canoe we began the descent of the Pelly on my thirty-eighth birthday. On his part, Campbell too had "constructed a raft, on which we embarked and drifted down a few miles on the bosom of the stream, and at parting we cast in a sealed tin can, with memoranda of our discovery."

At Hoole Canyon, a few miles along its "bosom," the river made a knee-like bend to the northeastward, and became rough and dangerous, and the canoe and that within it was rushed to the canyon's end, on the South side. On the portage terrace, a hundred feet above the river, we found traces of skids of timber which had been laid by the Hudson Bay people thirty years previous. Streams carrying clear, sweet mountain water – the Hoole, then the Ketza, named after the aforementioned faithful Indian companion of Mr. Campbell's, then the Ross – joined the Pelly from the South, and brought down great abundances of quartz-gravel. The next stream we came to from the south was anonymous, and so I called it the Lapie, Lapie being, as one will recall, another of the Indians in Campbell's party.

Our days on the Pelly River, and then later on the Lewes, were measured not in hours but in distance gained; yards were our seconds and miles our hours. From the Ross junction to the Glenyon River confluence was sixty-four miles by the bearing on my compass, but the minor flexures of the swift-running river increased that to eighty-two. For the first time, we saw black pines standing on the dry northern slopes as we finally hit tranquil water and rested our arms. A further ninety-one miles brought us to the junction, at a very acute angle, of the Macmillan River, a much more turbid affair of a yellowish colour and, on the 9th of August, registering a temperature of 54 degrees. Ten miles above the mouth of the Macmillan we encountered a couple of Indians, father and son, working their way up the Pelly with a small dug-out canoe. They were the first human beings we had met in the country since leaving the mouth of the Dease River, forty-three days previously, and it would take a poet of far greater skill than I to convey the landscape we had had to ourselves those long days, through a vast fragment of Creation that was truly awe-ful.

> We follow knowledge close from gain to gain
> But never touch the source of it all.

As we were totally unable to communicate with the Indians, and they with us, except by signs, it was impossible to obtain any definite local information of use from them. They were evidently quite at a loss to know whence we had come, and evinced a peculiar interest in examining our little canvas canoe.

About a mile and a half below the confluence of the brownish, muddy Pelly and the mouth of bluish, milky Lewes stood the ruins of Fort Selkirk, at one point the most important of the Company's posts to the west of Rockies in the far North, with, in 1852, one senior clerk, one junior, and eight men. But its very presence was an affront to the Chilkoot and Chilkat Indians, and Campbell had undergone an incident with robbers there that had forced him out for a winter, never to return though he had strongly wished to do so. The Post stood on a partly open flat, with one chimney built of basalt blocks. The blocks must have been brought across the river and cemented with clay that had been baked into brick by the combustion when the fort burnt down.

Our being at the mouth of the Lewes meant we had now joined the line of route used by the miners as they made their heavy way up to the richer gold grounds, and I had expected to find a pre-arranged memorandum from Mr. Ogilvie at this point with some useful information pertaining to our route. As we could find no such notice, and as the party of miners we met there had not seen him, we were forced to conclude that he had not yet reached this point. The miners also told us that in consequence of the discovery of much gold on Forty-Mile Creek, 200 miles down the river, most of the miners had gone there, and that Harper's Trading Post, where I had hoped to get an adequate supply of provisions if Mr. Ogilvie did not meet us, had also been moved to Forty-Mile Creek. From that point on the line of route we still had a journey of nearly 400 miles to the coast, with the swift waters of the Lewes River to contend with for most of that distance. If we had now to make a 200 mile detour to get provisions, it was doubtful we should reach the coast before the smaller lakes near the mountains were frozen over.

I therefore decided to set about the building of another boat, one suitable for the ascent of the Lewes, and on the second day after we had begun work, Mr. Ogilvie very opportunely appeared. After having completed the boat, and taking with us only Mr. Ogilvie's preliminary report and the map-sheets he had compiled back in Ottawa, we began the ascent of the Lewes, with four Indian packers. We were now following in the paddle strokes of men who already achieved this route, men such as Ketchum, Byrnes, and Labarge, explorers in the employ of the Western Union Telegraph Company.

The river seemed positively crowded after the lack of humanity we had witnessed on the Pelly. After a while spent on the river's easterly course, there came a turn to the direct south and soon we were on Lake Labarge, a body of water reputed to be a very stormy one, and the prevailing winds often were so strong that miners were detained in camp for many days. We lost almost the whole of one day on our way up the lake, owing to a muscular head wind. On the west side of the lake, a collection of modest hills sloped gradually back from the shoreline, and I named them the Miner's Range, for the miners met by us along the river, good fellows all of them.

The White Horse Rapid and Miles Canyon formed together the most formidable obstacle on the Lewes. Some miners had gone through the more dangerous White Horse rapids – generally accidentally – though we preferred to portage, and in Miles Canyon a sort of extemporized windlass had been rigged up by the miners for the purpose of hauling up boats. We then entered a series of lakes that, taken as a whole, constituted a singularly picturesque region, the calm after the storm, abounding in striking points of view. At the south end of one lake, Lake Marsh, I was able, in my continuing appellation of mountains, to honour both her Majesty in naming Jubilee Mountain, 1887 being of course the fiftieth year of her reign, and Mount White, referring not to its colour but to Mr. Thomas White, the Minister of the Interior, to whose initiative our Yukon expedition was largely due, and who most unfortunately died shortly after our return. As we moved out of Lake Marsh we passed, on the east bank, two roughly built stone houses belonging to the Tagish Indians. These were the only permanent houses seen along the whole course of the Lewes, and there the Tagish people, who roamed over that part of the country, resided during the winter months.

The final lake in the chain was Lake Lindeman, one of the smallest, being only five miles in length, and it is the extreme head of navigation when ascending the Lewes. We now had to abandon our boats and proceed on foot over the Coast Mountains, and we found a number of miners' boats drawn up at the shore at the beginning of the overland trail leading to the Chilkoot Pass. We were also fortunate to find a small party of Tagish Indians camped there, but as most of the Indian men had already gone over the portage with some of the miners, we were obliged to wait two days for their return before we could obtain the requisite assistance to carry over our stuff. Meanwhile we put our faithful boats in a place of security, and occupied ourselves in eliminating everything which was no longer of value from our outfit.

> The coals in the fire glowed red
> In the flames at the campment
> In the still Autumn night
> I saw the fair face of a woman, effulgent
> And I dreamed as I gazed
> At its tremulous light.

On the 19th of September we set out with four Indian packers, crossed the summit, where the trail led through a narrow rocky gap and the whole scene was one of the most complete desolation, and reached a point in the valley near what is known as Sheep Camp the same evening. On the evening of the 20th, after twenty-four miles of travel mostly downhill, we arrived at the head of Lynn Canal, a coastal inlet, and were hospitably received by Mr. J. Healey, who had established himself there for trade with the Indians and miners. We had at that time just completed our fourth month of arduous and incessant travel. No serious accidents had befallen us by the way,

The Indian crews on the boats we built, Yukon, 1887.

Looking up the Pelly River during the Yukon Survey, 1887.

and though, like the miners, we had arrived back at the coast with a deplorably ragged and uncouth aspect, we had with us, intact, our collections, instruments, survey-records, and notes. It was not the least pleasing moment of the entire journey when, from a distance of some miles, we first caught sight of the sea shining like a plate of beaten bronze under the rays of the evening sun.

Although I made no sign of it to the party, I felt some relief that we had come out of that country without seeing any sign of Indian trouble. The circumstantial account of the troubles from the two miners who had followed us in to Dease Lake back in early June had been a thorn in my thoughts. As it was impossible either to confirm or refute those reports without practically abandoning the scheme of work, I had determined to proceed according to the original arrangement, while remaining vigilant. As it turned out, on reaching the mouth of the Lewes River we had ascertained that the story was entirely false, but it had nonetheless kept me in a state of watchfulness during a great part of the summer.

On the way down from Lynn Canal to Victoria, I calculated what we had achieved in respect of travel. The entire distance covered during the exploration amounted to 1,322 miles. This meant that in those four months, taking into account the stretch of coast-line between the Stikine River entrance and Lynn Canal, we had circum-scribed an area of about 63,200 square miles, the interior of which was still at that time, but for the accounts of a few prospectors and reports of Indians, a *terra incognita*. The same description, with little qualification, still today applies to much of the surrounding region outside our surveyed circuit. It had been our mandate to make a large part of Canada better known, and we had done so.

Four and a half months after leaving Wrangell, I was back in Victoria and able to make contact with my dearest and not so nearest in Montreal. It seemed that news of my emergence from the "unknown regions into civilized society" as Mother called it, had preceded me, for Mother had mailed a letter from Montreal stating that a telegraphic notice in the *Witness*, dated October 2nd, contained a short sentence informing readers that "Professor Dawson's party will likely come out by the next steamer." She was much assured by this, for her imagination had filled with exaggerated dangers that had repressed her hope and she had for several months felt that writing to me was much like speaking in front of a high stone wall. She reproached herself for this, saying that Father by contrast had been a faithful friend, writing several times knowing that a reply could be months away.

It seems that the family had experienced ups and downs during the season, but the ups on their side of the scale outweighed the downs. The summer had been a warm one, which had modified into a drought throughout September, which in turn led to extensive forest fires, the smoke from which was so dense that the navigation on the St. Lawrence was stopped. The death of Bernard's father from an illness that began in June had cast a shadow over the months, and it meant that Anna and in particular the children had faced the prospect of summering at Métis without Bernard, and so Mother and Eva had gone down early with them. Rankine meanwhile had arranged for a substitute doctor on one of his steamer trips and had come home to Canada, in fact turning up on the heels of his letter in Montreal where Father was alone. After a week of Father hastening to finish his business, they too headed for Métis where Florence and her boy stayed throughout August, and then Rankine left for London at the end of September's first week, with two weeks' duty at the docks ahead of him before sailing on the *Massilia*. The coming winter was, he thought and hoped, to be his last as a wanderer and he was keeping a sharp lookout for likely openings. Mother thought Rankine found it hard to leave Métis and begin anew a life among strangers, but that was his choice as ever was. The latest family manoeuvre, occurring only a few days before the letter, was the departure direct from Métis for Scotland of Anna and Bernard. On the death of his father Bernard had inherited property in St. Andrews and there were numberless details to attend to there. I envied them, but the idea of organized travel, even to Scotland, was temporarily purged out of me.

On the journey back to Montreal I took out my notebooks and collated my gold findings in the Yukon District. Of the discoveries made there, the richest so far, was the Cassiar Bar, which was reported to have yielded in some cases $30 a day to the hand, and gold to the overall value of many thousands of dollars, most of it in the months before we got there. All along the Lewes River there were yields of $10 a day, as there was a long distance up the Big Salmon and the Upper Pelly. The Stewart was coming in big, reaching $100 a day to the hand in the rush of 1885 and 1886, with miners side by side on the river bank two hundred miles up from its mouth.

It was along the river called Forty-Mile Creek, it actually being neither a creek nor forty miles long, that we collected reports of activity almost everywhere. The gold coming out along a hundred mile stretch was often coarse and nuggety, and few of the men I met were content with a stake on ground that provided less than $14 a day, though several had taken $100 a day for a short time. Altogether I estimated a mining of $75,000 was taken out in the Upper Yukon region, by about two hundred and fifty miners, two hundred of those on Forty-Mile Creek, and one hundred of those had said they were going to winter over on the creek to be ready for Spring.

> With his gold pan and his shovel
> And little else besides
> He lit his pipe and left the camp
> To cross the Great Divide.

Forty-mile Creek was, as the miners called it, a "bed-rock" creek, one with no great depth of deposit below ground level. It was the only one I encountered with coarse gold, but I safely predicted that many more like it remained to be discovered. I could see that when the means of access were improved important bar-mining would take place all along the main rivers. The miners were facing and overcoming great hardships, the trail of the Chilkoot Portage being a formidable obstacle. That Spring of 1887 a trading post was established at the mouth of Forty-Mile Creek, serviced by small stern-wheel steamers that could not ascend the rivers till late in summer, and the slightest accident or detention could scupper their arrival altogether. Added to all that, beneath the mossy covering the ground was often frozen. However I could perceive that this problem of freezing was likely to be remedied by the general burning of the woods around the camps, allowing the summer heat to penetrate the lower layers of the soil.

I could sense then that this great inland country would not long go wanting for an easy means of connection between the coast and its great interior volume of lake and river waters, and there was every reason to believe it would support a considerable mining population.

But I was not quite done with the Far North yet.

—

A GREAT DEAL of my life has been about lines; lines on maps, lines separating one bed from another, contours, lines of reasoning, drawing the line, lifelines, deadlines, even lines of poetry. As a surveyor, I had long decided I was really in the business of casting lines around like nets, nets made of imaginary lines thrown down onto a blank map to allow one's country and its citizens to thereafter accurately claim their jurisdictions, be it a farmer's fences or a nation's borders. The progenitors of these lines were the explorers, and their legacy, in the wake they left, were the lines of subsequent settlement, the trails and the roads and the highways and the walls. I have contributed to Canada's stock of these lines myself, yet as I grew older my taste for places that remained as they were in the time before lines had grown stronger.

At times I have been called upon to take part in international efforts to make tangible and certain the imaginary lines, as in the case of the 49th parallel. In the case of the Bering Sea Arbitration, to which I was seconded by the Survey and which in the end occupied more than two years of my life, from 1891 till 1893, I was drawing the line for a herd of seals. Rather, I was helping decide quite where the line should be drawn in the waters of the Bering Sea so that the United States and Great Britain would know where they could and where they could not hunt those pelagic (sea-living) mammals.

> I cannot sound the depths of life and death
> They lie as infinitely deep today
> As when man first threw out
> His little line to measure them.

The genesis of the Bering Sea arbitration lay with United States President Harrison who, on receiving on his desk a disturbing report on the terrible reduction of the Bearing Sea seal herd by relentless hunting, had proposed to Her Majesty's government, and eventually won, a moratorium on the killing of seals in that region to last from June 1891 to May of the following year. He also was inclined to blame the Canadians for most of the sad diminution of a herd that, in 1880 around the Pribilof Islands alone, had been estimated at twenty-one million. In the course of the build up to arbitration, the United States had several times accused the Canadians of overfishing the seals in "their" waters, and therein was the rub; whose waters were where? For those of us seconded to the Arbitration then, the first order of business was to take a voyage of discovery to accurately ascertain the vitality or otherwise of the vast northern seal herds.

This trip took me as far north as I had ever been, even at the beginning of the journey, when we were anchored at the Pribilof

Islands, which sit out roughly in the centre of the Bering Sea, with not much else in the way of solid ground in any direction you choose to go. We immediately struck northward for Nunivak Island, taking me even "higher" up the latitudes than I had been before, then we zigzagged westward to St. Matthew's, a strip of an island like a deflated letter I, with a dot of land above it so small it was called Half Island. Here we found three men who had established themselves for the purpose of spending the winter hunting seals. The island was otherwise uninhabited by humans, and there was an entire absence of trees or bushes of any kind. Polar bears, however, abounded on it, and we saw about a dozen at different times, several being killed by a hunting party and served that night. We also had some shooting at walruses and sea lions along the shore, but without any known result.

From the polar bear hunting grounds we moved up to St. Lawrence Island, and then made for safe harbour at Plover Bay on the Siberian Coast, where we called in at a small village of reindeer people. All the way South from Plover Bay we had rough seas, the swell rollicking about in all directions, and for an entire day we had the worst time of rolling I ever witnessed, everything loose or that could break loose tumbling round all over, and it was impossible to cook or if you could cook something it was equally impossible to keep anything on a table. Altogether, as we rolled along, we expended six or was it twenty-four hours poking about in fog trying to make land. Unalaska Bay in the Aleutians, the port where we joined the combined Arbitrational United States and British fleets, was indeed a welcome sight. The *Nymph*, the *Porpoise*, and the *Pheasant* bore the Union Jack, and the *Porpoise* later guided us back to Seattle. There were several volcanoes along the Aleutian Islands – the chain of volcano peaks which stretches over a thousand miles and separates the Bering Sea from the Pacific Ocean – which were supposed to be active, but the two we sighted, on the rare occasions of partial lucidity, carried only little languishing brushes of steam.

On this dead crater's broken rim
The cold mists of the upper air
Fold and unfold their silent wings
Drift, and deploy.

By February of 1892, I was in Washington for the next stage of
the joint commission with the United States, and wishing that I
could get away from it, for it quickly became tiresome, with plenty
of time for work of one kind or another but no time for the people
I really wanted to see, rather a slowly turning wheel of returning
calls to people who had left cards. It was interesting to be enmeshed
with the inner movements of diplomatic matters, but the bloom
quickly went off the rose, and Sir George Baden-Powell was a bad
companion in respect of avoiding engagements. He was the senior
British member of the commission, shaping the case that we would
later make in Paris, and he never seemed to be happy unless involved
in a whirl of some kind. He spoke of his younger brother Robert, a
soldier who was pioneering the use of barrage balloons, and was
teaching the young men in his regiment something called "scouting." There was one engagement I enjoyed in Washington, when Mr.
Gardiner Hubbard (whose daughter Mabel, struck deaf by scarlet
fever as a young girl, had married Alexander Graham Bell) gave a
dinner for the Bering Sea commissioners and had secured a number
of well-known persons for the event. Mr. Hubbard was the head of
Mr. Bell's telephone companies, and by way of conversation I
described for them my recollection of the day in 1877 when Mr. Bell
had installed a pair of phones in Ottawa, linking the Prime Minister
with the Governor General at Rideau Hall.

By Spring, we commissioners had progressed to London, where
my head remained poised over a desk as I pegged away in the qui-
etude of a hotel room, preparing the report that would be the
bedrock of our case in Paris. I did receive a very kind invitation to
lunch with the Marquess of Lorne and Princess Louise, his lady

wife and the sixth of the Queen's children. I have to report, with
humble pride, that on that occasion I was the only guest. The
Marquess gave me a provisional invitation to spend two or three
days in the Outer Hebrides, should I find myself near there after
the arbitration proceedings were over. On another occasion I dined
with the man who, it was claimed, was the richest in Britain, Lord
Derby. Derby and the rather shy Canadian Governor General, Lord
Stanley, were of course brothers, and I had a lordly conversation
telling the one about my latest dealings with the other.

My own brother Rankine was due to arrive in London while I
was there. It was the family's fervent wish that I should try and do
what I could for him, get him to buckle to at something, even if it
was only hospital practice. When he did arrive in late June I was
able, despite most of my time being devoted to work, to see him
every few days. As was and is his nature he seemed to find it hard
to apply himself to an objective. We went to the Cooperative
together and he purchased some suits in a style Anna had mentioned to him as modern and suitable. I was privately glad that he
did not arrive until after I had gone to the "Venice in London"
exhibition, which quite took the shine out of the real Venice in
everything but actual size. A series of canals and bridges with
houses along them partly built and partly painted, and narrow dry
streets lined with stalls and shops had been constructed. The
canals were all connected and filled with water which was not only
real but clean and blue. The main feature was an enormous
amphitheatre, with a long stage at one side. Between the seats
and the stage lay a large basin of water, which connected with the
canals and into which, as a part of the performance, fleets of gondolas and barges of the most gorgeous character entered. The
performances were not like ordinary plays but rather like spectacu-
lar effects assisted by music and dancing which succeeded each other
in rapid succession, and the whole stage together with the floating
gondolas was thronged with performers, counted by hundreds.

After returning home in August for a respite at Métis, I left for England again in mid-December, from New York, where the countryside all about was snow-covered, and where Mother insisted on undertaking a general repacking of my hand bag and carry-all with gifts for my sister Eva and her husband Hope, then living in Rock Ferry near Liverpool and with whom I intended to spend Christmas. The ship left early Saturday morning and reached London at three-thirty the following Saturday afternoon, which was a record crossing for me. It seemed like I had never left, for there I was back in my usual quarters, with the bells of St. Margaret's in Westminster ringing out the usual prolonged Saturday evening chime while the Clock Tower of the Houses of Parliament noted the hours and quarters. I felt I had completed another of those circles I seemed to make with alarming regularity, returning to myself and cutting out a great loop of intermediate experiences. I stepped into another circle when, after a fine Christmas at Eva's, I crossed the channel to Paris for the final leg of the negotiations which had taken me from the very remotest parts of North America to the City of Light.

Over the months I spent there, while the points one had talked over and over in private rehearsal now came out in public argument, and rumours and suggestions from all kinds of sources suddenly turned up which required reference to London or to Canada, I can't say I particularly increased my knowledge of Paris, except at the lunch I took with Mrs. Crawford, the Paris correspondent of the *Daily News*, who knew several interesting specimens of various kinds in the large Anglo-French community. The meal was accompanied by very excellent singing by two young ladies training to be professional musicians. On another occasion, a party of us went to the Palais de Justice to see a system of identifying prisoners known as the "Anthropometric" Method. Persons convicted of any crime were carefully measured, photographed in full-face and profile, and all particulars were entered on a printed card to which the photographs were attached. The thousands and thousands of resultant cards were filed away like an immense library catalogue. To track someone down you began with the length of the head then the breadth and you gradually eliminated the unlikely persons, with a toss of the head, one might say. These two measurements alone probably got rid of three quarters of the whole number and with new measurements to hand it did not take more than five minutes to discover whether the individual in question had ever been convicted before. We had a demonstration of a man charged with a murder, who did not deny a previous conviction for robbery, but if he had denied it, it would not have done him any good, as the measure of him had already been taken.

In the end, despite their having initiated the process, the United States were somewhat miffed that, when the decision emerged, the British case went rather well. For my small part in that overall success, and perhaps simply for the length of time I had spent as part of the team, I was awarded the Order of St. Michael and St. George "in reward for services rendered to the Crown in relation to the foreign affairs of the Empire," and it was the Queen herself who presented it to me back in London. The acronym applicable to my medal was CMG, signifying I was merely a Companion and not a Grand Cross or such like. I overheard one gentleman at the ceremony drolly remark, *sotto voce*, that the letters stood for "Call Me God."

THE AGE OF THE DESK

—

I HAVE HEARD it said that contentment is the absence of ambition, and if that is so then I remained ambitious in my career when I rejoined my colleagues at the Survey direct from the arbitrations in Paris. At that point, 1893, I had been almost perpetually in the field for eighteen years since I joined the Survey on July 1st, 1875, and I had been its assistant director since 1877.

There had been a moment, the early months of 1888, after the success of the Yukon Territory expedition, when it seemed that Dr. Selwyn's superannuation and my appointment as Director of the Survey were in prospect. The Honourable Thomas White informed me that he had decided on just such a course, and that further he had obtained Sir John A. Macdonald's consent to it.

I had, in fact, been in charge of the Survey for most of the previous year, serving as the Acting Director during Dr. Selwyn's absence while he attended the Colonial and Indian Exhibition in London. A few days after raising my hopes, Minister White fell ill and died, in the April of 1888. Thus the matter ended for a time.

In mid-September 1894, while I was in a remote part of British Columbia surveying the interior in the Shuswap Lake area for Survey Map 604, Dr. Selwyn wrote to me requesting that I return to Ottawa as he intended to take a leave of absence and cross over to England again. Being to all intents unreachable, I did not receive the letter for a fortnight after it had been sent. Further, I had made a previous arrangement to meet my assistant, Mr. McEvoy, at Sicamous, and so I did not get back to Ottawa until the sixth of October, by which time Mr. Selwyn had already sailed, and I learnt I was Acting Director again. I now allowed myself to feel that this "absence," which Mr. Selwyn had taken, was a preliminary to retirement, and that it was generally understood among the staff and in the Ministry that I was to be his successor.

There was, however, another member of the Survey staff who was of a mind similar to mine – who felt that he too could soon assume the position of Director. That man is Robert Bell, and in naming him here I make it clear that this memoir must not be published, as I intended from the outset, until after my death – or his. Bell had returned from the field around the same time as I that October, and secured an appointment with Prime Minister Thompson, at which he intended to ply his own suit for the position of Director.

Bell, I believe, carried then and does still a grievance against me, perhaps more than one. He too had an enthusiasm for British Columbia, and yet I had adopted that region immediately on entering the Survey in 1875; Bell had been with the Survey eighteen years at that point, whereas I had been there a matter of mere days, which made his seniority over me indisputable. Thus being raised only to the level of Assistant Director in 1877, like myself, and no higher had lodged in his craw, and stayed there.

For my part, I chose a different avenue, procedurally the correct one as I understood it, and wrote a short memorandum to the new Minister of the Interior, Mr. Thomas Mayne Daly, saying that were the position to be offered to me, and so on. Mr. Daly met me within a few days of receiving my note and assured me the necessary papers granting me the directorship had been drawn up, and that the promotion was in the works. (I wonder now if my companions at the Rideau Club detected the elevation in spirits I made an attempt to suppress; a levity I was not then at liberty to explain. Certainly I was able to fully express my satisfaction to William, by

The Geological Survey building on Sussex Drive in Ottawa.

The overcrowded museum at the Survey, including a buffalo exhibit.

telephone. He had been resident in Ottawa since the year before, when he had been appointed head of the Department of Tides and Currents. Having a brother's ear nearby had on several occasions alleviated the strain of Survey service.)

Then events took an unforeseen and unfortunate turn, once again. While in England in December 1894, at Windsor Castle, awaiting audience with her Majesty, Prime Minister Thompson suffered a heart attack and died there and then, after only two years in office. The Queen held his requiem in the Castle, and readers will recall the battleship *Blenheim* painted stem to stern in black arriving with the body aboard at Halifax for the burial. I had made the better acquaintance of Mr. Thompson in the latter part of the Bering Sea hearings and knew him to be a fair man, and interested in female emancipation.

The new cabinet was, naturally, unaware of the contract Mr. Thompson and I had forged, and Mr. Bell, after the festive season had passed, now claimed that the Prime Minister, who could not now confirm or deny it from beneath the soil, had supported his candidature, not mine. There are no shortage of informants at the Rideau Club at the best of times, and I heard that Bell had described himself to the new Prime Minister, Mackenzie Bowell, as "the original and only living authority on a great part of what is known of the geology of this, the greater part of the Dominion." Bowell was faced with a decision similar to Solomon's, but, even before it was made public, I knew that I had succeeded, and that the requisite order in Council was to be issued on January 7th. The order recommended the retirement of Mr. Selwyn with a half pension and my promotion, immediate, to deputy head of department and Director of the Survey. When he learnt these facts, Mr. Bell wrote to Prime Minister Bowell and complained of a terrible injustice, which he took as a "most undeserved slur after a lifetime spent in faithful services to the country."

Poor Mr. Selwyn did not return from England until after my promotion. He landed at New York and proceeded to Ottawa, becoming aware only through the newspapers, which he read en route, that he was retired. The reporters were on him as his foot touched the platform at Broad Street, and he told them politely that he knew nothing of his supposed superannuation. As far as he knew, he said, he was still the director. The best light one can put on the rather shabby affair is that the death of Prime Minister Thompson while in office was a sufficient upheaval that some details were bound to be overlooked.

The situation was a little embarrassing for both Mr. Selwyn and me, and for his son, Percy, who was then acting as my secretary, but I must say that Mr. Selwyn took it very well. He had apparently completely forgotten his request for superannuation, and thought himself rather hardly treated, particularly in the want of due notice. His attitude to me personally was, as always, most friendly, and he took the courtesy to say so publicly at the Annual Dinner of the Logan Club which was held ten days later on January 17th. By then, I had been embarrassed by a flow of congratulations from home and abroad, and in my desk near to hand I keep the one from Father, dated January 12th, which reads, "All send congratulations and best wishes matters as usual here."

To achieve what one has long wished for is, in my limited experience, both a blessing and a curse. I had sought the Directorship, and now it was mine. Its dimensions were not unknown to me, but those occasions when I had been acting head were, by nature of the term "acting," finite. Now I was responsible for the employment of many and the deployment of a budget I would be forced annually to defend. If blame were being laid, it would nest on my desk and not migrate elsewhere.

The job quickly manifested itself as an ever-moving train of rather tedious details linked together by my sole authority to handle them. The desktop became my restricted field, and my hands its reluctant explorer. In my first week I found on it: requests for maps of almost all regions of the country as the population pushed out; letters with cleaned or dirt-encased miniature samples of this or that mineral enclosed for analysis; an enquiry from a gentleman in Victoria as to the merit of purchasing, at $15 each, two Peterborough canoes seen in Fort Simpson, to which I replied that a Peterborough canoe which is in my opinion "the very best boat for the trip you propose"; a gentleman residing in Blundellsands, near Liverpool, England, requesting a copy of my report on the coal deposits of British Columbia, no doubt towards making an investment; a letter from me to Henry Porter of Pall Mall, seeking a clock of the type that runs for a week; a purchase order for a barometer from Richard Frères of Paris that had been tested at Kew and came with a plain, solid beaten case and a shoulder strap; another letter from me to a Professor at the University of Prague asking questions about their new museum of natural history, its financing and design, as there were plans to build one in Ottawa (and still are, I might add).

That was one layer; below it lay the correspondence with the field surveyors and the beck and call of my political masters, mostly in matters of high and low finance. I recall one occasion relating to the latter when I had to talk to the Honourable Mr. Scott about twenty-five cents' worth of maps which a deadbeat in Nova Scotia was trying, by writing to Ministers, to force us to send him free! Running below all that, the joys and sorrows of my family, who were only two hours by train away. Sorrow was the first to make its presence known.

—

IT IS THE SUPREME tragedy for any parent to survive their child, and that such a fate should befall my dear sister for a second time fell hard upon the family in Montreal. It seemed that most of the Harrington children fell ill over the winter of 1894, and though he survived into the New Year, Eric, the eldest, then seventeen years of age, succumbed to influenza on January 24th. He was buried alongside his sister in Mont Royal cemetery. In the months that followed, I found myself constrained by work in Ottawa, and unable to visit Anna and Bernard and my remaining nieces and nephews as often as would have been wished, even on weekends. I wrote frequently, but for once in our correspondence Anna was tardy in her replies, saying in one letter that she had "not felt like writing much; I am unwilling to continue chronicling new disasters." The "domestic substratum" as she dubbed it was naturally uneasy, and her writings had taken on a sobriety that, despite the strength of her faith, conveyed the heavy weight within. As the Spring of 1895 turned to Summer, Anna's thoughts turned to the refuge of Métis, "the happy land" as she called it, where she and the children could revel in the seashore. Conrad, however, was still in the doctor's hands, and Lois had a catarrhal infection that required a diet of milk and lime juice together with constant poulticing, so she was delayed in her sojourn. The baby, by way of contrast to her elder siblings, was as jolly as possible, and greatly enjoyed being allowed to get dirty in the garden. On top of all these health concerns, or perhaps because of them, the Harrington household was, by Anna's own rare admission, hard up, but they always seemed to get, she believed, everything any reasonable creature should want.

My own time at the Survey during that first year was of necessity chiefly employed at the office, supervising the printing and publication of the reports and maps, such as the one of the Kamloops district, that had been completed within the twelvemonth, as well as a new list of the publications of the Geological Survey of Canada from the beginning of the work, in 1843, to date, making a pamphlet of fifty-two pages. In response to an invitation, a large number of archival photographs of geological features, coloured after nature by Mr. H. Topley, and including more than a few taken by myself, were transmitted for exhibition to London.

I was also employed in discussions relating to the possible entry into Confederation of Newfoundland. My counterpart at the Newfoundland Geological Survey, Mr. James P. Howley, wrote inquiring about such a union, and his potential position within it. In my reply I was enthusiastic, and assured him he would be invited to carry on within us. The negotiations at the political level, however, were unsuccessful, and the island remains outside Canada.

The gradual strengthening of my right arm was mostly due to the exercise of official correspondence, which for my Survey employees totalled close to eight thousand letters annually. I strove in my replies to give careful attention to placing consumers of mineral products and producers in connection. Inquiries relating to the geological structure and geographical features of different parts of the country were in abundance, and I personally embraced questions respecting coal, petroleum, gas, salt, water-supply, mineral-waters, stone, clays, lime, cement, peat, fertilizers, and many metallic ores, as well as heights of summits, watersheds, elevations of lakes, practical routes of travel, distribution of forest trees, and character of timber.

It was August of that first year before I got away from Ottawa, and I did not go far in time or distance, just a rather pleasant outing to the rural region west of Kingston, there to show my face in response to a request from the Mayor for a report on the local iron ore deposits, a file I had set aside for myself. The trip across to Kingston by the Rideau Canal, of which I had often heard but never travelled, was interesting and pretty, though the people and the accommodations along the way were rather primitive. I had set out with the vague idea that there were numerous sailing villages in the vicinity but only hamlets existed, and very often not even hamlets. The rural diet seemed to consist of bread and indifferent butter, potatoes, berries, and occasional eggs with milk and weak green tea, but the houses were fairly clean, and I met with several peculiar and therefore interesting people, which always spices up the trip. I found it pretty hard work walking up and down the country after having been so long at a desk, and my health was much better for the experience and fresh air.

All too soon, unfortunately, I was back in Ottawa, searching the desk for other tickets to other parts, while I assisted others in their plans for journeys I would not make, such as Mr. Joseph Tyrrell's second excursion into the Hudson Bay region. In September I did manage a visit of inspection to Athabasca Landing, in connection with the boring operations; the drilling there had reached a depth of 1,731 feet, passing through a great thickness of Cretaceous shales. The object of the experiment was to reach and penetrate the basal sandstone, which is charged with bituminous matter and is known as "tar sands." I predicted that the top of the tar sands would be reached at around 1,800 feet, and warned that impervious shales overlaying them might prevent the upward flow of petroleum. So the thickness of the shales over the whole area at the Landing would have to be fully tested.

Then, as every year, in the weeks when the weather grew colder, work began on collating reports and statistics for the Annual Report, which I was obliged to present to the Minister as early as possible in January. Looking back now on the summary report for my second year of office, 1896, which I submitted to my new Minister of the Interior, the Honourable Clifford Sifton, I register that, while I was anxious to speak well of our accomplishments, such as the supply of samples of our national mineral wealth to the Imperial Institute in London, an excellent medium of making known products likely to find a market there, the undercurrent in my summary was one of gentle complaint.

There was a summer session of Parliament that year, and the want of any appropriation to cover the work in progress in the field rendered my continued presence in Ottawa necessary, as I attempted to find the men their just wage from a declined budget from the Civil List. (Nineteen of the men had signed and sent me a memorandum, noting their discouragement at their salaries. One of them, Mr. Giroux, a most conscientious observer, died in November after fourteen years of service; his loss was sincerely deplored by all members of the staff.)

The number of visitors to the museum, housed within the Survey building on the third floor, that year passed thirty thousand, a notable increase, and I was wont again to point out the urgent need for double the space for display (there were many large mounted birds for which no room could be found in the cases) and the danger from fire, which was excessive. The destruction of the collections, I told the Minister, embracing as they did more than 2,000 unique specimens, with the entire supply of reports and maps and the manuscripts and notes representing over fifty years of work, would constitute an irremediable loss to the country.

As the first flowers began to bud on the slopes of Parliament Hill in 1897, I took the train to Montreal for a joyous family event. It was the Ides of March, at which time of year my parents celebrated another year of marriage; in 1897 they were able to give thanks, as Father put it, that they had both been spared to rejoice in their golden anniversary. Just the year before they had gone over to London to be at Rankine's wedding to Clorann, and now they were celebrating fifty years of their own union. My brothers, sisters, and I had commissioned a wedding cake that, as the newspapers reported, "was the pièce de resistance of the tea table, a cake of lordly proportions charmingly decorated." The house on University Avenue received an endless succession of friends and deputations all Friday, and Mother, as usual on special days of the calendar, had distributed in every nook and cranny the blossoms that had arrived as messengers of goodwill, all of them, golden, as to the occasion. Later that evening, when the house had cleared, Mother and Father told me the story of how they had courted and married.

In 1840, at twenty years of age, Father took a timber-laden sailing ship called the *Harvest Home* on a stormy traverse from Halifax to Newcastle for a short stay, then he went on to Edinburgh. A family council had decided that he should attend a scientific school, a form of institution that, for a young Nova Scotian in those days, could only be found abroad. The saying that one does not realize one has an accent until one travels was given an interesting twist among the steep streets and stairways of Newcastle when Father attended a young man's debating society in that city and was complimented on his spoken English; a young debater in question assumed that, since he was Canadian, Father's native tongue was Chippewa or Micmac or some such! Two days later he awoke from an uneasy sleep on the train to the sound of loud voices, speaking broad Scotch. After a winter's tuition in Edinburgh he returned to Pictou, as the family fortunes had taken a dip, and money was rationed and did not for the moment extend to foreign education.

Although he had perforce to leave Edinburgh in 1841 at the end of his first year, Father had not returned from that city empty-hearted. He became acquainted there with Margaret, the youngest of four daughters in the house of an old Scotch family, the Mercers. Mother said that when she had first seen Father, she was seventeen, and he was a long lean youth, five years her senior, winding his way up the Hill to their house in Edinburgh. One of her older sisters had turned to her as they watched him approach from the window and said, "You can have him, Maggie." She only thought of him vaguely at first, Mother said, but now they had been each other's for fifty years, so she supposed her sister was right. Father had come with letters of introduction to the family, as my paternal grandmother had made the acquaintance of my maternal grandmother before she left for Nova Scotia in 1811. He spent many an hour with my mother's mother, translating obscure Biblical passages for her from the original texts. When he could, he went for walks with Margaret about the town; one day, on Princes Street, he took her into a strange room with a strange little man, and she sat in a chair while she had her daguerreotype taken. I have seen this picture in the family albums, and Mother, at sixteen, appears more frightened than willing to smile. It is much the same face she wears now when confronted with the telephone.

When he left Edinburgh for Canada, all Father asked of Margaret Mercer was that she would answer such letters as he might find opportunity to send from Nova Scotia. Their subsequent correspondence only deepened his feelings of attachment, and at length, when he had to a certain extent assured his position and prospects, he ventured to ask her to marry him. He received a most emphatic rebuke, sufficient to have deterred anyone less interested and determined. Instead of declaring defeat, however, he apologized for too great a precipitance, and continued the correspondence, planning that next time he asked for her hand it would be while he was holding it.

At length the family finances revived, and Father returned to Scotland in 1846. In the winter of that year he resumed his studies in natural science at the University of Edinburgh. Unlike before, this time there was no warm welcome for him from Mrs. Mercer, Margaret's mother. Her perception of him, gained through his relentless correspondence, had changed from the safe role of companion to her daughter to the more dangerous one of suitor. That was out of the question. Should he succeed, her youngest daughter would be taken across the ocean to be swallowed up in a small town, and she might well never see her again.

Mother, she has told me, was not without other suitors at this time, the Scottish Academy painter James Lauder being one of them. He included her in one of his pictures, the one entitled *The Wise and Foolish Virgins*, Mother appearing in the former classification. Her heart had gone to Father though, and her father was not opposed to the union, preferring his daughter leave for foreign shores whole-hearted, than remain in Edinburgh broken-hearted. He also gave her some bills to buy travelling clothes, and Mother went with her already married eldest sister, Mrs. Jane Bell, to do just that. (Aunt Jane had thirteen children, my dear cousins, the dearest of whom throughout my life has been Ella.)

Mother would not be naysaid, and against the approval of her mother the date of the marriage was set, in April 1847. Mother rose very early on the day, picked some crocuses and set them in water on the table. Father kept one of the crocuses and pressed it in his notebook, where it lies still, in perpetual bloom. The wedding itself was clouded by Mrs. Mercer's sadness, but she did attend. Father's best man was Mr. Primrose, a fellow Nova Scotian also attending the University. Mother, on the advice of her sister who feared for safety of the colour white in the wild land, wore a grey dress. She was twenty-four. The service was over before noon, and Father and Mother left immediately for Glasgow for the transatlantic sailing ship. On arrival at the dock, there was a telegram from Mrs. Mercer; she had managed a change of heart and wished to say goodbye without any ill-feeling. The wedded couple returned to Edinburgh, where grandmother Mercer handed them a set of china and linen. Father wrote, much later in life, that to love worthily a good woman is the first feeling that raises a youth to real manhood, and so in that day he was borne up as a man.

Mother, as happened with many who journeyed from Old World to New, did not return to Edinburgh prior to the death of her parents; she never saw them again after the wedding. They died four years after her emigration, within three months of each other.

After six weeks of sailing, the newlyweds came into Halifax Harbour, where Mother remarked on the lack of stone buildings, so unlike Edinburgh, and she wondered if the houses were made of cardboard. A few days in the city and then they drove out to Pictou, in the aftermath of a snow storm. Mother told us one night at the dinner table that during this coach ride she saw pigs and geese wearing collars, as though dressed for an event, and Father had to explain that they were to prevent the animals passing through fences. It was almost dawn by the time they arrived at Grandpapa James' home.

—

THE REMAINDER of 1897 was marked not by union but rather by departure. The constant difficulty in endeavouring to run an office with professional men at starvation wages was most detrimental to good work, and several of them found better elsewhere: Mr. Brumell joined a graphite mining company in Quebec, Mr. Russell took up work in western Canada, and Mr. Eaton, a topographer, joined the Royal Canadian Regiment.

By year's end, with the strength of the staff at forty-eight, only one higher than when I had taken up the post, I was able nonetheless to assemble and publish the aggregate value of the production of minerals in Canada during 1897. The total was $28,661,430, a figure which received favourable comment in the House since it represented an increase of about twenty-seven percent over the previous year. The rise in wealth was largely accounted for by the great development of gold mining, particularly in the Yukon district. Though gold was king, lead revenues had almost doubled, silver was half again, copper the same, and cement, the raw material of a growing country, was up by a third. The work of the Survey in assisting in the mapping of these deposits prior to their exploitation was paying dividends, though our appropriation from the Civil list was stagnant.

In the summer of 1898, a dispatch from Mr. William Ogilvie arrived on my desk at the Survey. I had not laid eyes on Mr. Ogilvie for over ten years, although we had maintained contact. A Dominion Land Surveyor by trade, he had been a member of the Survey expedition that had gone into the Yukon Territory with me, back in 1887. Specifically, he had travelled the Lewes River to ascertain the location of the then still theoretical boundary of the Alaskan and Yukon territories, the 141st meridian. Ogilvie's dispatch, transported under his orders out of the Yukon by two men in a birchbark canoe, informed me that a town in the territory had been named in my honour. This eponymous act of township came about, he went on to explain, thus:

To aid him in his explorations in 1887, Mr. Ogilvie had employed as guides and packers the services of George Carmack, a Californian, his Tagish Indian wife, Kate, and a gentleman known as Snookum Jim Mason. They packed his supplies over the Chilkoot Pass and thence on to Forty-Mile Creek on the Yukon River, and hence on up to the meridian. Mr. Ogilvie was successful in his task, as was I, and after I returned to Ottawa, he decided he had found his place, and he remained at Forty-Mile Creek, working as a surveyor for hire.

Several years later, as fortune would have it, Carmack, Snookum Jim (a Chinook word meaning "strong" or "giant"), and Tagish Charlie (the nephew of the aforementioned Kate) were in a place called Rabbit Creek, prospecting for gold. As part of a salmon fishing trip, the trio had visited a friend, one Robert Henderson, who was himself involved in placer mining for gold in a locality he had hopefully named Gold Bottom Creek. The three hunters had staked a claim near Henderson and, in mid-August, 1896, they struck it rich, in a twist of fate that Henderson may not have appreciated. Their claim of coarse gold initiated what the papers later took to referring to as the Klondike Rush.

A few days prior to the Rabbit Creek strike, Mr. Henderson had paid a visit to one Joseph Ladue, to purchase some of the sluice boxes that Ladue was manufacturing in his modest saw mill. Henderson, according to Ogilvie, at that time showed Ladue the pinch of gold dust colour he had recently panned, and Ladue realized a way to make his fortune – not in gold panning but in town planning. Ladue hastily went to the confluence of the Yukon and Klondike Rivers, and set up camp there on a shelf of level land. Responding to Ladue's request, Mr. Ogilvie, who had settled several disputatious claims by miners, surveyed and mapped the grid of a township for him and, in anticipation of rapid municipal growth, Ladue erected a storage facility and a saloon. The nascent town needed a name, and Mr. Ogilvie suggested "Dawson," and Mr. Ladue did not object. And so there I was, and so I remain, in spirit if not in body, abroad on the streets of Dawson City, a town that has gone from a population of one man to several thousands in a single year, and is today chartered as the capital of the Yukon Territory. Yet not one square foot of it has ever lain beneath my feet.

While on the subject of objects bearing my name, it was during my duties as naturalist with the Boundary Commission that I was fortunate enough to collect a mouse bearing a red back. I sent off its skin for affirmation of its novelty to Dr. C. Hart Merriam, head of the United States Department of Agriculture's Division of

Ornithology and Mammalogy. Dr. Merriam duly pronounced it to be a new species, and gave it the title *Evotomy Dawsoni*, although I am certain the mouse itself, somewhere out on the prairie, remains in complete ignorance of this small fact. Father too was immortalized, but in something far more solid than a mouse. In 1874, some exploratory excavations on the site of the University, naturally, were monitored by the geology students, and one of the samples discovered in a limestone dyke proved to be unique. It was a rock composed of sodium aluminum carbonate hydroxide and it was a new mineral, which of course was named "Dawsonite," and is on view in the collection of the Museum. Father's name is thus truly written in stone.

When I arrived back in Ottawa after the Christmas holiday in 1898 in Montreal, late on New Year's Eve, it was a few minutes from Hogmanay. I could have pressed myself into the festive celebrations at the Rideau Club, but instead, after telephoning William and making sure the stalking influenza had not broached his home on Gilmour Street, made for bed. On awakening on New Year's Day 1899, I sat by the fire which I was able to rekindle and I wrote my felicitations to Mother, particularly asking her to convey the message to Father. I was on the edge of a cold, and stayed by the fire most of the day.

—

I AM NOT a man to consider events auspicious, but the month of January 1899, seemed determined to forecast a gloomy year. Near the conclusion of the month, Mr. Tyrrell, amid considerable publicity in the newspapers due to his cultivated reputation as a geologist and explorer, resigned. The genesis of the departure was my offer of a $200 salary increase to Mr. McConnell, who in the May of 1898 had been offered the increment as an inducement to stay and not leave to become the provincial mineralogist of British Columbia. I could not match the offer to Tyrrell, and he seemed at the time considerably miffed about McConnell's getting the increase which made his salary greater, and he so expressed himself. I tried to explain the special cause but he was not assuaged. The two gentlemen then had to work for several months side by side in the Yukon, where Tyrrell had taken the opportunity, outside of the Survey's work, to research future employment in the territory, should he have occasion to resign.

The despicable weather was extremely cold that winter, with little snow to act as a blanket. I fretted that my parents might find it difficult to keep comfortable in Montreal, and in particular I was concerned for Father's endurance after he suffered a stroke at the end of January. He was then still recovering from it, and in the same letter I reminded Mother that the balcony door in his room should be stuffed with cotton wool at the bottom and about three feet up on each side, as the cold slipped through the joints and along the floor like so much icy water. Also that Father should observe the doctor's instructions in regard to bananas and the other simple remedies that had been proscribed, as a temporary disagreement of the stomach under the circumstances was a small price to pay.

The entire family was under the weather then, taking turn and turn about, the prevailing colds and troubles having a grippish, tenacious character. Only William was faring well physically. Mentally, however, he was in need of a few months' leave, due to overworking himself. In a recent speech at Quebec, Sir William Van Horne, the President of Canadian Pacific, whose Empress boats were making such a success on the west coast, had spoken in regard to the future of a fast Atlantic service. The Empresses would, he hoped, soon be plying the Atlantic as well. This had made clear the pressing need for a hydrographic survey of the St. Lawrence, William's field of expertise, and his ongoing tidal survey of the Gulf had moved to the forefront of Sir William's plans. William was expected, indubitably, to take an active part in arranging the new work, and it would be unfortunate if he was off duty at the time, but of course he was first and foremost my brother, and if he needed the rest, I wanted him to have it.

The Survey understood that the more time I now spent in Montreal with Father, the better for both of us, but this did not make getting away any easier; no page of my Director's diary was ever less than full, and my struggles with budgeting seemed to grow extra tentacles the moment I left the desk. Certainly it seemed a greater monster than any I had heard rumoured in the lakes of the B.C. interior. As well, the privilege of being Director of the Survey carried with it a raft of speaking engagements. As past president of the Royal Society of Canada, and of the Ottawa Field-Naturalists' Club three years running, my face needed to be seen at meetings, and I was heavily involved with giving the national Ethnological Survey a firm footing. Some of the local engagements were less injurious than others; I was always ready to talk at Ottawa's May Court Club, as the audience was a small and select group of young ladies, including one Miss Dobell, with whom I find conversation to be an easy matter.

At the end of February, I was able to make a visit to Montreal and talk with Father, and only returned to Ottawa to attend a dinner given by the Rideau Club for the Governor General, at which I was to speak. While in Montreal, I spent a goodly amount of time dealing with Father's almost desperate proclivity for writing articles and tracts. He sensed, I believe, the end of his time on this earth was coming sooner rather than later, and he seemed anxious to commit his scientific experience and insight to paper and publication, as well as his unwavering religious convictions. I found it difficult to know how to treat his output, but thought it best to dam the production of the flood of articles at source rather than trying to intercept them once they had been produced.

One of the Nova Scotian Members of Parliament had suggested to me that a biography of Father was long overdue, and I conveyed this opinion to him. Father replied that such a document was in fact under way, under his own steam, and he intended to focus more on getting it finished. One of the ways I attempted to slow down his production with the pen was to find him plenty of reading material, such as the latest offerings from the Marquess of Lorne, who had remained a friend after his term as Governor General had ended in 1883. The Marquess produced not one but two handsome books that year, one on Windsor Castle (of which he was Governor) and one on the legends of Scotland, which Father most enjoyed and which Mother also bought me as a present.

Father, I had realized, needed to be led rather than, as had been the case the whole of my life, to be followed. I fancied he actually might take kindly to such a switch in roles, which indeed he did. The pathos involved in asking him to move from head of the family, to the shoulder, as it were, did not escape me, but the loving duty of raising children is a door that swings both ways; children should expect to take over from their parents when the time comes. By this same token, I urged Mother to award herself some rest, and as Spring came on she was able to get away with her granddaughter Clare and come up to Ottawa, and just spend her days reading, taking short constitutionals, getting up late and going to bed early, and most of all plenty of sleep, sleep in quantity in my experience being one of the best fundamentals for curing everything.

There was some excitement in the Survey that Spring at the arrival of the remains of a mammoth, found on the farm of Mr. Charles Fletcher, about a mile and a half northeast of Muirkirk, Ontario. When we opened the cases, we found: the lower jaw with the teeth in place; the upper molars with parts of the cranium; portions of the tusks; a few vertebrae and ribs; part of a scapula; two humeri; and all of the bones of the hind legs. Laying them out reminded me of the skeletons Father would bring me at McGill, puzzles that he would not help me solve. This osseous riddle, being writ large, was considerably easier.

One night in April, I got William to come around for dinner at the Rideau Club and we talked over the matter of his leave in its various aspects. I casually mentioned that Sir Davies, the Minister of Marine and Fisheries and William's superior, had remarked in a sympathetic way that he had had no idea William was unwell until he heard it in Council. At one point during dinner, William mused about going to Halifax and loafing about, and then on to Métis to join Mother. Then a notion to go to Bermuda crossed his mind, followed by some other idea to do with bicycles. Clearly he was in a state of flux, and was also suffering a bout of insomnia. I was anxious that the three months' leave that he intended to embark on, in May 1899, not be a waste of time, and that he find something of a pleasing interest quite out of line with his usual work.

William's state of mind took a turn for the better in May when Mother accompanied him on the short train journey to Ste. Agathe in the Laurentians, for a stay at the health spa of Mrs. Wand, overlooking the lake. Mother mentioned that while there she went to see the tuberculosis hospital that Dr. Richer had just opened and that was already attracting the attention of the country's physicians. With William ensconced in refreshing air, Mother and Father set off for the "resting place," the house at Métis, where Father's health had so much improved the year before, when he had had his smaller stroke.

There is a curious, almost contagious nature to the receiving of honours. The list attached to my own name began to grow with the speed of a prairie fire when I became Director. At the beginning of June I went to Toronto to show due appreciation for the honorary degree the University proposed to confer on me. It was really unlooked for and not a little embarrassing, but accept it I did, and attended both the somewhat protracted convocation function and the ensuing garden party, at which there was an enormous display of ladies' summer hats in all colours of the rainbow, before slipping away to catch the train. In all modesty I think I shall be glad of the extra volume when we do get our new building. I'll have some extra wall space to hang such certificates of achievement, my principal achievement being, I suspect, the refusal to simply disappear. While I was obviously, as the quantity of honours I was receiving seemed to indicate, nearing the end of my useful career, I was gratified to be able to give my nephew Matthew some Survey work for the summer on the Cambrian sections of Cape Breton, a relatively unworked field.

Father and I had a flurry of communication towards the end of July, which was a very broken month of weather, with the farmers hereabouts suffering badly from the wetness of it, no chance of curing their hay although the crop was good enough. The crop in Parliament was not yet in off the fields either, with new matters of dispute pushing up daily. Being at Métis did not seem to have slowed down the output from Father's desk at all, or the inquiring nature of his mind. One day he would send me a memo on the dredging of the St. Lawrence, and the next another wondering what the Geographic Board was, which I explained. (It was a committee of dragooned members from the various departments dealing with Canadian geographic matters for whom attendance was compulsory and the remuneration nil.) Yet another memo wondered if Hodder and Stoughton publishers had sent me, as he had requested them to, copies of the latest edition of his book *Salient Points in the Science of the Earth*, which he had updated and tightened as he continued his quest to refute Mr. Darwin's hypothesis. And there were the letters to the Montreal *Gazette*, in his own hand, in a steady stream, on matters of the day, of days past, and matters of the days to come. Many of them made print.

Mother, as always without fail, sent a telegram on my birthday (the day blotted its copy book when I learnt that there was to be no money for the new Survey building that year). William, thank heavens, was back in business, making a tour of his tidal stations in the St. Lawrence. All through August I kept threatening to escape Ottawa for Métis, but the thread tying me to the desk refused to snap. I felt uneasy about not being able to visit Father, and was relieved when Rankine arranged passage over in mid-August with the steamer company he worked for, intending to stay awhile. Having a doctor in the house night and day was fortunate, as Father was showing signs, just perceptible, of improvement. He was still unable to attend to business, and so, as eldest son I gladly took up the slack. For some reason I took it in my head to get nervous about the use of the oil stove at Métis, urging caution as the oil they could get at the local stores was of poor quality. Besides, I have no great faith in any of those stoves.

By mid-September, the family was back on University Avenue. The summer at Métis had not been of the best, the rain clouds winning out over the sun more often than not, and Father had not been able take a good quota of the long walks and rides by the water that in previous years were so reinvigorating. As Rankine was still at the house, I was able to go camping with a couple of fellows from the Survey and not feel overly guilty. It was just four days out in Hastings County in central Ontario under canvas, looking at a section that seemed to have a few secrets up its sleeve, but it was better than nothing, which was what I had suffered all year as my chances of field work were so strictly budgeted. The moment I returned I was plunged into the details for the next Paris Exhibition due to begin there in April, in which we were expected to make the maximum impact with very limited space. The Parisians were already proclaiming the electrical nature of the Fair – moving pavements and railways powered by direct current, and I would like to have attended, but the Survey's calendar would not allow it.

One of our Survey men, Mr. W. McInnes, had reported in October on the extraordinary activity in the extraction of iron ores just southwest of Port Arthur on the north shore of Lake Superior. There was some mining there already in the soft ores, for which there was a great demand just then. I felt a prompt map-sheet was necessary of the iron-ore bearing Animikie rocks in the vicinity, so I decided to seize the chance and go there myself, spending a few days in the Great Northern Hotel. This rather grand building had not been there when I spent a few raw days in Port Arthur back in 1873 at the start of my time on the Boundary Commission. Indeed, in small towns across the Dominion, much that was there now had not been there when I first stepped onto their muddy streets, although as I discovered, difficulty in getting a boat away from it remained the town's enduring feature. By the time I returned, Rankine had left for London again.

—

As Father's full recovery became less and less likely, the collective family wish was that he see another Christmas, with as many of the family at his side in Montreal as circumstances allowed. As usual, and to Father's preserving joy, there was a new grandchild around, William's daughter Cristall. As the photograph I sent to Rankine shortly after she was born proves, she is indubitably a Dawson, blessed with the expansive forehead that we all carry before us. Throughout October, though, the decline in Father was perceptible as pneumonia took hold. Yet I don't think two days passed that month without some request from him for information. One religious inquiry sent me scurrying to the Survey library to seek an article on "Ophir" in the *Journal of the Geological Society* from April, which he must have seen and needed again for cross-referencing. Ophir was a place, a city, or a land rich in gold, mentioned in the Old Testament to which Solomon's ships sailed and returned full of riches, but whose exact location was never determined. Father may have had a thesis as to its whereabouts – I believe southern Palestine was the main contender, although Father, if he did find something indicative, was soon thereafter too ill to take it any further. It may well have been the last intellectual puzzle he gave thought to.

> Throughout the land the maples flame
> The time has come, the leaf must fall
> Though still the day is blue, serene
> No storm nor wintry blast at all
> The time is ripe, and leaf by leaf

The garb of life is shed away
Not by the tempest's stress, but in
The dreaming azure eye of day
So, ripe in knowledge, ripe in years,
The pulse beats low, the eye grows dim,
And we, though blinded still with tears
We know the time has come for him.

Even in early November Father was still researching, but the discipline that had made him so formidable a scientist was gone. The pneumonia was gaining, but it was doing so almost with a gentlemanly courtesy. The gradual decay of his physical powers was evident, but his memory seemed undiminished, a fact Dr. Blackader, an admirer of Father's mental powers as well as his medical adviser, remarked on. On Sunday, November twelfth, Father attended church, the same one where he had once stood up during a service and decried the use of musical accompaniment, then took a ride in a carriage around the grounds of the University, up past the Redpath Museum where he had spent so much of his time in retirement the last six years, leaving each morning bag in hand to attend to his treasured collections. The nurses were now constantly present, and Anna and I barely left the room during the next week. On the Saturday night, Mother was in the room alone with him, and I heard him say, "I am dying, Lord Jesus into thy hands I commend my spirit." Then in a calm voice he said to Mother, to his golden wife, "Good night. If I leave you in the night, we will say good morning in a better world." (I recalled these words sometime later and wrote down an abbreviated version on a scrap of paper.) Then he moved into a coma, a peaceful one that seemed no more than an extension of sleep, and during that night of November the 19th, with Mother, Anna, and myself at the bedside, he passed away. Dr. Blackader explained that there had been a stroke and consequent effusion of blood on the brain. The passing was peaceful, and the lines on his face fell smooth.

The Principal of McGill, Dr. William Peterson, learned quickly of Father's demise, as did Lord Strathcona, one of the University's great benefactors, who cabled from the High Commission in London within hours of the public announcement. (It was Lord Strathcona who had funded the admittance of women that Father had pushed for in 1884, and indeed the first of the College's female professors, the botanist Dr. Derick, sent her condolences the same day.) At noon of the Monday, in the Old Library in Molson Hall, the staff and students met, while classes were suspended for the day. The notice of this meeting called on the campus to "testify their respect by their presence," which I thought a fine turn of phrase, and the testimonials and speeches lasted till suppertime. Of the original fifteen professors who had been there forty-five years earlier for Father's inauguration at McGill, three were in Molson Hall that day, and one of the trio, the Dean of Medicine, Dr. Craik, when his turn came, spoke of the "proud grief" that the assembly felt, which again was a fine piece of language; the language of bereavement being a difficult thing to master.

Father's funeral was the next day, the Tuesday. The casket, which had lain in the university main hall, with a flowery cross at its head and the words IN DOMINO CONFIDO florally inscribed at the foot, was moved from the Main building down the campus avenue in a sombre carriage. The avenue was lined on either side with undergraduates. Father's last journey continued from there to Park Avenue, then along Pine and onto the Mont Royal and into the family plot. Myself, William, and my nephews Victor and Owen, as well as Bernard and two of his boys, Conrad and Bernard Junior, acted as mourners, and Reverend Dewey from Father's longtime place of worship leading us. There were faces everywhere that I recognized from the many points of the compass of Father's past; from Mr. Primrose, of Pictou, surely Father's oldest acquaintance, to Mr. Whiteaves who had come down from Ottawa, representing the Survey. Anna and Mother had fretted, Anna I think more so, over the wording on Father's tomb, and in the end it read:

BLESSED ARE THE DEAD WHO LIE IN THE LORD
THAT THEY MAY REST FROM THEIR LABOURS
AND THEIR WORKS DO FOLLOW THEM.

In a day of sorrow, there was a sad footnote; news reached us the next day that Mr. Hugh McLennan, a governor of McGill who had walked in the funeral procession, had died just before midnight of heart strain.

The news of Father's death, at the age of seventy-nine, travelled with great speed. Within the day the Great North Western telegram office received an abundance of messages marked "Lady Dawson, 293 University." One of the most touching came from Little Métis and read "One hundred residents gathered in the Methodist Church at the funeral of the late Mrs. John Macnider send Christian sympathy." By a strange coincidence, Rankine cabled the same night with an abbreviated version of the same quotation that adorned Father's stone. "They rest from their labours, their works follow them." Sir William Van Horne, erroneously dating his letter a month earlier, told Mother "the ordinary expressions of sorrow and sympathy seem cold and formal in the face of the death of Sir William Dawson" and Lord Minto wrote personally from Government House to say that he hoped "the national sympathy in your loss and the grateful appreciation of Canada of all Sir William's great works may be pleasant to you to hear of." On the Thursday, in the *Gazette*, a poem of remembrance entitled "Perpetual Day" was printed in honour of Father, and signed with the initials B.D., whose identity no one could decipher. The poem claimed that Father was "Science and faith into a purpose brought," which was a worthy summation. These were the public expressions of condolence, and the time spent with them was a blessing, but it was never long before the private sorrow returned. I found myself in a flux of moments remembered; Father reading from *Pickwick Papers*, or counting the peppermints in the drawer of his desk to check we had not lifted any, or bringing some of Mr. Carpenter's shells to my sick room for me to catalogue.

Perhaps a week into December, a fuller letter arrived from Rankine that was, I see now, the first intimation of the division that would open up in the family, a division that no one wanted or expected, and yet has become imbedded and unmovable. In the letter, he said he had first heard of Father's passing in a short telegram from Eva's husband and it was not altogether a surprise. When he was in Montreal in the Autumn, he had told the nurse, who had made plans to stay until Christmas, that he doubted whether she would be required that long. Father had died, as he said, full of years and full of honours, unlike other very old men, and he gave Mr. Gladstone as an example, who were apt to ruin their life's record by displays of regret for the inevitable end of it.

Rankine then informed me that Father had told him, while he was nursing him at Métis, that he was anxious to have his biography prepared and published as soon as possible, and that it was Father's desire that I, the eldest son and the one closest to him in professional understanding, undertake this as editor. If he could be of any use in this project, pray let him know.

The bereavement letter I cherished the most was from cousin Ella, from Ivy Lodge in Scotland. Her message did not arrive until mid-December, but, as in all our correspondence, it was honest, concerned and, on her part, infused with her religious nature. She commenced by saying that she really did not know what to say, as her ideas of life and death were so utterly altered within the last few years; the things she could say truly at one time seemed worse than meaningless now. This was a strong echo of my own thoughts, and thus oddly comforting. In a dream she had once had, she wrote, she had heard a prosaic version of a quote from Shakespeare and awoken with the audible words ringing in her ears. The Shakespearian line was, "So unto thine own self be true and it must follow, as the night, the day, thou canst not then be false to any man" and I think that here, for the first time in our long relationship, Ella was not offering me advice or guidance towards the faith that had until recently sustained her. She was asking me to let myself be my own guide. Then,

A family gathering on the lawn at Métis. My brother-in law Bernard standing extreme left, myself, nephew Bernard Junior sporting a hat, Father behind him, Clare next holding her sister Eva, Conrad far right. Mother seated next to Anna, daughter Lois on her knee, Ruth sitting in front of Mother.

In my rooms at Victoria Chambers in Ottawa, letter writing as usual.

at the end of the letter, she wondered if I remembered showing her some of the constellations in the sky at Burntisland when we went rowing when we were no more than children. When she showed her own children the same constellations (at least she hoped they were the same) it always put me in her thoughts.

December dragged and the week before Christmas I was still detained in Ottawa. I was ready to leave as regards the holidays, and had collected the broach I had had made for Clare, which contained several of the freshwater pearls I had collected around the country in a gold setting. The Paris Exhibition was only a handful of months away, and our collective labours at the Survey resembled a hive as we strove to label, box, and dispatch by rail and sea the largest and most comprehensive collection of minerals of commercial value ever brought together in Canada. The space allotted for the exhibition in the Canadian Pavilion in the Trocadero Gardens was only 3,550 square feet, which was not enough for the 1,200 separate exhibits, and the ensuing compromises were my responsibility. In the end, the collection filled more than 325 boxes and barrels, and the weight of minerals contained in these was in all about seventy tons.

Concurrently, Mother and I, at our separate desks, had drolly designated ourselves "officers of letters," and we mailed off several times a day batches of signed replies to notes of condolence regarding Father. I did as many as I could at the Rideau Club of an evening, as well as devoting time to my personal writings, while she took the greater half in Montreal. I sensed the endeavour was part of Mother's effort to keep occupied at the surface, while her faith buttressed her below. Indeed there was no lack of work to hand, and work it was. I was able to handle, through the auspices of the Survey, the requests for reproduction cabinet photographs of Father to be placed in the journal of the many societies he had led, created, or joined. I had contacted a clippings agency, but as on previous occasions they had proved unsatisfactory, with much repetition and providing little of use.

He had great love for this green world
To plant and tend, to pray and toil
And seek increase from barren soil
To see the germ, the leaf, the flower
And look for harvest's happy hour
He knew his task would be relieved
When God so willed
And that by other hands his garden
Must be tilled.

In April 1900 the Paris Exhibition opened, and over the following months I anxiously awaited with each mail reports of our reception. It emerged that the large series of valuable gold specimens, priced at some $30,000, was the greatest attraction of the whole Canadian pavilion, and the four protected steel and plate-glass cases housing it were constantly surrounded by an interested and admiring crowd. In the next case was displayed a fine exhibit from the principal gold-bearing creeks of the Klondike, including Bonanza, Eldorado, Hunker, Last Chance, Dominion, Sulphur, Gold Run, and Eureka. One great attraction was a rosary lent by the Rev. F.P.E. Gengreau, made entirely of nuggets in the rough from various diggings.

———

IT IS EIGHT MONTHS since I began this memoir, and the end of the first year of the new century is close at hand, and the anniversary of Father's death has just passed. I am recently returned from Albany, where I read a paper to the Geological Survey of America, of which I am President this year. Father held the position in 1893, so I am again in his footsteps. The paper, entitled "The Geological Record of the Rocky Mountain Regions of Canada," brought together my many years of study of Cordellian geology, the geology of the western mountains. In preparing the paper, I went over my many reports and notes from the West, and must admit I found the mental journey pleasing, indeed fulfilling.

The streets of Ottawa are blanketed with snow and Advent is about to begin, a season of conflicting emotions for me with Father gone. From my office at the Survey, I can see no further out of the window than to the wall of the building behind. The entire Paris collection, under Mr. Low's supervision, has been repacked and shipped to Glasgow for the coming exhibition in that city next summer. The irony of my position at the Survey is that while I order other men into the field, to scramble the face of Canada and report her hidden treasures, I cannot issue the same request to myself, though I am perhaps the most eager of us all to leave Ottawa, half a year past my fifty-first birthday. One becomes grateful for small mercies, such as the sojourn in mid-August of this year, a mere canter out West and back on business that did not take more than a few days and did not even require me to go as far as the coast. Before setting out I attempted, as in times before, to induce Anna to make the trip with me, as my guest. As before, she could not go; the odds these days of any one child being under the weather when one has that many are formidable.

Here in the corner of the Rideau Club, I am writing to Anna again, thanking her for the fine fur coat that should provide some armour against the Ottawa winter. Christmas in Montreal was not the time of mirth that it has been in the past, but the young ones do not allow spirits to flag too far, and Conrad was anxious to show me his prowess on the bicycle I bought him for his birthday, the one with the added fattened pedals. The sight of Natalie the cook carrying in the enormous plum pudding, more bonfire than bon appetite, and the children shouting to her to not go up in flames, raised a chorus of laughter.

However, the frustration with Rankine is as yet undispelled. The point of friction remains Father's biographical manuscript, the one he laboured so hard to complete and almost did, sometimes beyond his physical stamina to do so, with the St. Lawrence flowing past even as his pen flowed across the page. Rankine was there with us this summer (Anna and Bernard have now built a connecting passageway between our cottage and theirs, the one Father bought them), and he took the time to look over the manuscript, whereas I can only give scraps of time to it here. Even so, I have seen enough to feel strongly impressed with the wisdom of passing it through the hands of some outside, sympathetic literary man, and I have said so to all concerned. It seems destined, in all likelihood, to be the only extended biography of Father, and should be made as good as it can be.

Matters slid further into the quagmire a month back, when a letter from Rankine, then back in London with his Clorann and baby Margaret, demonstrated that he had quite misunderstood my views and was proceeding to make independent arrangements for getting the biography printed at once, unedited and unenhanced. Against my firm desire to keep Mother out of this sorry business, I felt compelled by Rankine's oxen behaviour to write to her, explaining my side of the story. If she did not want to interfere, I wrote, I intended to dissociate myself from the project, and would cable to Rankine and emphatically tell him so. I am convinced that we have not done the best under the circumstances with the manuscript; and I want us all to be mutually satisfied before going further.

Rankine's misunderstanding of the situation has become positively willful. He has now hatched a new way of getting the biography out, namely by printing it at our own cost in London without a publisher and putting it in the hands of some Montreal bookseller. He has something he called the "specifications" for this, and he therefore requires the typed copy forthwith, with my corrections and additions so it should be printed by the end of the year. I am still adamantly opposed to any premature publication, and there are obvious advantages to employing a Canadian publisher, Dawson Brothers being the obvious choice.

Attempting a modicum of tact, in the hope of inducing some restraint, I have cabled Rankine that he should not allow haste in the

matter to interfere in any way with his plans and movements. I hope
to give a little time to the copy I have here *after* the New Year, and
perhaps we might include some letters of a more intimate kind, such
as those between Father and Sir Charles Lyell, and others, most of
whom are dead now but we might be able to scare up what became
of some of their belongings. These are, of course, delaying tactics.

I seem to have been the author of an inordinate number of lists
in my life, and this month is proving no exception. I am a member
of the Geographic Board of Canada, and over the course of eleven
meetings, we have put together six lists of nearly 1,500 place-names
to decorate the many Survey maps in the course of preparation. The
maps will show only the features of greater geological importance,
so a large number of duplicated or otherwise objectionable names
have been excised. It is remarkable to note how many of the dis-
carded place-names I am acquainted with first hand. Another list
duly prepared is my annual weighty account of ores and minerals
subject to inquiry by the public over the past year. It reads alpha-
betically as follows: amber, apatite, borax, corundum, chromic iron
ore, chalk, dolomite, feldspar, plumbago, haematite, limestone, magnetic iron sand, magnetite, manganese, marbles, molybdenite,
nickel, ochre, onyx, petroleum, platinum, peat, pyrites, shell marls,
soapstone, vanadium, and wolframite.

The silver lining has appeared on the cloud! Today, February 8,
Minister of Works Tarte has informed me that the forthcoming
Survey budget is to include the sum of $50,000 for the building of
a new museum. The stuffed birds and dinosaur bones will at last
have a suitable display, and my office will resemble less a tide wash.
I am impatient to see the earth turned on the new site.

———

I FEAR I HAVE COME to the edge of my temper, a place I rarely
if ever reach, and am compelled to recount Rankine's latest
chicanery. A letter from him has arrived, written on stationery
from the library of the Royal Colonial Institute, detailing the

"specifications." I shall record them as written: "The title page of Father's <u>auto</u>-biography (Rankine's underlining) will announce 'Edited and published by either "His sons" or by (our names in full).' For an edition of 1,200, well done, with four plates, the total cost including printing, binding, paper, proofreading will come to about $500. If you wanted to go half shares with me, you could do so, otherwise I am quite prepared to do it 'all alone,' as baby is fond of saying." My goodness.

When Rankine was in New York, almost twenty years ago, studying for the medical exams he would eventually pass not there but at McGill, he was entranced by the "prizes" he saw the commercial life had to offer, and from then on he sometimes referred to himself as an "amateur financier." He has striven to maintain that status since. In the letter he continues, "With packaging and freight we can easily supply a bookseller in Montreal with books at under 50 cents a copy, and they would sell for 75 cents in Montreal and $1 elsewhere." The bookseller he has in mind is Renouf, Dawson Brothers head clerk for twenty years, whom he considers a decent, honest little man and who always looked after Father's order and accounts. He claims to be quite satisfied with the manuscript just as it is, and if Mother and I are not satisfied, "why not put it right at once" but equally "procrastination and delay served no purpose" as far as he can see.

Now that I am back at my desk, and drafting my letter to Minister Sifton to accompany the Annual Report, Anna and I are writing daily in the matter of Rankine, a frequency of communication I don't recall between us since she married. The storm of letters I must say blows mainly in one direction, from Ottawa to Montreal, and I think it best to continue recording my thoughts on this matter, as I am thinking matters may yet come to some form of legal steps being required.

With great alacrity, it seems, has Father's death turned the skies from blue to grey, and things have remained in that sad hue ever since. Though I doubt that Rankine had a hand in it, the skies have darkened further with the news that yesterday, January 22nd, 1901, the Queen passed away. The announcement was made to the watchers at the Palace gate by a sergeant of the police, minutes after she died at half past six in the evening. Her Majesty, who not so long ago visited Dublin, retired to the Isle of Wight five days ago, to Osbourne House, in grave health. She expired after occupying the throne for all of my life, and she was two years older than Father when he left us. She is to be buried next to Prince Albert, and so an era, the Victorian Age I presume it will be called, has ended, and the Edwardian has begun.

At last, now when it is too late, I have heard from Eva. Rankine sent her a copy of the book! She is about half way through (by now she will have finished it). It brings Father very clearly to mind, she feels, and is nothing to be ashamed of. In her letter of January 31st, which is twelve days ago, she states that no one had, up till I wrote her, mentioned the matter. She had no idea Rankine was acting against the wishes of the other members of the family. In fact, she has seen him; he stayed for two nights in Rock Ferry before leaving from Liverpool. She feels that Father would be deeply grieved to know there was a break in the family circle. Better that than nothing at all was Rankine's reply when she said that, and Eva was frankly glad, when they spoke, that he was working at anything at all. In doing so she hopes he might derive a lesson from Father's life of useful and self-sacrificing labour for the benefit of those around him.

Eva wonders whether Rankine's judgement was not a little unbalanced by an incident he related to her that happened years ago when he was lost in the woods, a reference I think to a time when Rankine wandered from camp on the Queen Charlotte Islands. Eva says that to her, who was so much his companion during their early years, he has seemed an entirely different character ever since.

I am guessing, but I think Rankine has had the book printed by Ballantyne's on some private agreement, and is himself responsible for the cost. If it has indeed been mentioned among Books of the Week in the *London Times*, as I am told, I have not seen it referred to in any papers here. This leads me to think he may be arranging to import the printed sheets to Canada, and is meeting with difficulties he did not foresee in Canadian Copyright law, which calls for printing in Canada. In addition, Rankine has expressly excluded William from getting involved. I have in the meantime dropped the idea of taking legal steps, since that would involve Mother as she is the manuscript's executor. The great shame of all this is that I have no desire to go to Montreal just now, being fearful of what I might say about Rankine in Mother's presence. For the first time in my life, I do not want to go home.

The new year has got off to a poor start at work, as well, with the tendered resignation of Mr. Low, after twenty years as a geologist with the technical staff. He had been in Paris most of the previous year with the Exhibit. I will be forced to accept, and he is to take three months' leave prior to the resignation taking effect in June, so I will have to seek a replacement, with no money to do so. He says in his letter that "this step will sever the cordial relations which he has always had with me," and he will look back "with pleasure on the happy if impecunious years spent with my scientific confreres." He leaves to work with the Dominion Development Company, there to undertake the location of their minerals on the Hudson Bay.

———

THE WALK FROM Victoria Chambers to the Survey today, the last day of February, took a little longer than it usually does to perform, even with the heavy weather being taken into account. The Potsdam sandstone of the Parliament Buildings caught what little light broke through the clouds, and I was fine along Wellington Street, but crossing Sapper's Bridge I felt as though my brain had suddenly lightened, even as the air seemed to become heavier, more liquid, and to settle in my lungs and not want to leave. I paused for a moment, pretending to watch a boat pass through one of the locks in the Rideau Canal, but in fact I needed a moment to collect my thoughts, which were in danger of subsuming. After several deep breaths, I found my way down Sussex and in through the Survey door and to my desk, all the while feeling as though I was moving through a London fog. I have not been able to achieve much all morning, except to open my notebook and make these brief observations. An absence of a mental ability to make pertinent decisions and reach the end of lines of thought has quite come upon me. A page that will not remain steady on the desk is not a useful platform, so I will confine myself to reviewing some accounts, and put in abeyance stressful thoughts of fraternal friction. I cannot recall the last time I did not complete a day's work that I had started, so I intend to work till twilight and then take a meal at the Rideau Club, where light companionship may prove remedial.

—

I AM IN MY ROOMS, it is the following morning, and I can hear the clock of the Peace Tower striking. Despite it being a Friday, and one day's work away from week's end, I fear that, for the first time since joining the Survey as a young geologist, my fellow employees will have to forgo the pleasure of my company. The grippe has me in its grip, so to speak, and completing even so short a journey as that from here to the Survey lies beyond me. I was undoubtedly less than prudent to venture to work yesterday, and I am paying the price today.

Dr. Powell has left just the room – the same Dr. Powell who a decade ago issued his infamous one-line note at sunrise as the Prime Minister approached death at Earnscliffe: "Sir John Macdonald is still alive and more cannot be said." He informs me that my malady shows a distinct desire to turn bronchial. I believe in fact it already has, a clue being the sudden weight that the pen and my eyelids have gained as I write. Sleep beckons.

The heat of my brow has awoken me. It is morning, so the birds tell me. I can hear Dr. Powell informing me that the notary is waiting in the drawing room as requested, together with a clerk, and though I have no recollection of making such a request, I obviously must have. Changes to my will have to be made; it will remain much as before, except that I will set up a trust fund in the name of Rankine's daughter, until she is twenty-one, then it is hers to do with as young women of the twentieth century will then do.

—

THE NOTARY, a Mr. Monk, an apt name for a man in such a position, has left, and I hope I dictated everything as I had planned. Anna and William to be executors, yes, and my notebooks of travels, sketches, papers, printed books, and such disposed of by them, guided by dear Mother's wishes. Mother to have investments from whatever I am worth, liquefied, less the money my sisters and William will receive, quickly, I hope. Done.

I believe William appeared several times at the bedside in the night, or perhaps it was one extended vigil. Now he has come again to tell me, before stepping out to telephone home, that Mother has been called in Montreal and has boarded a train. She should be at my side before sunset. I have been searching in my bedside table for a note I made when Father passed, a line he had quoted from somewhere. I have it. "Today's good night is God's good morrow."

Suddenly, I remember a good morrow, like it was yesterday. We were on the prairie, myself on Sampson, riding out to visit some limestone on Turtle Mountain. The wind strong and chilly. We rode, halted for lunch, let the horses feed. A while later, we came upon a Boundary mound in poor condition, a shabby piece of work. At day's end, we stopped at a pretty little sheet of water with high wooded banks, built a fire, ate a hearty supper, chose the sleeping places, unstrapped, and turned in. There was a brilliant aurora.

Up at sunrise, and we went east, ascended a ridge to a high point and saw a view like no other. At the next lake, there was no place shallow enough to ford, unless we had been on giraffes. I urged Sampson in. He was not at all afraid, and he took me to the other side safe and sound, wet up to the waist and water in the saddle-bags. Our camp that night was by a small swamp among tall poplar woods, the leaves yellow and falling one by one while we dried the clothes. Owls were answering each other from tree to tree, and a partridge drummed to keep himself warm. The sound of Indians shooting ducks brought us awake. We quickly broke camp and soon after came on two tepees, the dogs barking. A squaw came out to quiet the dogs, and was transfixed by astonishment at the sight of us. Then an old man and some children appeared. They were much astonished to hear that King George was dead, by which they meant George IV, who had been dead a good while. I told them, "A woman is now our Chief" and they were silent for some time. Then one asked, "Is she married to the Great Spirit?" We dined with them on freshly slaughtered partridge and a ruffed grouse I had bagged earlier as it fed on catkin buds of hazel. In the late heat of the day we arrived back at the main party and someone asked me, "Was that a good day?" Yes, it was a good day. They were all good days. Out there.

And now, I am very tired. Sleep, I think.

My life is short, the threads of life
A tangled skein, I cannot sort
But count it gain to live
To live and die – to see and know
And pass to the unknown
If I might live anew and plan
Throughout, and shape again
So far as men may do
The web of life – would I
Or would I not pursue
The self-same scheme?

MONDAY, MARCH 4, 1901. THE CITIZEN, OTTAWA, CANADA

EMINENT GEOLOGIST

Dr. G. M. Dawson, C. M. G. Died on Saturday After Brief Illness

---

Dr. George M. Dawson, Director of the Geological Survey of Canada, died in his rooms in the Victoria Chambers at 6:15 o'clock Saturday evening, from the effects of acute bronchitis, after forty-eight hours illness. He was in his office on Thursday and at night dined at the Rideau Club. On Friday he was taken seriously ill and although a hard fight was made for life he proved unequal to cope with the disease which had attacked him in a virulent form. His brother Mr. W. Bell Dawson, of the department of marine and fisheries and Dr. R.W. Powell were present when the end came. His mother, Lady Dawson, was telegraphed for Saturday morning and arrived on the 6:30 express fifteen minutes after he had passed away. She was accompanied by her daughter the wife of Prof. Harrington of McGill university.

The announcement of Dr. Dawson's death caused a great shock in the community. He was widely respected and honored, not alone for his great talents but because he was a man of an exceptionally genial and loveable character. His colleagues on the staff of the Geological survey were almost prostrated with grief. There was a warm attachment between the Director and his staff and his unexpected demise has caused a genuine sorrow. In the Rideau Club there is also grief. There he had dined for many years and formed warm friendships. He was a delightful companion. His fund of knowledge seemed inexhaustible and he could converse on nearly every subject.

His death was stated by several last night to be a national loss.

Ivy Lodge,
Trinity, Edinburgh
4 – 3 – 1901

Dear little Auntie,

It seems almost like an intrusion to write to you just now, but you know that your boy's welfare was very dear to me, and I can't resist sending just a few lines.

It must have been a bitter disappointment to you and Anna not to be with him at the last, but we know dear that God cannot err, & He would never have given you that added grief unless it had been quite unavoidable.

George was so absorbed in the interests of Science & such an unwearying worker & His Saviour may perhaps have longed for a quiet uninterrupted talk with him, and so kept the last few hours for Himself.

And Auntie dear, do not look upon the parting as a long one: everything at present seems to indicate the very near return of our Lord, so we may have a happy reunion much sooner than most people seem to expect.

And think how glad dear George will be to have his mother see him tall and straight, as she never had the joy of seeing him on earth: won't it be delightful!

With love to you all,

Your affectionate Niece,
Ella.

GEORGE MERCER DAWSON
(1849–1901)
is buried in the family plot, Lot 100, Section C
of Mount Royal Cemetery,
Montreal, Quebec.

BY WAY OF ACKNOWLEDGEMENT

—

AN EXPEDITION INTO THE PAST, mounted in the hope of returning with a book, cannot be accomplished single-handed. So I am pleased, at this end of the book, to express my gratitude to the following, who rode alongside me for all or part of the way.

The original backers of the expedition were Jan Walter and Gary Ross, and for their faith and the too brief time we had together I am indebted. Would that we had finished what we started as a team.

While researching at the McGill University archives, I felt as if I had been allowed into the attic to go through the Dawson family chest. Mary Houde, Kathi Murphy, and Johanne Pelletier gave me the keys and their time. Also in Montreal, Skipper David Gerstel provided maps and shelter along the way.

In Ottawa, the staff of both the library and the resource centre of the Geological Survey of Canada were all ears and hands whenever I spent the day there. At Library and Archives Canada, Kara Quann never failed to return with exactly what was needed whenever I sent her on a fact-finding mission. I thank them all. I am obliged to say, on behalf of my fellow researchers present and future, that despite the staff's best efforts, the systemic and logistical obstacles at the National Archives, though under assault, remain frustrating. Would that the path was smoother. No doubt underfunding is the problem. The past is a minor deity in the Canadian coffers.

As always, my thanks to those who pay tax in Canada, through whose generosity the Canada Council and the Ontario Arts Council provided funding for this project.

There were several relatives of George's within a morning's ride of my tent who were solicitous and encouraging, namely Peter Geldart, Penelope Geldart, Joan Harrington, and especially Anne Byers, George's great-niece, who joined the party of her own free will and was more than gracious and generous with her memorabilia. I dedicate this book to her.

Dinah Forbes, as editor, withstood the storms and patiently made my report a much better thing. I love the cover and design of the book; how often do you hear an author say that? Thank you, Mr. Richardson. Dean Cooke, agent extraordinaire, I owe you a bread pudding.

Liette, my faithful, wise listener, *merçi*. Mum, ta for the literary DNA. Ken, the next one is ours. And to everyone who in the last decade has asked me, "How's George coming along?", here you go.

—

The illustrations in this book appear through the kind permissions of the agencies listed below.

The photographs: GSC 1616, which shows a man gold mining in the Yukon; GSC 311, at Fort McLeod, with George Dawson and party standing in front of a building in 1879; GSC 243, the Haida village in the Queen Charlotte Islands; GSC 199634, the overhead of Telegraph Creek; GSC 842, the Francis River Canyon; GSC 858, the Indian crews; GSC 201736b, the Geological Survey building on Sussex Drive in Ottawa; GSC 109124, the museum collection within that building; the etching from a photograph of the Athababsca River in 1879; the triptych of fossil drawings; the map of the route taken by the Boundary Commission; and the detail map of George Dawson's route in the Yukon in 1887 are from the collections of the Geological Survey of Canada.

The cameo of James Dawson, number PNOOO330; the sketch of the Indian coat of arms dated 1861; the sketch of the *Lake Erie*; the page from George Dawson's mining school notebook; the two sketches from the Europe notebooks; as well as PRO29135, the photograph of George Dawson in his rooms at Victoria Chambers, and PRO27302, the family gathering on the lawn at Métis, were harvested from the ever-helpful Archives of McGill University.

The photograph of James William Dawson and his family on the Arts building steps at McGill College, about 1865, is from the Notman Photographic Archives, access number MP-0000.90 in the McCord Museum.

The photographs of George Dawson as a boy; Anna Dawson as a young girl; George Dawson standing at the North-west Angle Monument; the Boundary Commission of the move; the odometer party in the deep prairie; the *Wanderer* in the Queen Charlotte Islands; and the panorama of Waterton Lake are from the private collection of Anne Byers.

A NOTE ABOUT THE TYPE

Beneath My Feet is set in Monotype Van Dijck, a face originally designed by Christoffel van Dijck, a Dutch typefounder (and some-time goldsmith) of the seventeenth century. While the roman font may not have been cut by van Dijck himself; the italic, for which original punches survive, is almost certainly his work. The face first made its appearance circa 1606. It was re-cut for modern use in 1937.

Born in London, England, in 1951, Phil Jenkins immigrated to Ottawa with his family just six months later. The family moved back to England in 1961, but Jenkins returned to Canada in 1978 and has stayed ever since. Jenkins has written for a number of magazines, including *National Geographic Traveller*, *Equinox*, and *Heritage Canada*, and was a feature writer for *Ottawa Magazine* for five years. His first book, *Fields of Vision: A Journey to Canada's Family Farms*, a national bestseller, was published in 1991. His second, *An Acre of Time*, published in 1996, won the Canadian Authors Association Lela Common Award for History, jointly won the *Ottawa Citizen* Non-Fiction Award, and was made into a play nominated for a Governor General's Award. His third book, *River Song: Sailing the History of the St. Lawrence River* was published in 2001. From 1991 to 1996, Jenkins was the book columnist for the *Ottawa Citizen*, and he currently writes on interesting city rooms for the newspaper. He lives in Ottawa.

ALSO BY PHIL JENKINS

River Song
An Acre of Time
Fields of Vision

available from www.philjenkins.ca